KIMBERLY WAS HOLDING SOMETHING IN HER RIGHT HAND.

Actually, she wasn't exactly holding it. In death, her hand had relaxed. So what she'd been holding just before she died was now resting on the floor beneath her fingers. I leaned a little closer, peering at the thing.

It was a scrap of paper obviously ripped from the cover of the *Redbook* magazine lying on the floor right next to Kimberly's hand. On the torn scrap of paper was just part of the magazine's name. It was, however, a pretty significant part. The *R* had been ripped away, along with the part that said *BOOK*. That left just two letters.

ED.

My breath caught in my throat. Without a doubt the only letters on that torn piece of paper were *E* and *D*. *ED*.

A shiver went down my back. I turned slowly to stare at my ex-husband. Ed.

TWO-STORY FRAME

A Schuyler Ridgway Mystery

Tierney McClellan

A SIGNET BOOK

SIGNET
Published by the Penguin Group
Penguin Books USA Inc., 375 Hudson Street,
New York, New York 10014, U.S.A.
Penguin Books Ltd, 27 Wrights Lane,
London W8 5TZ, England
Penguin Books Australia Ltd, Ringwood,
Victoria, Australia
Penguin Books Canada Ltd, 10 Alcorn Avenue,
Toronto, Ontario, Canada M4V 3B2
Penguin Books (N.Z.) Ltd, 182–190 Wairau Road,
Auckland 10, New Zealand

Penguin Books Ltd, Registered Offices:
Harmondsworth, Middlesex, England

First published by Signet, an imprint of Dutton Signet,
a division of Penguin Books USA Inc.

First Printing, May, 1997
10 9 8 7 6 5 4 3 2 1

PUBLISHER'S NOTE
This is a work of fiction. Names, characters, places, and incidents either are the
product of the author's imagination or are used fictitiously, and any resemblance to
actual persons, living or dead, events, or locales is entirely coincidental.

TWO-STORY FRAME

Chapter 1

I was already angry, even before the phone call that sent me hurrying out into the rain. In fact, on that damp Tuesday in early October, I'd spent practically the entire morning sitting at my desk at Arndoerfer Realty, working very little and, more than anything else, glaring at the wall clock across the room. I couldn't seem to stop watching the stupid thing as it steadily ticked away the minutes, moving closer and closer to the dreaded three o'clock.

I was alone in the office, but that was okay with me. In the mood I was in, I didn't want to see anybody. I was angry at my boyfriend, Matthias Cross. I was angry at my ex-husband, Ed Ridgway. And I was angry at both my sons, Nathan and Daniel. I was angry at all of them for talking me into doing things that every one of them knew very well I didn't want to do.

Most of all, though, I was angry at myself. In fact, I think I might've been angrier at myself than I was at all of the others put together. The thing I kept asking myself over and over again was, why was I such a wimp? Why couldn't I do like all the drug posters said, for God's sake, and just say no?

Heading the list of people I should've said no to was Matthias. I mean, okay, so Matthias had the greenest eyes I'd ever seen. And so he also had a wonderfully thick beard, peppered here and there with gray, that I loved running my fingers through. And so he also had a slow, lazy smile that could turn my knees to jelly. So what? I was not some love-struck teenager. I'd passed the Big Four-O two entire years ago, and I do believe at this age when warning bells start going off in my head, I should listen.

Those bells had sounded like a four-alarm fire last night, right after Matthias had asked me to do him "a little favor." Oh, yes, that's what he called it, a *little* favor. If Matthias considered this a little favor, I'd hate to see what he thought qualified as a big one. It would probably involve organ donation.

Actually, now that I thought about it, I believe I'd much rather donate a kidney than do what Matthias had asked. "I'd really appreciate it," he'd said, "if you'd go with me to meet Barbara at Standiford Field."

Standiford Field is the main airport here in Louisville, Kentucky. Recently, Standiford Field changed its name to Louisville International Airport, but so far I've yet to hear anybody—except television newscasters—call it that.

Before Matthias mentioned Barbara and Standiford Field, he and I had been sitting quietly on a wicker bench out on my screen porch, enjoying a cool evening breeze already hinting of rain on the way. After Matthias spoke, I stiffened, and for a long moment, I just looked at him. Barbara? He wanted me to meet *Barbara*?

Even though Matthias and I had been dating over a year, I had yet to meet either Barbara, Matthias's ex-wife, or their daughter, Emily. I didn't think there was anything particularly ominous about my not having met these two, however. After all, Barbara and Emily did live in Boston these days, and the last time I checked, Boston *was* quite a distance from Louisville.

Mother and daughter had moved back to Barbara's hometown right after she and Matthias split up. According to Matthias, Barbara had insisted that she was moving back home mainly to be near her aging parents. In case they needed her. However, since Barbara up and married a guy by the name of Phil Coleman a mere two days after her and Matthias's divorce was final—and this Phil person happened to own a house in Boston—it seemed to me that Barbara might've exaggerated her concern for her parents a bit.

Shortly after establishing residence in Boston, Barbara had opened a boutique called—what a surprise—Barb's Boutique. From what Matthias had told me, Barb's Boutique didn't run very well without Barb. Emily, on the other hand, was attending Boston College not only during the regular semesters, but during summer school, too—and holding down a part-time job to boot. So, it didn't exactly take a genius to figure out that, in the last year or so, neither Barbara nor Emily had really had any time to come down for a visit.

Until, of course, *now*.

I cleared my throat, and immediately asked the first incredibly stupid question that came to mind. "You mean, Barbara is coming to town?"

If I were Matthias, I'd have been tempted to reply, *No, I just thought we'd go hang around Standiford Field on the off chance that she might show up.*

Instead, Matthias just gave me a quick glance, and then nodded. "Her plane arrives at three tomorrow afternoon." He ran his hand over his beard, and looked out into the night. "I can't imagine why Barbara has suddenly decided to come down for a visit."

I didn't say a word, but what Matthias had told me a few days before did immediately spring to mind. He'd mentioned that his ex-wife had just filed for divorce from the Phil person. Now, maybe Matthias couldn't imagine why Barbara would be dropping by all of a sudden, but *I* sure could.

This whole situation, in fact, is covered by a Mama-ism. Mama-isms are what I call all the little down-home truths that my mother has sent winging my way ever since the seventh grade when I went out on my first date with Johnny Guthrie. Some Mama-isms Mama was told by her own mother, and some Mama-isms Mama has just observed all by herself over the years. Mama must be one keen observer, because she has always seemed to have a Mama-ism ready to pass on to yours truly. Like, for example: *Opposites attract . . . arguments.* And, *If your boyfriend ever tells you that he thinks you and he should start seeing other people, he already is.* The Mama-ism applying to Barbara was: *When you break up with a guy, whoever you were seeing just before him will start looking like God's gift to women.*

"I'd sure appreciate it if you'd come with me," God's gift was now saying. "I really don't want to meet Barbara all by myself."

I took a deep breath, and forced myself to smile. When Matthias and I had first started dating, I'd been pretty curious about Barbara. Mainly because I couldn't imagine what kind of deranged female would let a man as wonderful as Matthias get away. Now, though, suddenly faced with the prospect of meeting Barbara face-to-face, I didn't feel anywhere near as enthusiastic. This was the woman who'd spent far more years with Matthias than I had. The woman with whom he'd had a child. The woman who today might very well be deeply regretting her decision to leave him.

Lord. If I never met Barbara, it would be too soon.

My smile was beginning to feel like something I'd pasted on my face. "You won't be all by yourself," I told Matthias. "Emily will be there, too, won't she?"

I thought I sounded positively casual as I asked the question. I must not have sounded quite as casual as I thought, though, because Matthias's green eyes darted once again in my direction. "It's almost time for midterms," he said, looking at me unwaveringly, "so it looks as if Emily won't be able to find time to visit."

I blinked, and looked away. Barbara was coming down *alone*? Correct me if I'm wrong, but wasn't it a little odd that only Barbara would come down for a visit? Leaving Emily behind?

These weren't the only questions that occurred to me, either, as I sat there on the screen porch, avoiding Matthias's eyes. Another was this: Where exactly was Barbara going to stay while she was in town? I was not, of course, about to broach this particular subject with Matthias, but it definitely weighed on my mind.

What also weighed on my mind was how I'd recently turned down Matthias's invitation to move in with him. I'd turned him down for several very good reasons, not the least of which was that I just wasn't quite ready to give up my independence. That particular reason had sounded perfectly logical at the time, but now I couldn't help thinking that if I hadn't turned Matthias down, I'd at least have some say in where Barbara would be staying.

I wasn't looking at him, but I could feel Matthias's eyes.

"So," he said, "how about it? Will you come with me, Sky?"

Sky is Matthias's nickname for me. Short for Schuyler. Every time he says it, it reminds me of the only other person I've ever heard of whose name was Sky—Sky King. Sky King was this cowboy/airplane pilot on television back in the fifties. As I recall, when Sky wasn't riding the range or flying his plane, he was catching criminals. It was a little hard to take Sky seriously because—even though he played a tough guy—he often wore an embroidered Western shirt, a string tie, and spurs that jangled merrily every time he took a step. Whenever Matthias calls me Sky, though, he says it so fondly I've never had the heart to tell him that I've always thought Sky was a boy's name. And a geek boy's name, at that.

I looked back over at Matthias, and gave him another smile. "I'd be glad to go with you to the airport," I lied. "In fact, I'm looking forward to finally meeting Barbara."

I was surprised to hear my own voice. I actually sounded sincere.

That, of course, was how I ended up on this rainy Tuesday, sitting at my desk, gloomily watching the clock on the opposite wall march toward three o'clock. Apparently, I'd sounded so sincere, Matthias hadn't even questioned it.

I don't know why I should've been surprised. Hadn't I sounded every bit as sincere two weeks ago when I'd agreed to do what my ex-husband, Ed, had wanted me to do?

As a matter of fact, Ed was the next name on my list of people—right after Matthias—to whom I should've just said no.

Actually, I guess my sons, Nathan and Daniel, should be listed on the same line with Ed, because it was my sons who'd done the actual asking. Ed had evidently known that what he wanted me to do was pretty outrageous, so—basic coward that he is—he'd gotten Nathan and Daniel to discuss the entire thing with me.

I've got to hand it to my sons. They don't beat around the bush. "Yo, Mom," Daniel had said the second he'd walked through my front door. *Yo* accounts for a major portion of Daniel's vocabulary. I should never have taken the boy to see all those *Rocky* movies when he was little. Those movies obviously hit him hard. "Nathan and I have got something to ask you."

Nathan was right behind Daniel, and he jumped in at this point. "How about helping Dad and the Kimster house hunt, okay?"

The Kimster was the boys' name for Kimberly Metcalf, Ed's fiancée. I would've said *current* fiancée—Ed has gone through quite a few fiancées in the years we've been divorced—except that it looked like this one might actually turn out to be the real thing. Ed and Kimberly had set a wedding date—in a scant four weeks—and mailed out the invitations. None of Ed's former fiancées had ever lasted long enough to lick a postage stamp.

Unlike Barbara and Emily, I *had* met the Kimster. Several times. In fact, I suspected Ed had gone out of his way to make sure I'd met her. Kimberly, Lord love her, was just twenty-seven, only five years older than Daniel, Ed's and my oldest. Kimberly was also very petite, and very curvy, with shoulder-length blond hair and blue eyes so large, she looked perpetually surprised. To be cruelly honest, Kimberly was not quite as pretty as some of Ed's previous fiancées, but from what I gathered from Ed, she had something that none of the others had—something I knew the second he mentioned it that Ed would find wildly attractive.

Connections.

Ed had told me more than once that Kimberly was one of *the* Metcalfs of Lexington, Kentucky. I don't really keep up with Who's Who in Kentucky, but even I had heard that particular name. Around the Bluegrass state, the Metcalf family name meant money so old, nobody really knew how they'd first come by it. What everybody did know was that the Metcalfs had spread a good deal of their money liberally around Kentucky, making endowments to the Louisville Ballet, the arts, the University of Kentucky scholarship fund, and various other charities.

Ed had also told me several times that he'd met Kimberly at the opening of a regional art exhibit at the J. B. Speed Museum. Ed seemed to feel that Kimberly's appearance at such a function was further proof of Kimberly's superior bloodline. It was, no doubt, not a bit kind of me to think such a thing, but Kimberly's pedigree certainly explained why good old social-climbing Ed might've decided to really get married this time.

Kimberly, for her part, seemed to believe that marrying somebody twenty years older automatically put you in their age group. Shortly after she met me, Kimberly told me in all seriousness not to worry—that she had no intention of trying to replace me as a mother figure in the boys' lives. Really. She actually said this. I, of course, immediately assured her that I wasn't worried. I mean, the Kimster might try to be a sister figure to Nathan and Daniel. But a mother figure? To Daniel, age twenty-two and Nathan, age twenty-one? I didn't think so.

I had known, of course, the second that Nathan and Daniel popped the question, so to speak, that I would regret giving in to them. And yet, I couldn't think of a good excuse not to help Ed and Kimberly with their house hunt. Not without sounding as if I had a problem with Ed getting married again, anyway. In fact, it was while I was talking to Nathan and Daniel that I—in an effort to convince them both that I had no problem whatsoever with their father's upcoming nuptials—actually agreed to kick back part of my commission as a wedding present.

Kick, of course, was the operative word here. I'd been kicking myself ever since. Too late, I'd realized that this was what Ed had, no doubt, wanted me to do in the first place—reduce my commission. This kind of maneuver was just like cheapskate Ed. He was, after all, the very same man who'd insisted back when we were still married that I wash out plastic sandwich bags and reuse them.

Lord. What a sweetheart that man had been to live with.

Knowing all this, however, I still couldn't exactly renege. Not after telling Nathan and Daniel that I would do it. A promise was a promise. So, honorable person that I was, I'd spent the last two interminable weeks escorting Ed and his child bride-to-be all over Louisville and surrounding counties.

During those two god-awful weeks I'd listened to Ed lecture Kimberly on everything from the quality of carpet to how many bathrooms they'd need. Lord, that man had staying power. Listening to him go on and on had been a painful reminder of all the times I myself had listened to Ed's lectures back when he and I were married. That had been over fourteen years ago, and yet apparently Ed was still laboring under the delusion that it was his personal duty to enlighten the womenfolk. By the time I'd spent two weeks herding the happy couple through countless houses, I firmly believed what up till then I'd only suspected: The *Ed Encyclopedia* could rival the *Britannica* easy.

Kimberly didn't seem to mind Ed's lectures nearly as much as I did, however. In fact, the young woman seemed to hang on Ed's every word. Kimberly even told me during one of our first house-hunting expeditions that she considered Ed to be absolutely perfect. I believe the Kimster's exact quote was, "Ed is so wise, so mature." I'd just stared into those huge blue eyes. Only somebody in her twenties would think that Ed, of all people, was mature.

Kimberly apparently believed that Ed was so perfect, she couldn't understand how he ever came to be divorced. She'd actually taken me aside one afternoon and bluntly asked why Ed and I had split up. "Was it really because you two had just grown apart? Like Ed says?" Kimberly asked.

I'd had to bite my tongue to keep from telling Kimberly about Ed's joining the Girlfriend of the Month club during the last years of our marriage. Or, at least, that was what I thought he must've done, since a new girlfriend seemed to show up about every four weeks or so.

I did not feel, however, that it was my place to drag out all Ed's dirty laundry. If Ed wanted Kimberly to know what a jerk he'd been, it seemed to me that he should be the one to tell her. Besides, what did I know? Maybe Ed had finally finished sowing his wild oats, and was ready at last to settle down. It could happen. It might be shortly after pigs became airborne, but it *could* happen.

"I guess Ed and I just grew to be two very different people," was what I finally ended up telling Kimberly that afternoon. Hey, I was telling her the truth. *I* had grown to be someone who was faithful. And Ed, on the other hand, had grown to be someone who wasn't.

Ed had also grown to be someone who based his judgments of people pretty much entirely on what they drove, where they lived, and whom they could claim as ancestors. Or maybe Ed hadn't grown to be like this. Maybe he'd always been this shallow, and I just hadn't noticed until I'd been married to him for a while.

When Ed and Kimberly at last made up their minds about a house, it was all I could do to keep from weeping in sheer relief. Naturally, the house that Ed and Kimberly finally decided was perfect for them turned out to be one of the first houses I'd shown them on day one of their house hunt—a two-story frame on Willow Avenue.

The two-story house was a listing of mine that I'd been trying to sell for some time. It was a charming Victorian with a wraparound porch, a stained-glass inset on the second-floor landing, and lacelike gingerbread at the windows and eaves. Inside, it had some wonderful extras—a claw-footed bathtub and a pedestal sink in the master bath, three marble fireplaces, and two staircases—a narrow one just off the kitchen, and a wide one with a curved oak banister just off the living room.

The house was in pristine condition, and the only reason it had been on the market for so long was that it was being sold as a result of a pending divorce. From what I understood, the separation agreement stipulated that the wife, Adrienne Henderson, a petite blond in her late forties, could stay in the house until it was sold. Adrienne's estranged husband, Frank, had already moved into his own condo, but Adrienne apparently had not wanted to move. *Ever*.

Whenever I'd tried to sell the house, Adrienne had followed along in back of me, telling the prospects anything and everything to discourage them from buying. Unfortunately, it had taken me a while to catch on to what Adrienne was doing.

As a matter of fact, it was only after Adrienne had told Ed that she was "sure that Schuyler had mentioned the roach problem," but for him not to worry, she was "fairly certain it had been taken care of," that it had finally gotten back to me what was being said behind my back. In fact, it had taken me several minutes to convince an indignant Ed that I was not—as he put it—"trying to unload a roach motel."

Having been through a divorce myself, I admit I felt sympathetic toward Adrienne. Judging from the framed photos I'd noticed around the house, the Hendersons had two grown children, both married with children of their own. My guess was that Adrienne herself had probably never worked outside of the home. And had never expected to. The poor woman often had the disoriented, frightened look in her eyes of someone who'd just been in a terrible automobile accident.

It was abundantly clear that the divorce was all Frank Henderson's idea—and that poor Adrienne was doing everything she could to keep from having the thing finalized. In the months since I'd listed the Hendersons' house, Adrienne had taken to wearing skintight, above-the-knee skirts and clinging, low-cut knit tops. These outfits might've looked adorable on a teenager, but on a woman in her late forties, they looked sad. Not that Adrienne didn't have a good figure. She was in great shape for her age, no doubt about that. No, it was just that she looked as if she were desperately trying to look sexier and younger—as if this alone would be the answer to everything.

The worst part of it was that Adrienne's husband, Frank, didn't even seem to notice. In fact, if Frank ever gave his wife more than a passing glance, the look on his face was always hostile. Judging from these occasional glances, I'd say the man was more than a little anxious to untie the knot. In fact, I wouldn't be surprised if he had somebody on the side waiting for him.

Not that all of this was any of *my* business. My business was to sell the Hendersons' house. Period. Toward that end, I was pretty much duty bound to tell Frank how Adrienne had been sabotaging sales. After all, the two-story frame was *his* house, too.

The afternoon I told Frank, he'd just stared at me for a long moment while a red flush slowly crept up his neck from beneath his collar. A broad-shouldered bear of a man, with thinning brown hair and a dusting of gray at both temples, Frank was usually soft-spoken with an easygoing grin. I'd known that he worked for a local paint company as their collections manager, and up to that afternoon, I'd wondered how somebody as easygoing as Frank Henderson could possibly hold down a hard-nosed job like that one. How could somebody so soft-spoken be successful calling people up day after day, hounding them for payment?

That afternoon, however, I saw how he did it. I saw the steel beneath the affable, easygoing exterior. "Mrs. Ridgway," Frank had told me quietly, "I assure you that this will never happen again." Looking into his eyes, I believed him.

Whatever Frank said to Adrienne, I didn't know, but after that, Adrienne always kept to herself whenever the house was being shown.

After Adrienne's input, it seemed practically a miracle that Kimberly and Ed had finally decided that the Henderson house was the one for them. Kimberly and Ed had already written a contract on another house before this one, only to back out at the last minute because Kimberly had decided she didn't like the people next door. Rednecks, Kimberly had called them. I personally wasn't sure how she'd arrived at this conclusion. The people next door did have a Ford pickup parked in the driveway, but surely just owning a truck didn't qualify you as a redneck.

Kimberly's little discovery that their prospective

neighbors were of the redneck variety had cost Ed his five-hundred-dollar deposit. And yet, Ed—can you believe it—hadn't even acted as if he minded. This was a surprise. The man who'd yelled at me for leaving a light on whenever I'd left a room—the man who, as I mentioned earlier, had pioneered the concept of the washable plastic sandwich bag—*this* was the same guy who simply shrugged when the Kimster blew five hundred smackers? What's more, the Henderson house on Willow Avenue cost fifteen thousand dollars more than the first house. And yet, Ed still had not seemed to mind.

It could very well be that the man was in love.

Ed and Kimberly's offer on the Willow Avenue house had been accepted the day it was made, and the closing was set for the end of the month. I'd made a note on my calendar so on the day of the closing I'd remember that the Hendersons were to be kept apart. And, just to be on the safe side, I'd already scheduled two separate rooms in the closing attorney's office. So that Adrienne and Frank would be able to sign their respective papers without once running into each other.

This is one of the things that all my years in the real estate business has taught me. In the case of divorce, for God's sake, *separate* the unhappy couple. Otherwise, you stand a pretty good chance of ending up seated at a table with two angry people shouting at each other and nothing getting signed. You also stand a pretty good chance of seeing your neatly typed papers torn into tiny pieces and thrown in a trash can.

Along, incidentally, with your commission.

With all the preparations made and the closing finally set, I guess I should've been elated. And yet now, as I sat at my desk, listening to the rain pattering on the roof overhead, and continuing to glare at the wall clock across the room, I was still angry at myself for agreeing to give up any of my commission. Hell, I'd earned every penny. Twice over.

What was wrong with me, anyway? Why did I let all the men in my life walk all over me? If this kept up, I might as well just lie down and stencil WELCOME on my chest.

When the phone rang a little before noon, I remembered just as I reached for it that this was the day that Adrienne was supposed to let Kimberly come in and measure for drapes and such. I was suddenly sure that this had to be one or the other of them, no doubt complaining about something.

"Schuyler?"

The second I heard the tremor in the voice, I knew that, sure enough, something was wrong. "Kimberly?"

"Look, you've got to get over here right away."

My first impulse was to tell Kimberly that I was busy. "I'm pretty tied up—" I began.

Kimberly interrupted me. "Look, there's a problem here, understand?"

"A problem?" It crossed my mind that Adrienne Henderson might've been up to her old tricks again. Had Adrienne told Kimberly that something else was wrong with the house? "Let me speak to Mrs. Henderson," I said.

Kimberly's answer was quick. "Mrs. Henderson's not here. She left."

"She left? What do you mean, she left?"

Kimberly went right on, as if I hadn't said anything. "Look, Ed's going to be mad, and I don't think I should have to deal with this all by myself—"

"Deal with what?"

Kimberly was now sounding angry. "Just get over here *now*, okay? I'm afraid—"

The phone suddenly went dead. It was so unexpected that for a moment I just sat there, staring stupidly at the receiver. Had Kimberly hung up on me? Or had she been cut off? I looked up the phone number for the Henderson place in my current listings file, dialed it as fast as I could, but nobody answered.

I double-checked the number, and then I dialed two more times, only to hear the phone ring again and again.

The last time I couldn't help sighing. My boss, Jarvis Arndoerfer, didn't like his office left unmanned, but he did make an exception when a client called with a problem.

There seemed to be only one thing to do.

I put on my coat, grabbed my purse and umbrella, and cursing under my breath, I hurried out into the rain.

Chapter 2

I've heard that when it rains in Paris, the city looks even more charming. I'm talking about the Paris located in France, you understand, and not the one located here in Kentucky. I've never visited either Paris myself, but I have been told by those who have traveled to the French one that during a rain, the air actually smells sweeter. The wet streets all but glow, and you start noticing quaint architectural details in the newly washed buildings that you hadn't seen before.

When it rains in Louisville, what you start noticing is how bad the city needs a good hosing. As I drove as fast as I dared through the downpour toward Willow Avenue, streams of dirty brown water seemed to keep pace with me, running along the sides of the road into the storm drains. I wish I could say that all the stores, restaurants, and homes lining Taylorsville Road suddenly looked quaint and charming, but to be honest, everything looked about as charming as the inside of a car wash. That is, if the inside of the car wash were painted gray. The road ahead of me was gray, the sky above me was gray, and everything I passed—from Mazzoni's Restaurant to the Jewish synagogue—seemed to be a uniform shade of gray.

I felt a little gray myself. Now I was not only dreading the upcoming meeting with Matthias's ex at the airport, I was also dreading the upcoming meeting with the Kimster. The only good thing about this last appointment was that I wouldn't have as long to dread this one as the one at the airport. Even with the weather being what it was, I would be there in less than ten minutes.

I braked at the ever-busy intersection of Taylorsville Road and Bardstown Road, pumping the pedal when I felt the car start to slide a little on the wet pavement. While I sat there, waiting for an opening in the steady stream of traffic so that I could make a right-hand turn onto Bardstown, I wondered what Kimberly's current problem could be. Could there really be a roach problem, after all? That certainly would account for Kimberly sounding so agitated over the phone. Maybe while she was measuring for drapes, she'd come across a few creepy-crawlies.

That was possible. And yet, Kimberly's reaction had seemed a little extreme for it to be just that. She'd sounded as if it were taking all her strength to remain calm. Would she have sounded that upset if her problem was only that her new home needed a quick visit from the Orkin man?

Okay, so maybe it wasn't bugs. Maybe the Kimster had gotten a good look at her new neighbors-to-be, and once again decided that they were too red in the neck. I gripped the steering wheel a little tighter. If Kimberly's aversion to rednecks really turned out to be the reason that she'd insisted I take this little trip in the rain, I might finally lose all control and slap her silly.

Traffic had thinned out enough so I could finally make the turn onto Bardstown. I eased into the left-hand lane, and wondered for what seemed like the millionth time why in the world I'd ever agreed to help Ed and Kimberly house hunt. Oh, my, yes, I was back to kicking myself for being such a wimp.

Something else also flashed through my mind as I made my way down the wet street. I wondered if maybe Ed hadn't gotten wind of the first conversation Kimberly and I had engaged in this morning. That's right, Kimberly's little problem phone call had not been my first chat of the day with her. The first time we'd spoken had been shortly after I'd arrived for work. The phone had started to ring just as I sat down at my desk. Stowing my purse in back of the lower file drawer, I picked up the receiver on the second ring and said all in one breath, "Arndoerfer Realty, Schuyler Ridgway speaking."

Kimberly didn't even bother to say hello. "If I told you that I thought Ed was running around on me, would you be surprised? I mean, is that the kind of behavior you yourself pretty much expect out of him?"

The first response that occurred to me was, of course, Is the Pope Catholic? Somehow, though, I managed to refrain from saying this out loud. As a matter of fact, it took me a moment to answer—mainly because Kimberly had caught me off guard and I had to scramble around in my mind for a more suitable reply.

"Well?" Kimberly pressed. "Did Ed ever run around on you?"

I hedged. "What do you mean?" Can you believe I actually tried to sound as if I weren't any too clear what the term *run around* meant?

"Come on, Schuyler." Kimberly now sounded a little disgusted. I didn't blame her. "I'm asking you straight out," she went on. "Woman to woman. Was Ed ever unfaithful to you when you all were married? I need to know."

Kimberly may have needed to know, but I certainly didn't need to be the one to tell her. After all, she *was* talking about the father of my two sons. While Nathan and Daniel were hardly impressionable youngsters anymore, there were still a few things about their father that I didn't think I ought to be blabbing around town.

Not to mention, Ed did have something of a temper. If he ever got wind that I had burned the Kimster's delicate ears with the sad saga of his misdeeds, I'd never hear the end of it. I had no intention of spending any additional minutes of my life listening to Ed bellow. Lord knows, I'd spent far too many already. I took a deep breath. "Kimberly," I said, "you really should ask Ed about this. He—"

Kimberly cut me off. "I'm asking *you*."

I blinked. Thank you so much, Kimberly dear, for pointing that out to me. I opened my mouth, intending to pretty much repeat what I'd just said, and then I found myself hesitating. If I were a real friend of Kimberly's, I'd tell her the truth. In fact, I was surprised to find that I actually felt a little guilty, knowing that I was about to withhold information that any woman really ought to have about the man she intended to marry.

And yet, how could I tell Kimberly? How could I possibly fill her in on everything I knew regarding Ed's Girlfriend of the Month club? For one thing, it would take quite a while. Did Kimberly have a few *days*?

For another thing, how would I go about it? Should I just blurt it all out? Like, for example, how I'd always known whenever Ed had roped in a new one because my phone would start ringing again at all hours of the day and night? Should I clue the Kimster in on exactly how much fun it was to answer that stupid phone again and again, only to hear silence—even though sometimes I could plainly hear someone breathing on the other end of the line? Should I describe exactly how baffled Ed had always managed to look? Once he'd even had the nerve to say, "You know, we're going to have to call the phone company. This has got to stop."

Oddly enough, he never did get around to calling the phone company. And yet, in the end Ed turned out to be right. It did stop, all right. Right after he moved out.

"Schuyler?" Kimberly prodded.

I tightened my grip on the telephone receiver. Lord, I felt like such a jerk. Because I knew, of course, that it was my silence—and the combined silences of all the other women just like me—that permitted the Eds of this world to keep on doing what they do. Lord. How convenient could we make it for these guys? They could make passes at us with their wives only a room away, and they knew damn well that there wasn't a chance in hell we'd immediately go find the missus and tell. These guys could even phone us from their offices and ask us out, and it didn't concern them for even a moment that right after they hung up, we'd be dialing their wives with a little news bulletin. Hell, even years later—even after we were divorced, for God's sake—we could still be counted on not to say a word to Prospective Wife Number Two.

Why was this? Why exactly do we women so often keep our mouths shut? I suppose it could be that we're all afraid that somebody might get the idea that *we* were the ones who got things rolling—that somehow we encouraged all these straying husbands' advances. Then, too, there was always the chance that we wouldn't be believed. Hell, we have trouble convincing twelve total strangers that we've been raped. How on earth are we supposed to convince some guy's wife that he's been making moves on us?

It seems then, in the end, that we women are drawn into a silent conspiracy whether we like it or not. In fact, from what I've observed, the only time a woman ever does spill the beans is when she wants to hurt the wife. It is something almost never done out of kindness, but out of malice.

"Schuyler?" Kimberly prodded again. "I mean it, I really do—"

I interrupted her. "No, Kimberly, *I* mean it. You really do need to ask Ed."

Kimberly drew a short, audible breath. "Then you won't tell me?" she said.

I could feel my face growing hot as I gripped the receiver even tighter. Oh, yes, I was slime. No doubt about it. And yet, maybe telling Kimberly everything I knew about Ed wouldn't be fair. For all I knew, Ed had turned over a brand-new leaf. I hadn't lived with the man in over fourteen years. In that length of time Ed could've turned over an entire *tree*. "Kimberly," I said, "I really don't believe I should be—"

Kimberly must've known where I was headed with this. She cut me off. "Well, *I* believe if Ed had not ever run around on you, you'd just say so. Straight out." Kimberly sounded even more disgusted. "So I guess he did. Right?"

I took a deep breath. Then I slowly repeated once again what I'd said before. Only this time I emphasized each and every word, so much so that you might've thought each was a sentence by itself. "Kimberly. You. Should. Ask. Ed."

Even as I said this, I knew very well that Ed was not

going to be satisfied with my just keeping quiet. He would, no doubt, expect me to out-and-out lie for him. My lying for him had, after all, been something he'd pretty much counted on during our eight years of marital bliss. Back then Ed had apparently felt that, as the patriarch of our little household, he ought to have ample opportunity to chase after every skirt that caught his eye. He'd also apparently felt that I, as the matriarch, ought to have ample opportunity to cover up for him.

What a guy.

I hate to admit it, but I actually went along with this little scenario of Ed's for most of our marriage. I lied to his parents, I lied to my parents, and I lied to our friends. I told them all what a wonderful husband Ed was, and how lucky I was to have him. I'd like to say that I did this because, taking a cue from Tammy Wynette, I'd felt as if I should stand by my man. The truth was, I'd simply found it too humiliating to admit to anybody that I couldn't keep my man at home.

It had taken an unbelievably long time for it to finally occur to me that *I* wasn't the one in control of Ed's behavior. So how could I possibly be the one responsible for it?

"I'm right, aren't I?" Kim pressed. "If Ed had never run around on you, you'd just say so, wouldn't you?"

I had to repeat myself two more times before she finally gave up. As soon as I got off the phone, of course, I headed for the tiny kitchen in the back of the Arndoerfer Realty office. There I poured myself a long, tall one. A long, tall Coca-Cola, that is. Very heavy on the ice.

For me, Coke is a sort of liquid pacifier. I always reach for an icy Coke when I'm feeling tense. It's not any big deal. I just happen to really like Coke, that's all. I like it for breakfast, for lunch, for dinner, and for snacks in between. Just hearing it fizz as I pour it over ice is enough to lift my spirits.

Strangely enough, there are those who have tried to make the comparison between my desire for a Coke and a smoker's craving for a cigarette. To which I must say: You have *got* to be kidding. The last time I looked, there was no surgeon general's warning on my two-liter. Believe me, if I ever do see a message from the surgeon general there—or, for that matter, any words to the effect that drinking Coca-Cola could contribute to heart and lung disease and should be avoided by pregnant women— that's the day that I quit. Cold turkey.

Until then, however, I intended to drink large, icy glasses of Coke to my heart's content. I'd finished in a matter of minutes the Coke I'd poured right after I got off the phone with Kimberly, I'd polished off another as I worked at my desk—and even now, as I parked my Tercel at the curb in front of the two-story frame on Willow Avenue, I had a tumbler of Coke-on-the-rocks sitting in the driver's side cup holder of my car.

I took a quick sip, looked over at the house, and immediately frowned. Because the first thing I saw, naturally, was Ed's car in the driveway. These days Ed drives a candy-apple red, brand-new Lexus, so you can't exactly miss it. I was pretty sure, in fact, that your not missing it was the entire idea behind Ed's buying this particular vehicle in the first place. If I'd had any doubt about that, Ed's vanity plate would've immediately removed it. The plate said, ED'S TOY. Oh, my, yes. I'd say Ed wanted you to notice, all right.

There was also something else I noticed. Adrienne Henderson's car—a silver-blue Honda Accord—was nowhere in sight. As I looked up and down Willow Avenue, I recalled Kimberly telling me over the phone that Adrienne had left. Had Adrienne not returned yet?

Of course, not seeing Adrienne's car didn't necessarily mean she wasn't home. The Henderson house did have a matching detached frame garage out back. Large enough to take up a good chunk of the narrow backyard, the garage opened onto an alley so narrow only one car could travel down it at a time. You couldn't see inside the garage from the front of the house, so for all I knew, Adrienne's car was parked in there.

Sitting there in my lowly Tercel, staring at Ed's Toy, I could feel my stomach constricting. If Ed himself was waiting for me inside, then it definitely looked as if my suspicions had been correct. I had indeed been dragged out of a nice warm office into the cold pouring rain to discuss my and Kimberly's first little chat this morning.

I took another deep breath. If given the choice, I would definitely prefer *not* to discuss Ed's infidelities in front of Adrienne Henderson. Or anybody else, for that matter. I took my keys out of the ignition, dropped them into my purse, and then—noticing that the rain now seemed to be coming down with a renewed intensity—I twisted around in the driver's seat, looking for my umbrella.

I try to keep an umbrella in my car at all times. The problem is, though, using the thing generally involves taking it out of my car. And once an umbrella's out of my car, it's apparently subject to the same mysterious, cosmic forces that make socks disappear in washing machines.

I'd tried solving my disappearing umbrella problem once by buying three identical Totes umbrellas and putting every single one of them in my car. The week after I'd done this, it had rained for four days straight, and all three umbrellas had been gone by the second day.

Now, sitting outside the Henderson house on Willow Avenue, I could see that cosmic forces had been at work once again. The little black collapsible umbrella that I was sure I'd put in my Tercel a few days ago was not where it was supposed to be—that is, next to the back window in the wide groove in front of the rear speaker. A quick glance around the back told me that the umbrella had not fallen forward onto the rear passenger seat or the floor.

I leaned sideways, being careful not to impale myself on the gearshift or knock over my glass of Coke, and checked under my seat and under the passenger seat beside me. After that, I checked my glove compartment, the pocket on each door, and even behind both visors where an umbrella couldn't possibly hide. I found nothing. That is, if you didn't count lint, two fuzzy pennies, and some fossilized Fritos.

Finally, I had to face facts. If there was an umbrella anywhere in my car, it had to be in the trunk.

I leaned back against the driver's seat, took still another deep breath, and stared glumly at the rivers of rain streaming down my windshield. Obviously, I had a decision to make. I could jerk open my door, run as fast as I could to the back of my car, open my trunk and rummage frantically around in there for my umbrella—while, no doubt, I found out what it felt like to be in a wet T-shirt contest. Or I could just give up on the damn umbrella and stay right where I was, high and most assuredly dry, until the rain subsided—regardless of who was cooling his heels inside, waiting on me.

I was pondering these weighty choices—and, yes, quietly sipping my Coke—when a sudden noise made me jump. I immediately turned and looked in the direction of the noise—toward the front entrance of the Henderson house. Right away I could see what had happened. Ed, Lord love him, had flung open the Hendersons' front door with such force that the door had smacked against the exterior wall. Ed was now hurrying straight toward me, his broad shoulders hunched against the rain.

My throat tightened. From the set of his shoulders, I could tell I was about to be treated to another Ed lecture. What was it this time? Had I taken too long getting out of the car? Had he been inside this whole time, watching me conduct the Great Umbrella Search, and now he was heading my way to tell me to forget the damn umbrella, for God's sake, he didn't think I needed one?

Ed obviously didn't think *he* needed an umbrella. The rain was making the shoulders of his navy blue designer suit even darker and turning his sandy hair dark brown as he headed my way.

I stared at him, making up my mind. Maybe Ed wanted to do an impromptu impression of Noah, but I sure didn't. I rolled down the window next to me and shouted loud enough to be heard above the rain, "For God's sake, Ed, you don't have to come and get me! I'll be inside in just a minute. I'm just waiting for the rain to—"

Ed was close enough by then for me to get a good look at his face. The words died on my lips.

Good Lord. What was wrong with him?

Ed, even I will admit, is usually a very good-looking man. He is often taken for our sons' brother, rather than their father. In fact, at six feet one—an inch shorter than both boys—Ed looks much like what you'd get if you mixed our two sons' best features. Ed has Daniel's long lashes, square jaw, and broad shoulders, and he has Nathan's muscular build and sandy brown hair.

Like I said, Ed is *usually* very good-looking. At the moment, though, his face was drawn and drained of color, and he looked quite a bit older than his forty-three years. When Ed got up to my car, he just stood there for a long moment, staring at me, his eyes wild. His mouth was moving, but no sound was coming out. He didn't even seem to notice that he was standing in the rain.

Under other circumstances, I might have been tempted to say something about not having the sense to get in out of the rain. The way Ed was acting, though, gave me a chill that had nothing to do with the damp weather. "Ed?" I said. I'd never seen him behave like this before. "Ed, what's wrong?"

Ed continued to stare at me. For a second there it looked as if he wasn't going to be able to speak.

"Ed, what is it?" I asked.

He ran a trembling hand through his hair. "In—inside," he said finally, directing an uneasy glance at the door in back of him. "I—I couldn't even look at—I just walked in, and—and—I *saw*—I mean, *right there* on the—"

Ed was not making a whole lot of sense, and I had no intention of just sitting there, waiting for him to have a moment of lucidity. I put the glass of Coke back in the cup holder, grabbed my purse, got out of my car, and took off through the drizzle for the house. I knew Ed was following me—I could hear his footsteps sloshing behind my own on the wet sidewalk—but I didn't look back.

Ed had left the front door of the Henderson house standing ajar. I didn't even pause as I hurried through it. I did, however, come to an abrupt halt right after that. Mainly because it was then that I got my first look at what had caused Ed to act so strangely.

Oh, my God.
Oh, my dear God in heaven.
It was Kimberly.
I stifled a scream.

Chapter 3

I couldn't move. I just stood there, as if frozen, in the middle of the foyer of the Henderson home, taking in the whole terrible scene directly in front of me.

Kimberly was lying on her stomach at the bottom of the oak staircase leading to the second floor. Her arms were outstretched, and her left leg was twisted beneath her in a position that would've been excruciatingly painful had she been able to feel it. It was obvious, though, that poor Kimberly was beyond feeling anything. Her blond head was turned to the right, facing the front door. So that as soon as you walked in, you could see that her eyes were fixed and staring.

For a minute there, I couldn't seem to tear my own eyes away. I took a step closer, and that's when I noticed the ugly wound on the back of Kimberly's head. Matted with hair, it was a couple inches behind her right ear and such a dark red it almost looked black against Kimberly's pale blond waves. I stared at the thing. How had Kimberly managed to fall face forward and still get a wound like this on the *back* of her head?

I had barely formed the question in my mind when I spotted the flashlight. It was large and metal, and it was lying on the first step of the stairs. There was a runner in a richly colored Oriental print tacked in the middle of each hardwood step, leading up to the second-floor landing. The flashlight was lying half on the runner and half on the hardwood. Even from where I was standing, I could see that the flashlight's glass was cracked, its metal rim bent, and a large dark red splotch marred its shiny surface.

I swallowed against the nausea rising in my throat. My God. Kimberly hadn't accidentally fallen. She'd been *murdered.*

Just thinking such a thing sent a chill down my back. "Ed?" I said, and I realized, even as I spoke, that I was whispering. It wasn't something I'd planned to do, it just seemed as if talking out loud would be somehow disrespectful of poor Kimberly. "Are we here all by ourselves? Or . . . or . . ." I let my voice sort of trail off, because I really didn't want to put into words what I was thinking. Which was, of course: *Or is there a murderer somewhere in this house waiting for his chance to kill again?*

I wasn't sure if Ed ever really understood my drift, but he shook his head distractedly, his eyes still on poor Kimberly. "Nobody else is here," he said. "Nobody."

I could tell he wasn't any too sure whether he should count Kimberly as being here or not.

A small mahogany table was lying on its side right next to Kimberly's left shoulder. On the wood parquet floor near the table were several magazines—I could see, among others, the covers of a *Good Housekeeping*, a *Family Circle*, and a *Woman's Day*.

What had happened seemed clear. Kimberly must've been upstairs on the landing when someone had come up behind her and struck her with the heavy flashlight. She'd tumbled down the stairs, and when she'd reached the bottom, she'd collided with the table. The magazines now littered around her must've been stacked on top of the table, and they'd all hit the floor when the table went over.

I didn't really want to, but I couldn't seem to help myself—I looked again at poor Kimberly's face. Her eyes were as blank as if they'd been made of blue glass. I swallowed again, feeling a little dizzy. My God, how could this be? I'd just *talked* to Kimberly. How could this have happened?

I was dimly aware of Ed now moving past me, heading straight for Kimberly. He dropped to his knees at her side, stared at her without moving for a long moment, and then abruptly looked back up at me. "She's dead." His voice was oddly flat. "Kimberly is dead," Ed repeated. He sounded as if he himself didn't quite believe what he was saying.

I moved across the foyer to stand right behind Ed. My throat tightened up again, and I had to swallow once before I could speak. "Ed, are you sure there's nobody else here?"

He was staring at Kimberly again, and for a moment, I thought he hadn't even heard me. "There's nobody."

"Where's Adrienne Henderson?"

I'm not sure what I was getting at. I suppose I was afraid that we'd find Adrienne in a similar condition.

Ed, however, looked up at me and immediately shook his head. "She's not here. She was gone when I got here. I—I don't know where she went—" His voice faded as his eyes traveled back to Kimberly.

I cleared my throat. "Ed, listen to me, we have to—" I'd been about to tell him that we needed to call the police, but as I spoke, I spotted something that up to then had escaped my notice.

Kimberly was holding something in her right hand.

Actually, she wasn't exactly holding it. In death, her hand had relaxed. So what she'd been holding just before she died was now resting on the floor beneath her fingers. I leaned a little closer, peering at the thing.

It was a scrap of paper obviously ripped from the cover of the *Redbook* magazine lying on the floor right next to Kimberly's hand. On the torn scrap of paper was just part of the magazine's name. It was, however, a pretty significant part. The *R* had been ripped away, along with the part that said *BOOK*. That left just two letters.

ED.

My breath caught in my throat.

Steeling myself, I stepped around Ed and moved even closer to Kimberly. Surely I must've read that piece of paper wrong. Bending over a little to get a better look, though, I could plainly see that I'd made no mistake. The scrap of paper in Kimberly's hand was a piece torn from the cover of the *Redbook* on the floor beside her, all right. And, without a doubt, the only letters on that torn piece of paper were *E* and *D*. *ED*.

Another shiver went down my back.

I turned slowly to stare at my ex-husband.

At that moment, however, Ed was not looking at me. He'd followed my gaze, and he was also leaning forward a little, hands on his knees, peering at the scrap in Kimberly's hand. "Why," he said, "what's that she's got in her—"

I could tell the exact moment Ed realized what it was and what it said. That was when his voice stopped abruptly like a tap suddenly shut off. It was also when what little color that was still left in his face instantly drained away. "Oh, my God," Ed said. He turned and met my eyes.

I tried to just return his gaze and keep my face expressionless, but I guess I couldn't disguise what was going through my mind.

Ed's eyes widened. "Oh, now, wait a minute," he said, holding up his hand. "You can't think that *I*—"

Actually, I wasn't sure what to think. Unless I missed my guess, I'd say that what Kimberly now held in her hand was what was often referred to in mystery movies and detective novels as a "dying clue." It certainly looked as if Kimberly must've realized that she wasn't going to be around to convey this little message verbally. I swallowed again, not wanting to think even for a moment about what coming to that kind of conclusion must've been like. God. She'd only been twenty-seven.

Before Kimberly had lost consciousness, she'd evidently used what strength she had left to reach for the *Redbook*. From all appearances, she'd managed to tear off the part she wanted, and then she'd clutched the incriminating piece of paper until death had finally released her grip.

Her leaving this clue, in all honesty, seemed pretty gutsy. I'm not sure that if I were suddenly facing the prospect of imminent death, I'd have the presence of mind to try to leave some clue as to the identity of my killer. Not to be speaking ill of the recently deceased, but I might as well say it—I wouldn't have thought that Kimberly had it in her, either. Apparently, beneath that big-eyed blond facade, there had been a young woman of remarkable courage.

Of course, I would've been a lot more impressed except for one tiny detail. Kimberly's final courageous act did a pretty good job of implicating the man next to me—the man, I might add, to whom I'd once been married for eight entire years, and who continued to this day to be the father of my children. And who, not incidentally, was at that moment beginning to look as if he might explode as he got to his feet and turned to face me.

"You *cannot* possibly believe that I had anything to do with this."

I cut him off. "Now, Ed, I didn't say that—"

Apparently, I didn't have to say much at all. Ed didn't let me finish. "Oh, well, this is great." On the up side, Ed had gotten his color back. A crimson spot had appeared in the middle of each cheek. "This is just *great*," he said, running his hand through his sandy hair. "Somebody kills my fiancée, and right away my ex-wife starts thinking that *I*—"

I followed Ed's earlier lead and held up my hand. "Ed, listen to me, I'm not thinking anything." Okay, I was lying, I admit it. Because, believe me, I was thinking a lot. To begin with, forgive me if I'm being picky, but it seemed to me that Ed was not nearly as distraught as he ought to be. As he'd just pointed out himself, he *had* lost his fiancée, the woman he'd been counting on claiming as his beloved wife in a scant four weeks. So why wasn't he crying—or cursing—or *something*? I knew very well that men were supposed to be strong and all, but this was stoic beyond belief. Not to mention, this was also Ed. The man who, if I remembered correctly, became upset when a light bulb burned out.

"What I'm trying to tell you," I hurried on, "is that if you say that this is an accident, then it's an accident. No doubt about it. It's just that even *you* have to admit that your name being on that piece of paper could possibly give somebody the weird idea that—"

Ed interrupted me again. "Schuyler," he said, "I am telling you the truth; I only just got here, okay? Kimberly and I had a lunch date—and this is the way I found her. I only arrived a few minutes before you did. So, if Kimberly is holding a piece of paper with my name on it, somebody else put it there!"

I nodded, trying again to look as if I didn't question— even for a moment—what he was saying. The problem was, though, when some guy has lied to you so many times in the past that you've lost count, you actually begin to get the idea that he's a liar. Funniest thing.

And, as it happened, I not only believed that Ed was a liar, I also believed that Ed was very good at it. Judging from past experience, I knew for a fact that Ed could look you directly in the eye, speak with a voice that seemed to vibrate with heartfelt emotion, and then fabricate a story that could possibly be featured as a TV Movie of the Week.

I drew a long, shaky breath. And yet if Ed was lying this time, then what he was trying to cover up was something far worse than being unfaithful. If he was lying now, he'd actually taken the life of another human being. And if he'd taken one life, what would prevent him from taking another? Like, oh, say, *mine*, for instance?

I darted a glance in Ed's direction. Lord. Was I supposed to be afraid of *Ed*? The idea seemed preposterous. I knew Ed. I'd known him since I was a freshman in college. And up to now, I'd been pretty sure that I knew what he was capable of. He would—without a moment's hesitation—lie his head off to cover up an infidelity, but did it necessarily follow that he was capable of taking the life of another human being?

I suppose I really didn't want to believe that the father of my children could really be capable of murdering his fiancée. And yet there was something else I also knew about Ed. I believe I mentioned this something else a little earlier—the man did have a temper.

Over the course of our marriage I'd seen Ed totally lose it over things as trivial as stubbing his toe. Ed didn't confine his tantrums to trivialities, either. The time I'd made a tiny error in addition and ended up bouncing seven—count them, *seven*—checks in our joint account, I'd thought Ed would pop a vein before he'd finished yelling.

So, the question was, could Ed have gotten mad over something or another that Kimberly had done? Could he have lost control for one horrible moment? I couldn't help remembering Kimberly's last words to me over the phone. "I'm afraid—" Had she meant just that? Had she been afraid of *Ed*? She had said, "Ed's going to be mad—"

Ed was looking pretty angry right this minute. "Schuyler," he said, his tone clipped, "you have *got* to believe me. I did not do anything to Kimberly."

I gave him a quick little nod, as if to say, *I know you didn't*. But the truth was, I didn't know. True, Ed had never raised a hand to me. But then again, as I also mentioned earlier, I hadn't lived with the man for years. Had what had been a bad temper over a decade ago turned into something much, much worse over the years? I gave poor Kimberly another quick glance. She certainly wasn't going to be able to tell me the answer to that one.

And I certainly didn't want to continue to think about Ed's possible homicidal tendencies with Kimberly lying right there on the floor, in plain sight. Not to mention, Ed himself at my elbow. I spun on my heel, turning in the direction of the kitchen where I knew from previous visits that the Hendersons had a wall phone.

I wasn't just running from the sight of poor Kimberly, mind you. There were people who really did need to be notified. "We've got to call 911," I sort of mumbled in Ed's direction. Before he could say anything, I stepped carefully around Kimberly and headed down the hall.

Ed followed me. "Wait, Schuyler," he said.

I didn't slow down.

"Before you start phoning anybody," Ed hurried on, "we've got to decide some things. I mean, you're a *lot* more familiar with situations like this than I am—"

My chin went up at that last little comment. It didn't take a genius to figure out what Ed was referring to. In the last year or so—through no fault of my own, I want to make clear—I've been involved in three separate homicide investigations. First, I was left over one hundred thousand dollars by a man I'd never met, but whose body had been found in Cherokee Park, not far from my home. Next, I'd stumbled across a dying man in one of the houses I was showing. And, finally, a few months ago a fellow real estate agent had been murdered, and I'd been unfortunate enough to discover the body.

Three deaths in just over a year, and now the count had gone up to four. Hey, nobody had to tell me that this seemed like an awful lot of homicides for just one woman. I believe, in fact, I was beginning to rival that poor Jessica Fletcher woman on *Murder, She Wrote*. And yet, what was I supposed to do? These things just happened, that's all. I certainly didn't appreciate Ed acting as if lately I'd turned into some kind of homicide groupie.

"—so," Ed finished, "I need you to tell me what I should do."

I gave him a look over my shoulder just as I was going through the archway that opened into the kitchen. "Well, let me see, speaking from my *vast* experience with this sort of thing, I'd say you should call the police." I headed straight for the phone, picked up the receiver, turned and held it out to Ed.

I don't know how I could've made myself any clearer. Ed, however, didn't seem to understand. He just continued to stand there, staring at me dumbly and making no effort whatsoever to take the receiver out of my hand.

"Ed," I said, "I'm telling you, you need to call the police. Now. This minute. *Immediately.*" I held the receiver out toward him again.

Ed just looked at me, unblinking, and crossed his arms. "I'm not calling anybody until you promise me something," he said.

At that moment the phone in my hand began making an intermittent beeping noise, indicating that it, like me, was tired of waiting. I turned back around, hung the thing up, and then turned to face Ed again. "Okay, what am I supposed to promise?"

"Before I get the police over here," Ed said, "I want

you to promise that you won't tell them anything about that piece torn off the magazine cover."

I guess maybe seeing poor Kimberly in the condition she was in had scrambled my brain. I just stared at Ed for a moment. "Ed, I don't think I'll have to *tell* them a thing. I think they're going to notice it right off without me having to—"

Ed didn't let me finish. "Oh, no, they're not," he said. He turned around and started back the way we'd come, heading back toward the foyer and Kimberly. Over *his* shoulder, Ed said almost casually, "The police can't see what isn't there."

I didn't hesitate. I took off right after him, caught up with Ed in a matter of seconds, and grabbed his arm. "Oh, no, you don't." The vehemence in my tone actually surprised me a little.

It must've surprised Ed, too. He stopped dead in his tracks. "Schuyler," he said, shrugging off my hand, "I'm going to get rid of that piece of paper." His tone implied that he was explaining the obvious to someone not terribly bright.

I shook my head. "You're not getting rid of anything," I said. "I mean it, Ed, if you take that piece of paper, I'll tell the police that it was there, anyway. So, you'll just be wasting your time, and you'll be getting yourself into a lot—"

Ed's reaction to what I was saying was a surprise, to say the least. He shrugged off my arm and turned to face me, eyes blazing. "You have *never* once backed me up on anything!" he said. He was now amply demonstrating the temper I mentioned earlier. "Every single time I have ever depended on you for anything, you've let me down! And now, *all* I'm asking—"

I just stared at him. Wait a minute. Correct me if I'm wrong, but I believe that *all* Ed was asking me to do was a little something called obstruction of justice. A little something that could actually put me behind bars, thank you very much. Not to mention, if he removed that paper before the police could test it for fingerprints, and Ed was

innocent, then we might never find out who really had
done this awful thing to poor Kimberly. "Ed—" I began.

He interrupted me *again*. This was getting irritating.
"Schuyler, listen to me," he said. "The very least you can
do is back me up. I am telling you that all this—" He indicated the awful scene out in the foyer with a wave of his
hand. "—*all* this is some kind of awful mistake. I—I
don't know why Kimberly would have my name in her
hand." He ran his hand through his hair again. "All that I
know is that it's a mistake. Or it's a setup. One or the
other. So, don't be stupid, Schuyler. Keep your mouth
shut and let me take care of everything."

I could've told the man that when you're trying to convince somebody to do something, it's probably ill-advised
to call them stupid. "Ed," I said, now starting to sound
angry myself, "you'd better leave that scrap of paper
where it is, understand? You'd better not touch it. Now,
I'm calling the police."

That said, I turned and went back into the kitchen,
heading for the phone again. Ed stood there for a split
second, and then once again he was at my heels. I had
every intention of dialing 911, but for a man whom I once
couldn't get to mow the lawn, Ed can really move when
he wants to. The moment I picked up the receiver, Ed was
at my side, grabbing it out of my hand. "I *said*, you can't
get the police over here—not until we fix everything," he
said, hanging up the phone. "Damn it, Schuyler, don't you
see what's going on here? Somebody is trying to make me
look guilty!"

What could I say? Somebody was doing a terrific job.

"I mean it, Schuyler, I'm being framed!" Ed went on.
"Kimberly wouldn't be trying to implicate *me*, because I
didn't do this. Understand? So somebody else must've put
that paper in Kimberly's hand! Just to make the police
think that she was naming me as the . . . as the . . ." Ed
couldn't seem to bring himself to say the word. He
cleared his throat and hurried on. "If you don't let me get
rid of that piece of garbage, Schuyler, you'll be helping
whoever it is who's trying to frame me!"

I gave him a flat stare. Ed was making it sound as if all

this was somehow my fault. Boy, did this ever feel familiar. In eight years of marriage, whenever anything went wrong, Ed had blamed me. When the paint started peeling on the back porch, it was because *I* had bought cheap paint. When the brakes went out on our car, it was because of the way *I* drove. Once he'd even blamed me for the weather. He'd actually said if *I* hadn't gotten the car washed, it wouldn't have rained.

Accusing me of helping a nameless someone frame him for murder, however, took the cake. I stared back at Ed, trying not to grind my teeth. "Ed," I told him, "if you're innocent, you don't have anything to worry about. You just need to tell your story to the police. That's all."

I wasn't completely sure that even I believed what I was saying. Almost immediately, however, I was sure that Ed didn't believe it. The words were barely out of my mouth when he turned on his heel once again and ran out of the kitchen.

I thought for a minute that he was going to make a quick stop in the foyer and grab the paper out of Kimberly's hand. But he went right past her without even a downward glance, and picking up speed, he headed straight for the front door.

Chapter 4

There was a time when, if I'd found out that Ed was in trouble with the police, I would've laughed out loud—and cheered the police on. Back then if you'd told me that one day I would actually be going out of my way to keep Ed from getting arrested, I would never have believed you.

Of course, the time I'm thinking of was right after Ed and I had gotten divorced. I'd just found out about all the charges he'd put on our joint MasterCard, buying gifts for his Girlfriends of the Month. I'd also just found out from a neighbor that the last time I'd taken the boys to visit their grandparents, and had been gone all day, Ed had taken advantage of the opportunity by inviting one of his little friends over. Judging from what lights in our house went out where, my neighbor was pretty sure Ed had slept with his little friend in our bed. And, as if that wasn't enough, I'd also just found out that Ed had told his parents that he was the one who'd wanted out—because *I* had a boyfriend on the side.

Oh, yes, back then, if I'd thought Ed was in trouble with the law, I'd have hoped that they called in Robo-Cop.

I guess I hadn't realized how much my attitude toward my ex-husband had changed over the years. When Ed took off for the front door, I actually surprised myself a little when I didn't hesitate for even a split second. No, in one quick motion, I made a wild grab for his arm.

And missed him entirely, wouldn't you know.

Even after I missed, though, I didn't give up. I immediately sprinted after him. "Ed! For God's sake," I shouted, "where the hell do you think you're going?"

Ed didn't take the time to give me an answer. He just put his head down and picked up speed. I tried to pick up speed, too, so at least I'd have a decent chance of making another grab for him. Unfortunately, I was severely hampered by a little thing called gravity. I was also severely hampered by having much shorter legs than Ed. Ed had already put quite a bit of distance between us by the time I got out on the front porch. In fact, once I was out there, it was clear that I wasn't going to be able to catch him. I wasn't even going to come close. Ed at that moment was only a few steps from his Lexus. "Ed," I yelled, "don't be an idiot!"

The words were barely out of my mouth when it occurred to me that it was probably as ill-advised for me to call Ed an idiot as it had been for him to call me stupid. Neither approach was exactly destined to win friends or influence people.

I decided a change in tactics was clearly in order. "Ed, please," I said, my tone coaxing, "come on back here now. Running away is not a good idea. It's only going to make you look that much more guilty!"

I thought I sounded positively conciliatory, considering what was going through my mind. Which was: Good Lord, hadn't the man watched even *one* made-for-TV movie? I mean, where had he been, for God's sake? I thought everybody out here in TV land knew that, if you ever got in trouble with law-enforcement types, the one thing you did not do was run. Running was practically the same as signing a confession. Hell, if Ed didn't believe me, he could ask the host of *America's Most Wanted*.

Ed now had the door of his Lexus open, and he was getting in.

"Ed!" I yelled. "You *moron*, stop this minute! Get right back here, you *idiot!*"

Okay, so I lost it for a second there and completely forgot that calling somebody names is not exactly a sure-fire persuasive technique. Proving this point, Ed had to have heard me, but he certainly didn't act like it. He didn't even glance in my direction.

"Ed!" I yelled again. *"Edward Daniel Ridgway!"*

Without even thinking, I'd slipped back into an old pattern. Back when we were married, and I'd wanted to make sure I had his attention, I'd always called him by all three of his names. "Ed, I mean it, you had better not leave me here all by myself! You had better not!"

Oh, my, yes, that put the fear of God into him, all right. Ed was obviously terrified that I might get mad at him. Uh-huh. Sure. Hell, if he wasn't careful, I might even *divorce* him.

Ed still hadn't so much as given me a glance. He was too busy sliding behind the wheel, slamming the door shut on the driver's side, and starting up the Lexus. A second later, he was careening down the street, tires squealing all the way.

Right after he took off on the wet pavement, Ed fishtailed for a wild moment. I was sure that he had lost control and was going to wrap the front end of Ed'$ Toy around a streetlamp, but he righted the car in a heartbeat. Ed then sailed down Willow Avenue, rounded the corner with another ear-piercing squeal of tires, and kept on going.

While I, of course, just watched helplessly, standing out there on the Henderson front porch. When Ed was completely out of sight, I sighed and headed back inside, intending now to make the phone call myself that I'd told Ed to make earlier.

I should've known that Ed would just take off. I believe I've already mentioned how world-renowned the man is for his bravery. I mean, Ed couldn't even ask me face-to-face to help him house hunt. So why on earth would I think that he'd stay around to face the police?

As a matter of fact, as I recalled, it had been only a little over a year ago that Ed had amply demonstrated his amazing strength under pressure. It had been around September, if I remembered correctly, when Ed had discovered that one of the women he'd been dating for several months had neglected to mention a certain tiny, insignificant detail—that she was married. I'd heard the whole sordid tale from Nathan, who—as a carrier of sensational news—could give the *National Enquirer* a run for its money. According to Nathan, Ed had found out his lady friend had a husband when the said lady friend's husband stormed into the front office of Ed's insurance business and broke the news. At the top of his lungs. While the guy was in a breaking mood, he'd also broken one of the panes in Ed's front door, and threatened to do the same to Ed's neck.

Ed—referred to by Nathan from that point forward as Captain Courageous—had responded predictably. Ed had tippy-toed out the back door. Ed had also seen fit to take an immediate two-week vacation—out of state.

Oh, my, yes. Ed doing this latest fast fade certainly should not have been a surprise. What bothered me most about it, in fact, was that in the past, when Ed had refused to face repercussions, Ed really had been guilty. He really *had* been dating the married lady friend that Nathan had gleefully told me about. So did that mean since Ed was running *now*, he really was guilty this time, too?

I had just stepped across the threshold of the Henderson house as all this was going through my mind, and now I paused just inside the front door, trying not to think the unthinkable. Could Ed really be a murderer? It was hard to believe that such a thing could be possible. I mean, my God, if I'd seriously thought that Ed could really kill somebody, I most certainly would not have stood there, right in front of him, and told him to his face that I intended to tell the police about the paper in Kimberly's hand—whether he took it or not. Lord, if Ed had killed Kimberly, I'd been almost inviting him to kill me, too, in order to shut my mouth for good.

This last, of course, brought up another question. Since I was still alive to tell the tale, so to speak, did that mean that Ed must be innocent?

My head was beginning to hurt. I'd started moving again, but very slowly, as all these things chased themselves through my mind. I was now in the middle of the foyer, getting ready to step around poor Kimberly. I was careful to avert my eyes as I went past her. I certainly didn't need to refresh my memory. In fact, I'd say the way Kimberly currently looked was pretty much burned into my brain. It wasn't *remembering* that was going to be difficult. It was forgetting.

Once past Kimberly, I quickened my pace, hurrying down the hall to the kitchen. There, I made a beeline for the wall phone and dialed 911. I told the woman who answered what had happened, and then I stayed on the line until the 911 woman confirmed that someone was indeed on their way.

After I hung up, I started to go back out to the front porch to wait for the police. I certainly didn't want to hang around inside the house with only Kimberly for company. I'd only taken a few steps, heading toward the front door, though, when I came to an abrupt halt, did an about-face, and headed right back to the phone in the kitchen.

There was no telling how long I was going to be tied up here. So, what do you know, there might actually be a faint silver lining in this otherwise dark cloud. My goodness, it looked as if I wouldn't be able to meet Barbara's plane with Matthias after all. What a shame. How terrible. Say it wasn't so.

I did feel a little guilty at the quick surge of relief that washed over me at almost the exact second that this particular silver lining popped into my mind. After all, silver lining or no, Kimberly did continue to be dead. And yet, here I was, actually feeling a little glad that I got to put off meeting Matthias's ex for a little while longer. How petty and insensitive could I be?

Apparently, monumentally petty and extremely insensitive. I found myself suppressing a little smile as I dialed Matthias's apartment.

I had no intention of telling Matthias why I was going to be tied up. For one thing, I didn't want to get into it over the phone. For another, I was afraid that Matthias might echo what Ed had said earlier. That's right, Matthias might mention how lately I seemed to be the realtor equivalent of Typhoid Mary. If Matthias said such a thing, with me being in the terrific mood I was now in, it might be the second time today I called somebody a moron.

Better not risk it.

I knew, of course, that I'd have to tell Matthias all about this sooner or later. The whole mess was going to be in tomorrow's paper, without a doubt. But for the moment it seemed best just to explain to Matthias that I was tied up with a client. Which was the absolute truth. Kimberly *was* a client of mine. She'd signed a contract hiring me, and she certainly hadn't fired me since she'd signed it. Nor did it seem at all likely that she was going to.

I gripped the telephone receiver a little tighter. The phone on the other end of the line rang three more times before it was finally picked up. By that time I'd almost convinced myself that I was doing Matthias a favor by not telling him everything right away. The poor man had enough on his mind, what with his ex-wife about to visit and all.

"Hello?"

This was definitely not Matthias. In fact, it was a throaty female voice that sounded a lot like Kathleen Turner. Up until I heard that voice, I was pretty sure that I'd dialed correctly, but maybe what had happened to poor Kimberly had rattled me even more than I thought. "I'm sorry," I said, "I think I've gotten a wrong—"

The throaty voice interrupted me. "Who were you calling?"

"Matthias Cross," I said, "but I guess I—"

The throaty voice interrupted me again. "This is the Cross residence. May I help you? I'm Barbara Cross."

My mouth suddenly felt as if I'd swallowed sand. What was Barbara doing at Matthias's apartment? Answering *his* phone? Not to mention, wasn't she here a little early? And, while I was asking questions, what was she doing still using the Cross name? Had Barbara gone back to using the name she'd had before her most recent marriage? Apparently she had. A thing like this could actually give you the idea that old Barbara here was trying to forget that the entire Phil episode had ever happened. It sort of made you wonder if she might want to encourage Matthias to forget it, too.

I cleared my throat. "Is Matthias in?" I said. "This is Schuyler Ridgway."

"Oh, *Schuyler*," Barbara said, "it's you." Her throaty voice now gushed warmth. "Matthias has told me *so* much about you, why, I feel as if you and I are friends already."

Uh-huh. Sure. She and I were buddies, all right. Lord knows, we had a lot in common. I forced myself to sound considerably more amiable than I felt. "Matthias has told me a lot about you, too," I said. Like, for example, he told me that you were coming in at three this afternoon. "I was looking forward to meeting you at the airport today," I added.

Barbara laughed, as if I'd said something terribly funny. "Oh, well, you know how it is."

No, I thought, how was it?

Barbara hurried on. "I decided I just couldn't wait a minute longer to begin my little visit." Her voice dropped, as if she were confiding a personal secret. "I was really looking forward to seeing everybody again."

I didn't say a word.

Barbara didn't seem to notice. "So I took an earlier flight. Then, when I got here, I just phoned my husband to pick me up." She stopped here, and then laughed again. A little tinkling sound, like bells. "Oh, I mean my *ex*-husband, of course," Barbara added.

Of course. My head was starting to throb. "May I please speak to Matthias?" I said.

Too late, I realized I sounded a bit abrupt. Barbara, on the other hand, sounded amused. "Well, now, Schuyler, that's going to be a bit difficult. You see, that sweet man simply insisted on running out to the store to pick us up some wine."

Wine? Matthias was out getting them some *wine*? What on earth was he doing, getting them wine? There was a moment of silence during which I was sure that old Barbara was mentally daring me to say something, *anything*, about this little wine excursion. Instead, I took a deep breath and changed the subject. "Oh. Well, I'm sorry I missed him," I said, my tone now unnaturally cheery.

"Would you mind telling Matthias that I'll call him later?"

"Oh, of course, Schuyler," Barbara said, sounding amused again. "I'd be glad to."

"Thanks so much," I said.

I had every intention of hanging up right that second, but before I could, Barbara went on. "It's such a shame that you missed Matthias." She still sounded amused. "But, well, you know Matthias when he gets an idea in his head. There's no stopping him. He's such a doll, he simply *insisted* on going out and getting wine for me. Why, he even remembered my favorite—Cabernet Sauvignon. You know, I'd forgotten what a big old sweetheart he can be."

I was now trying not to grit my teeth. Evidently, Barbara's opinion of the big old sweetheart had improved by leaps and bounds during her marriage to the Phil person. "Matthias is a doll, all right," I said, trying to keep my tone even. "Now, if you'll let Matthias know that I—"

"Of course, I should've expected it," Barbara said. "I mean, I guess you've noticed it, too, haven't you?"

She'd lost me. "Noticed what?"

Barbara went from an amused tone to outright laughter. Evidently, there was very little that didn't crack this woman up. "Why, surely you've noticed how thoughtful Matthias is!" she said. "He is *such* a baby doll!"

The knuckles of my hand were now turning white, I was gripping the phone so tightly. As much as I would've loved pointing out to her that it was a wee bit inappropriate to refer to a grown man as a "baby doll," it did occur to me that there continued to be a dead person out in the foyer. Only a few steps away. And the police were going to show up any second now. I needed to get off this damn phone.

"Matthias is thoughtful, all right," I said through clenched teeth. "Now, if you'll let him know that I—"

Once again Barbara interrupted me. "You know, I am *so* looking forward to meeting you, Schuyler. I do hope we get to be good friends."

Okay, so call me standoffish, but all I could think of

was: Oh, yeah, *that's* likely. Maybe we could form a Matthias Cross fan club.

"I mean," Barbara went on, "any friend of Matthias's is a friend of mine."

I couldn't be sure, but I thought that Barbara put a little extra emphasis on the word *friend*. Was I getting paranoid here, or was this woman trying to let me know in her own syrupy-sweet way that all I'd ever be was one of Matthias's friends? Or could it be that having a dead person in the vicinity put a distinctly negative spin on everything I was hearing? "Yes," I said, "well—" I knew I should probably say something more, but I couldn't think of anything. I decided to go with the tried and true. "—well, it was nice talking to—"

Unbelievably, Barbara interrupted me *again*. Would this woman never let me off the phone? "Oh, Schuyler, by the way—"

I took a deep breath. The way things were going, Kimberly's funeral would be over by the time Barbara let me hang up.

"What?"

I guess I must've let a tiny bit of my impatience slip into my voice, because Barbara didn't sound amused anymore. She sounded startled. "Well, *all* I wanted to know was if you'd be coming to dinner at Mother Cross's tomorrow night."

I blinked. "Dinner?"

Matthias hadn't said a word about dinner at his mother's. Of course, there could be a perfectly good explanation. Such as, oh, off the top of my head, I'd say that it could possibly have something to do with the way Harriet— that is, Mother Cross, to call her what Barbara apparently did—had made it abundantly clear that she hated the sight of me.

Yes, if I were to hazard a guess, I'd say this might possibly be the reason I had not yet received an invitation. Harriet hated me for what some might consider a pretty good reason—because she continued to believe to this day that I really had murdered Ephraim Benjamin Cross, her husband and Matthias's father.

Can you believe that? At this very moment there was an actual person behind bars who'd confessed to the crime. An actual person who I myself had helped put behind those very bars, for God's sake. And yet, Mother Cross still clung to the belief that *I* was the guilty one. She'd made up her mind, and she was *not* going to let little things like facts make her change it.

Barbara had now gone from startled to flustered on the phone. "Oh, my, I do hope I haven't spoken out of turn. Matthias *has* invited you, hasn't he?"

I suspected that Barbara had a pretty good idea that Matthias had not said a word to me about the dinner, but I didn't want to give Barbara the satisfaction of admitting it. On the other hand, I couldn't exactly tell her that I was going to attend an event to which I had not been invited, either. "I've told Matthias that I'm not sure I'll be able to make it," I said.

"Oh, that's too bad," Barbara said. She did not sound the least bit distraught. If anything, she sounded remarkably cheery. "But I'm sure that we'll see each other before I go back to Boston. I intend to have a nice long visit down here, so—"

I was halfway tempted to interrupt *her* this time. I wanted badly to ask her how she defined "a nice long visit." Specifically, that is. As in, how many days does it take to make a nice long visit? Unfortunately, at that moment the doorbell sounded.

"I've got to go," I said hurriedly. "Please tell Matthias that I—"

Barbara must've been determined never to let me finish that sentence. "Oh, I certainly will," she said, cutting me off. Her throaty voice was sounding amused again. "Good-bye Schuyler."

There was a click, and the dial tone sounded in my ear.

I stood there, motionless for a moment. Barbara's voice had undergone a not-so-subtle change as she'd said those last two words. If I wasn't mistaken, Matthias's ex-wife had told me good-bye with undisguised malice.

I didn't have any time to think about it, though. The doorbell sounded again. This time whoever was ringing it must've been leaning on the thing. The doorbell rang again and again and again.

I hung up the phone and hurried toward the front door.

I already had a good idea, of course, exactly who I'd find standing out there on the Henderson front porch. As I mentioned earlier, I have had the misfortune of being involved in the investigations of three homicides in the last year or so. Wouldn't you know it, each of those cases was investigated by the same two policemen—Detectives Murray Reed and Tony Constello.

The salt-and-pepper cops.

At least that's what I call them. Behind their backs, of course, like the proper Southern lady I was brought up to be. Detective Murray Reed is short and muscular with pale blue eyes, pale skin, and blond hair so light it looks white. Detective Tony Constello, on the other hand, is tall and thin with dark brown eyes, a thick mustache, swarthy skin, and brown hair so dark it looks black. Reed always seems to wear light-colored suits, and Constello always seems to wear dark-colored ones. When these two guys stand side by side, you can't help but think of salt-and-pepper shakers.

Before I opened the front door, I took a quick peek through the peephole.

Sure enough, it was Murray Salt and Tony Pepper.

If I hadn't just had a little chat with Matthias's ex, seeing these two again would probably have made my stomach feel as if I'd just struck a match and swallowed it. Now, though, after the truly entertaining conversation I'd just had with Barbara, the prospect of talking with Reed and Constello for a few minutes seemed like a cake walk.

I held the door open wide. "Detectives," I said. "Thank you for getting here so fast."

Lord. I actually sounded sincere. I was getting good at this.

Chapter 5

Thanking the detectives for coming was, I quickly found out, a waste of breath. In fact, judging from the way Reed and Constello behaved right after I thanked them, I'd say good manners were not a high priority with these two.

It was starting to sprinkle again—what my Kentucky kinfolk have always called spitting rain—but Reed and Constello must've enjoyed being spat upon. Or maybe they were accustomed to it—a possibility that would not surprise me. The detectives made no move to come inside. Instead, they just kept standing out there on the Hendersons' front porch, staring at me, their hair getting damper and their eyes getting smaller by the moment. By the time Reed finally uttered a sound, his eyes were pale blue slits.

"You." Can you believe that was all Reed said? Just that one word. After the big wait, it was a definite let-down. Reed paused right after he said it, too, for another long moment. I had a pretty good idea, of course, why Reed paused. He was leaving space for a word that he didn't say out loud, but that I believe all three of us mentally added: *Again.*

I may have been a bit oversensitive—running into the police on a regular basis can do that to me. However, it did seem to me that both Reed and Constello looked even less pleased to see me than I was to see them. A thing like this could definitely hurt the old ego.

"I can't believe it." Constello found his voice right after Reed had found his. "I just can't believe it." With his swarthy skin and dark hair, Constello may have looked like an extra from a *Godfather* movie, but he sounded like somebody who'd grown up in the hills of eastern Kentucky. He made *can't* sound as if it rhymed with *ain't*, and he pronounced *it* as if it started with an *h*. "Don't tell me you've gotten yourself involved in *another* one."

Constello didn't have to worry about my telling him anything like that. I was already shaking my head before he'd even finished his sentence. "I'm not involved in anything," I said. "All I did was call 911; that's the total extent of my—"

Reed interrupted me. He'd pulled a Bic pen and a small spiral notebook out of an inside coat pocket, and he pointed the Bic at me. "Are you not involved this time, ma'am, like you weren't involved *all* those other times?"

I caught my breath. Obviously, I'd been mispronouncing Reed's name ever since the first day I'd met him. It should've been *Rude*.

I folded my arms across my chest and glared at him. Reed knew very well that during "*all* those other times"— as he so eloquently put it—I'd actually been of some help in bringing the guilty parties to justice. Which, correct me if I'm wrong, was a significant part of his and Detective Constello's job description. Not mine. So, shouldn't Reed be treating me with—at the very least—a grudging respect? Instead of acting as if I were Bonnie in search of Clyde?

"Look," I said, and yes, I'll be honest, I did sound testy. "I don't want to be here. This is not my idea of a good time. But I thought I really ought to let you all know about this—this *situation*." I'd been standing in the middle of the doorway, blocking Reed's and Constello's view of the foyer, but now I stepped to one side. So that the salt-and-pepper shakers could get a good look at the specific situation I was referring to. The overhead light in the foyer wasn't on, so it was pretty dark over where Kimberly was, but once I was out of the way, Reed and Constello didn't seem to have any trouble at all spotting her.

One thing about it. If you show a dead person to the police, they get pretty excited. Reed and Constello actually had a little footrace as they hurried over to poor Kimberly. From where I was standing, the race looked to me like a dead heat. No pun intended.

For my part, I left the racing to the salt-and-pepper shakers. I held my ground, letting Reed and Constello run right past me, and then I busied myself fastening the screen door and making sure the front door was shut tight against the drizzle outside. That done, I turned and made my way over to where the salt-and-pepper shakers were now looking Kimberly over. If I could've moved any slower, I would have. Lord knows, I'd already seen far more than I ever wanted to.

Constello had his own Bic and spiral notebook out by the time I got over there. He and Reed had stopped looking at Kimberly, and they were at that moment looking at the bloodied flashlight lying on the stairs.

"Looks like she never even saw it coming," Constello said.

Reed nodded agreement. Apparently, Reed and Constello's footrace had turned into a scribbling race. At my approach, neither detective even glanced in my direction. Reed's eyes, in fact, were still fixed on his notebook when he said, "Ma'am? Do you know this woman?"

Reed was now doing a fair-to-middling imitation of Joe Friday, the detective that Jack Webb played in the old classic fifties TV show *Dragnet*. I'd been expecting it. Reed has done Joe Friday every single time I've run into him. He starts speaking in short staccato bursts, he says everything in a flat, emotionless monotone, and he gets a lot of use out of the word *ma'am*.

The first time Reed did Joe Friday, I'd been sure that he had to be joking. Surely no cop would sound like that on purpose. Not unless he was going for laughs. Now, of course, I knew better. To my knowledge, in the time that I've known him, Reed had never done anything to indicate that he possesses even a semblance of a sense of humor. So I knew that *joking* would never be on Reed's list of Things to Do Today. "Ma'am?" Reed prodded.

I swallowed, deliberately turning my eyes away from poor Kimberly. Instead, I found myself staring at an electrical outlet on the opposite wall. "Her name is Kimberly Metcalf," I said. "She phoned me to meet her here. She was a client of mine."

Constello looked up from his notebook just long enough to give a low whistle. "*Another* client?"

I gave Constello a sharp look. Maybe Reed wasn't the only rude one here.

Constello was continuing to write in his notebook. "Lordy, mercy, how many is this now?"

I caught my breath again. Constello made it sound as if I were *notching* something. I was not about to dignify his question with an answer.

Constello apparently didn't require one. He went right on. "Lands' sake, you have got to be just about the unluckiest woman I have ever run across."

The man actually said this with Kimberly lying at his feet. I decided it probably was not worth pointing out that, in the bad luck department, Kimberly had me beat hands down.

"I mean," Constello went on, "it seems like every five seconds you're discovering another body."

"I didn't discover this one." I hadn't meant to just blurt that out, but Constello was making me sound like some kind of ghoul who hung around morgues for kicks. I immediately regretted my big blurt, too, because it instantly got both Constello's and Reed's eyes off their notebooks and onto my face.

"If you didn't discover the body, ma'am," Reed said, running his hand through his white-blond hair, "who did?" His eyes were blue slits again.

I hated to answer that one. If I'd suspected earlier that Ed would've wanted me to lie to Kimberly, imagine how absolutely positive I was that Ed would want me to concoct a tall tale for the police. I swallowed, and then said as casually as I could, "Well, I believe that would be my ex-husband, Ed Ridgway. He was here when I got here. Kimberly was his fiancée."

As I mentioned Ed's name, I felt a quick rush of guilt. I mean, why didn't I just tie Ed up and hand him over to the salt-and-pepper shakers? My own sons' father. What's more, what if Ed had been right earlier? What if I really was helping somebody frame him?

"Did you say, *Ed* Ridgway?" Constello asked. Something had evidently caught his eye, because he was now moving a step closer to Kimberly. Squatting down, he peered at the scrap of paper in Kimberly's hand.

Uh-oh. I shifted my weight uneasily from one foot to the other.

"That's Ed, right? As in, capital letter *E* capital letter *D*, Ed?" Constello glanced over at Reed, saw that he had his partner's attention, and then pointed with his Bic pen at the scrap torn from the *Redbook* cover.

When Reed peered at the paper scrap, his eyes stopped looking like slits. In fact, they widened considerably. "Ma'am," he said, turning toward me, "where is Mr. Ridgway?"

I hated to answer that question even worse than the one earlier. I stood there, reminding myself that Ed had done some pretty terrible things to me in the past. After all, he *had* slept with another woman. In my own bed. And he hadn't even changed the sheets.

I cleared my throat. "To tell you the truth, I'm not exactly sure where Ed is right now. He was very upset." I decided it wasn't necessary to mention that Ed seemed to be more upset over my reluctance to get rid of a certain item than he was over what had happened to Kimberly. "Ed just got into his car, and—"

That was all I got out before Reed interrupted me. He was still talking in a monotone, but there was now an urgency in his voice that hadn't been there before. "Ma'am, what kind of car does Mr. Ridgway drive?"

I just stared back at the detective for a moment while another wave of guilt washed over me. I tried reminding myself again that Ed *had* been unfaithful to me—that he, no doubt, deserved what he got—but this time I didn't believe me. So Ed had run around on me. So what? It had been over fourteen years ago. It could very well be that the statute of limitations for the crime of infidelity had run out by now.

Not to mention, even if it were abundantly fair to pay

Ed back after all this time—a thing that I tended to doubt—I wasn't at all sure that the punishment fit the crime. Let me see now, how would that go? First, Ed sleeps with somebody in my bed. And then I put him in prison for the rest of his life. Uh-huh. Oh, my, yes. That would definitely be an eye for an eye. I suppressed a sigh, cleared my throat, and then, because I really couldn't see any way to avoid it, I sort of mumbled, "Ed drives a red Lexus."

Hey, it wasn't as if I were telling the shakers anything that they couldn't find out on their own. There was, I believe, such a thing as the Department of Motor Vehicles in Kentucky.

"Where's a phone?" Reed said. He must've been thrilling to the chase and all, because he seemed to have forgotten to say *ma'am*.

I directed him to the wall phone in the kitchen, and Reed disappeared down the hall. In no time at all, I could hear him out there. From what I could tell, he was putting out an all points bulletin on Ed, and he was calling the coroner to get over here and pronounce Kimberly what we all already knew she was.

I didn't get to hear all of what Reed said, mainly because even though I took several steps away from Kimberly, moving closer to the kitchen, Constello followed me. The moment I stopped moving, Constello started talking to me, his deep voice drowning everything else out. "Well, then," Constello drawled, scratching his mustache with his Bic, "that over there must be who your husband left you for, huh?" He jerked his head to indicate Kimberly. "That there's the other woman, I reckon."

I just looked at him. "You reckon wrong."

Constello sort of blinked when I said that. It occurred to me then that it was probably not all that great an idea to antagonize anybody carrying a handgun on his person. I softened my tone. "Ed and I have been divorced for almost fifteen years, Detective Constello," I went on. "That would've made Kimberly all of twelve when we split up."

Constello stopped blinking after that one. In fact, he

just stared at me for a long, long moment. I wasn't sure if he didn't quite get what I'd just told him, or if he was trying to make me uneasy. I took a deep breath and hurried on. "What I mean is, Kimberly could not possibly have been the other woman. The most she could've been back then was the other *girl*."

Constello still stared at me.

"Ed has had a lot of girlfriends since we were divorced," I added. The word *legions* came to mind, but I decided I'd probably already said too much.

Constello's dark eyes seemed to be shrinking. "Had your ex ever actually set a wedding date with any of these other girlfriends of his? I mean, before this one?"

I swallowed once before I answered, not sure what he was getting at. "Well, no," I said, "now that you mention it. Ed *has* been engaged before this, of course." Hell, Ed's ex-fiancées could get together and form a support group. "But I guess Kimberly was the first one Ed ever made definite plans to marry."

Constello nodded, his tiny dark eyes solemn. "Well, then," he said.

It was my turn to stare at him. *Well, then?* What did that mean? Unfortunately, Constello explained. "You know," he drawled, scratching at his mustache again, "you could've torn that magazine cover yourself." The man actually said this as casually as if he were suggesting that I might've seen a certain movie. "You could've torn it after your ex had already left. You could've conked that little lady with the flashlight, come downstairs, made sure she was really dead, torn out those letters, put the paper in her hand, and then you could've called us."

I rolled my eyes. Oh, for God's sake. Would these guys never stop trying to pin a murder on me? Did I look like the quintessential criminal type, or what? "Detective, why on earth would I do such a thing? Ed and I are divorced. He is perfectly free to marry anybody he wants."

Constello shrugged. "This one, though, sure is awful young, isn't she?"

She *was*. The thought made my throat tighten up.

"How much younger than you do you figure this little

lady is?" Constello went on, once again in that I'm-just-making-casual-conversation tone.

I frowned at him. "I don't have to *figure*. I know she was fourteen years younger than me. What's that got to do with anything?"

Constello scratched his mustache with his Bic yet again. The way he kept doing that made you wonder if maybe he had little creatures living in there. "Well, it appears to me," he drawled, "it must've made you real mad, your ex getting ready to marry somebody so much younger than you and all."

I was glaring at him by the time he finished. He was making me sound like Methuselah. Another few minutes and he'd have me in a nursing home. "Look," I said, "I couldn't care less whom Ed was marrying, okay?" I started to add that, in my opinion, the only kind of woman who *would* marry Ed would necessarily have to be somebody extremely young. Otherwise, the bride-to-be might actually notice that Ed obviously adored the sound of his own voice, and that he appeared to be incapable of passing a mirror without checking his hair. The blushing bride might also begin to wonder if Ed was so terribly sure about all his opinions—as he endlessly insisted that he was—why, then, did he have to convince everybody within a five-mile radius that he, and he alone, was right?

Not to mention, the young have real staying power. If you were in your twenties, Ed might not even start to grate on your nerves for another ten years or so. And, finally, if you were just starting out, you might not even mind being lectured every five minutes. Mainly because if you were young and inexperienced, you might actually be persuaded for a little while that Ed really did know more than you did.

Hey, it could happen.

Believe it or not, all this flashed through my mind as I stood there next to Constello. I decided not to say any of it, though. Mostly because I was afraid that the only thing Constello would hear was that I was terribly hostile toward Ed, and little else. If Constello started believing that I was hostile toward Ed, he would probably have no trouble at all believing that I was capable of doing this terrible thing to Kimberly—and trying to get Ed blamed for it.

I confined myself instead to just saying, "Look, I have just spent the last two entire weeks house hunting with Ed and Kimberly. Do you think I'd have done that if I had a problem with the two of them getting married?"

Constello scratched his infestation again. "You might have if you'd been planning all along on killing her and implicating him. Helping them house hunt would be a real good cover."

Like I said earlier: Oh, for God's sake. I wasn't sure if Constello was serious, or if he was just trying to get me so worried about whether or not I myself was a suspect that I'd throw Ed under the bus without thinking twice. I guessed it was probably no accident that the very next thing Constello asked me was if Kimberly had ever said anything about Ed and her having arguments. "You know," Constello drawled, "did she ever mention being afraid? Anything like that?"

If Constello had been trying to scare me, it must've worked. I didn't even hesitate. Suddenly terribly anxious to divert attention away from myself as a possible suspect, I found myself repeating word for word what Kimberly had told me over the phone. In fact, I blurted it out almost before I realized what I was doing.

"Miss Metcalf told you that your ex-husband was going to be mad at her?" Constello said. Reed was just returning after making his phone calls, and his slit eyes got rounded again at that one. He immediately started scribbling away in his little notebook.

I shook my head. "No," I said, "Kimberly just mentioned that Ed was going to be mad. She didn't say about what. She also didn't say *who* he was going to be mad at." I was trying to make it clear that Kimberly hadn't said that Ed would be angry with her, but this must've been a nuance that the salt-and-pepper shakers didn't pick up on.

Reed stopped scribbling just long enough to point his Bic at me. "She did tell you that she was afraid of him, though. And for you to come right away?"

I shook my head again. These guys were not listening. "No, she said she was afraid, but she didn't say of what."

"But just before that, ma'am, didn't you say that the victim had told you that Ed Ridgway was going to be mad?"

I swallowed once before I answered. "Well," I said, "yes, I suppose I did say that."

Reed and Constello exchanged a look. These guys are always doing this around me. I am never quite sure what these dumb looks mean, but I always know that whatever they mean, it isn't good.

I tried again. "Kimberly didn't finish her sentence. She started to say that she was afraid of something, but then the phone went dead before she could finish."

My mouth went dry. Good Lord. That must've been when her killer had struck her with the flashlight.

And I'd been on the phone with her.

"Ma'am, you said the phone went dead?"

My mouth had gotten so dry, all I could do was nod.

Reed exchanged another maddening look with Constello, and then both of them began looking around the foyer. Right after that Constello headed up the stairs. At close to the top step, he said, "Yep, it's here, all right. A cordless. She must've dropped it when she fell."

Reed shrugged. "To disconnect it, all the killer had to do was unplug the base unit."

I stared at him. That's why the phone still rang when I'd called back. It hadn't been pulled out of the wall or anything. It had just been unplugged. As I recalled, the Hendersons had another extension upstairs in their bedroom, so that phone must've continued to ring even with this one out of commission.

Constello came back downstairs, nodding. "You know," he drawled, staring unrelentingly at me, "I'd bet, as a real estate agent showing this here house, you'd know exactly where the base unit of that cordless was kept."

He made it sound as if I were privy to top-secret information. "It's on a little table in the upstairs hall," I said. "Out in plain sight. *Anybody* could find it."

Constello opened his mouth to say something, but he didn't get the chance. The front door suddenly swung open, and we all turned to see who was standing there, framed in the doorway.

It was Adrienne and Frank Henderson.

"Oh, my God," Frank said. His eyes traveled to my face, then over to the salt-and-pepper shakers, and finally ended up on poor Kimberly. As he stared at her, Frank's face went so white, his mouth looked like a gash.

Adrienne, I must say, took the whole thing a lot better than Frank. She, too, took one look at all of us and then zeroed in on Kimberly. After that, though, she turned back to her husband. "See? *See?*" she said. "I told you! *I told you!*"

You could tell that little pronouncement caught Reed's and Constello's attention. Both detectives immediately began to move toward Adrienne. I, on the other hand, just stood where I was and waited. For the shakers, of course, to begin insisting that Adrienne tell *them*, too.

Chapter 6

I didn't have to wait long for Reed and Constello to begin with Adrienne. Detective Constello had no more than asked the Hendersons their names and found out that the Hendersons owned the house that we were all standing in—a thing he would, no doubt, refer to from this point forward as *the crime scene*—when Reed started in. "Ma'am," he said, taking a step closer to Adrienne, "what did you mean when you said, 'I told you so'?"

Adrienne was wearing one of her teeny-bopper outfits—a stretch denim skirt, a navy blue sweater tight enough to significantly reduce circulation, and matching navy blue opaque hose. Her shoes were those big clunky-heeled things that were supposed to be the height of fashion, and yet have always looked to me like army boots. Adrienne shifted her weight to her left army boot, and said, "Well, I told Frank that something awful was going to happen, that's what. I could see it coming. Clear as day. None of this is a surprise to me. *None* whatsoever."

As Adrienne spoke, I couldn't help staring at her. From the neck down she looked as if she were in her early twenties. From the neck up, however, she looked every bit the forty-something matron she really was. It was a little disconcerting. Looking at her, you got the feeling that maybe when she was getting ready this morning she'd made a mistake and put on the wrong head.

Standing next to her husband in his severely tailored gray flannel suit, Adrienne could easily have been mistaken for his daughter—if, of course, you viewed the couple from a distance. Now Adrienne gave her shoulder-length blond hair a little pat as she turned to her husband. "Tell them, Frank," Adrienne said. "Tell them what I told you. About how something awful was going to happen."

Frank seemed to realize about a beat late that every-body had turned to look at him. His eyes sort of flickered, and for a second he had the same expression on his face that I remembered seeing in high school when friends of mine were suddenly called on in class—and they hadn't done the homework. Frank cleared his throat before he spoke. "Uh, yes, that is what Adrienne said, all right." Frank's face was still very pale. "Adrienne, uh, said that something bad was going to, uh, happen."

I just looked at him. Thank you, Frank, for that in-depth analysis.

Even the salt-and-pepper shakers looked a little disap-pointed. Until Adrienne turned to me and patted my arm. "You know, Schuyler, I really am terribly sorry," she said. "I do hate to do this to you."

That little comment reached out and grabbed the shakers' attention. Both detectives suddenly looked con-siderably more alert as they turned to stare at me.

I, on the other hand, turned to stare at Adrienne. I immediately voiced the question that, I believe, was now on the lips of both detectives. "What do you mean?"

"I mean, I'm sorry, that's what I mean." Adrienne lifted her chin and brushed a stray blond curl away from her face. "I really am. But I do have to tell the truth."

I was still not getting it. The implication here seemed to be that I didn't want Adrienne to tell the truth. And yet, why wouldn't I?

Not to mention, what the hell was she doing, suggesting in front of two policemen that I wanted her to lie? I mean, thank you so much, Adrienne, but I can get into enough trouble with these two without any help from you. As if to illustrate my point, Reed and Constello at that moment had taken a break from staring at me and were once again exchanging one of their meaningful looks. Once again, the meaning of this look was beyond me. I gave Adrienne a weak smile. "Oh. Well. Of course you've got to be honest," I said. I tried to sound as if this was something that went without saying. A self-evident truth.

Adrienne shrugged her shoulders. "I mean, I know Ed's your husband—"

I had to interrupt. "Ex-husband," I put in. "He's my *ex-*husband."

I know. I know. I was the rat deserting the sinking ship. However, I would like to point out that I'd deserted this particular ship a long time ago. What's more, I'd been reminding people long before this that Ed and I were no longer a couple. Every once in a while, particularly after he'd had a little too much to drink, I'd even reminded Ed.

Adrienne shrugged again. "Whatever," she said, waving one hand in the air carelessly. "You two still seem to be friends—"

I wasn't sure how she'd come to this conclusion. I wasn't even sure I myself would call Ed a friend. Of course, I knew that there were those who felt that if you and your ex could stay in the same room with each other for more than five minutes without reaching for weapons, then you two had to be friends. Adrienne must've been one of these people. Evidently, she'd decided that Ed and I must be buddies or else I wouldn't have been showing this house to him and his fiancée. "—and I know that Ed Ridgway is your boys' father and all," Adrienne went on. I suppose I'd mentioned this sometime or another, in passing. "But, Schuyler, you've got to understand," Adrienne hurried on, "under the circumstances, I cannot keep quiet—"

I just looked at her. So, all right already, don't keep quiet. Who was asking you to? A quick sideways glance at the salt-and-pepper shakers seemed to suggest an answer to this last. Both Reed and Constello were looking directly at me again.

I immediately looked back over at Adrienne.

So did Reed. "So what is it exactly that you wanted to tell us, ma'am?" he asked. Joe Friday sounded impatient.

Adrienne put a hand on one hip and took a deep breath. "Well, Ed Ridgway is an asshole. That's what."

I blinked. Did Adrienne think this was a news flash? Tell me something I didn't already know.

Adrienne was now nodding her head. For emphasis, I suppose. "He's the biggest know-it-all in the entire world."

I swallowed uneasily. I might've described Ed that way myself. Only I don't think I would've said the entire world. Western hemisphere, maybe.

Adrienne was warming to her subject. "And it was so pathetically obvious why he was marrying that little girl."

Little girl? I recalled telling Constello that Kimberly would've been twelve when we'd gotten divorced. To hear Adrienne talk, you'd have thought Ed really had been carrying on with Kimberly back then.

"Ma'am?" Reed asked. "What was obvious?"

Adrienne shrugged her small shoulders. "Well, I even hate to say it, it's such a cliché. But, you know, the reason something gets to be a cliché is because it happens to be true a lot of the time."

"Yes, ma'am." Joe Friday sounded as if he had no idea where this was going, but he wished that Adrienne would pick up speed getting there.

I glanced over at Frank. He, on the other hand, looked as if he knew precisely where his wife was headed. He knew, and he was not the least bit pleased about it.

Adrienne twisted a blond curl around one finger. "I mean, everybody knows that some men get to be forty or so and, well, they just go crazy. They start worrying about getting old. I mean, my God, you hear the same sad story on all the daytime talk shows over and over again. It's like some idiotic rerun."

"Yes, ma'am." Reed wasn't looking so pleased now himself. In fact, he looked as if he'd opened a Pandora's Box, and it was now too late to get it shut again. He was going to have to just stand there while everything flew out.

"So off these assholes go," Adrienne said, "dumping their wives—the women who've stood by them during all the lean years—and they go off and get themselves a trophy wife. That was obviously what was happening ᵛwith Ed Ridgway. If he only knew how ridiculous he looked!"

There was an odd silence during which I suspected the detectives were thinking exactly what I was. Was she talking about Ed now? Or her own husband, Frank?

I gave Frank a quick glance to see how he was taking all this. He was staring at the floor.

Even Adrienne seemed to realize that what she'd just said could apply to her husband, too, because she sort of coughed, and then patting at her hair again, she said, "Ed Ridgway picked out a sweet young thing he could bully. That's what he did." She glanced over at me. "And, Schuyler, you're better off without him."

I just looked at her. Once again, she was telling me something I already knew.

"He treated women like dirt. And he had an awful temper." As Adrienne said this last, she lifted her chin and gave me a pointed look. It was a look that practically dared me to argue with her.

This is one of the things I used to hate about being married. People seemed to think that you and your husband were the same person. Evidently, when they say *joined* in holy matrimony, they really mean it. After you're married, anything your husband does, you're held accountable for. Sometimes it seemed to me that the very last time I ever said, *"I do,"* was during Ed's and my wedding ceremony. After that, it was strictly, "We do." Everything Ed did seemed to be interpreted as a group effort. I had to answer for his actions even when he did things that I totally disagreed with.

Of course, in a way, I suppose my being held accountable for Ed did make sense. After all, Ed was the man I'd chosen, the man supposedly embodying all the attributes of what I considered the ideal man. Apparently, then, the qualities I valued most highly in the opposite sex were a bad temper, a wandering eye, and the ability to tell convincing lies.

Even now, even after Ed and I were divorced, for God's sake, I was still having to answer for Ed's behavior. In fact, right then Adrienne, Frank, and the salt-and-pepper shakers all seemed to be waiting for me to say something. I stared back at them, not sure what to tell them. I couldn't exactly testify that Ed had never lost his temper with me, because he most certainly had. So what could I say? *I don't think Ed could possibly be violent, because the only thing Ed ever did to me was sleep with other women?*

Somehow, I didn't think this testament to Ed's sterling character was going to help his case with the salt-and-pepper shakers.

I took a deep breath. "Ed could be difficult, yes, but I spent a lot of time with Ed and Kimberly, and I never saw them argue even once."

Adrienne looked skeptical. "Oh, Schuyler," she said, shaking her blond head. Her tone sounded pitying. In fact, if you didn't know better, you might've thought I'd just told a bald-faced lie. Adrienne glanced over at the salt-and-pepper shakers. "Ed Ridgway and that poor little girl bickered all the time. And then, of course, this very morning they had a huge fight."

Reed and Constello perked up again, their light and dark heads jerking in Adrienne's direction. "What?" Constello said. "What was the fight about?"

"Well, if you must know," she went on, fussing with her hair again, "they quarreled about me."

My mouth almost dropped open. Constello's dark eyes widened, and Reed's white-blond head instantly swiveled in Adrienne's direction. "*You*? Why would they quarrel about you?"

Adrienne lifted her chin even higher. "Ed Ridgway made a pass at me." As she said this, her eyes traveled around the room, once again practically daring any of us to question whether she was telling the truth. "Today wasn't the first time, either. He'd done it several times."

"Several times?" Reed repeated

Adrienne nodded.

Constello let out a low whistle. I think it was louder than he expected, though. Adrienne jumped a little at the sudden shrill sound. She frowned at him, and then went on. "I think Ed Ridgway thought his fiancée was on another floor, measuring for drapes, but as it turned out, she most certainly wasn't."

I stared at Adrienne, not sure whether to believe her or not.

Adrienne was now patting at her blond curls still again, her hand fluttering around her head like a moth. "I really wasn't expecting it. I was out in the kitchen, about to unload the dishwasher, and he—well—he just grabbed me. And then, that—that *jerk* tried to kiss me!" Adrienne at this point wiped her mouth with one hand, as if she were trying to wipe away the memory. "I was just pulling away when Miss Metcalf walked into the kitchen."

Reed was now scribbling away in that notebook of his. He didn't even look up when he asked, "Ma'am, what happened then?"

"Why, the two of them started yelling at each other!" Adrienne said. She shook her head. "My goodness, the names they called each other. Really, it was awful." Adrienne wrinkled her nose at the thought. "I thought that little girl was supposed to be this big-time society type, too. At least that's what Ed Ridgway said. Well, believe me, she sure didn't sound high-class!" Adrienne looked around the room, and finally ended up looking directly at Constello. "That's, of course, why I left. I didn't want to be a part of an ugly scene."

I stared at Adrienne. She may not have wanted to be part of that ugly scene, but she didn't seem to be particularly eager to shy away from *this* one. Unless I missed my guess, it looked to me as if old Adrienne here was enjoying herself. She certainly seemed to be deriving a malicious pleasure out of trashing Ed.

Of course, Ed's despicable behavior might've given Adrienne good reason to enjoy trashing him. I had not been here earlier. I peered at Adrienne a little closer. Was it possible that Ed really had made a pass at her? Adrienne Henderson *was* an attractive woman, even if she was wearing someone else's head. She was small and curvy, and she had shoulder-length, pale blond hair and large blue eyes. Obviously, Ed *was* attracted to Adrienne's type.

Of course, now that I thought about it, there were very few types that Ed was not attracted to. Offhand, I couldn't think of any. Unless, let me see, the Golda Meir type might be one. The Mother Theresa type might be another. And, possibly, the Margaret Thatcher type. All these types might not make Ed's A-list.

Although, I have to admit, I wasn't all that sure about Margaret Thatcher.

And yet, even if Ed had been attracted to Adrienne, would Ed really have jeopardized his upcoming marriage to one of *the* Metcalfs for the sake of a quick smooch in the kitchen? I mean, I knew that Ed had always done a significant portion of his thinking with the little head, but I wasn't sure even Ed could be that dumb.

I also wasn't at all sure that Adrienne wasn't making everything up in order to look more desirable in her estranged husband's eyes. If she was, it seemed to be working. Frank was now staring at his wife, his blue eyes intense.

"Once the yelling started, I left to go get my husband." I noticed Adrienne did not put any adjectives in front of that last word. Like, *ex*, or *estranged*. Even if he was living in his own apartment these days, he was still her husband. "It was after twelve, and I knew my husband would be having lunch. He always ate at home, so I just headed over there." As Adrienne said this, she moved closer to Frank, linking her arm through his. "To be honest, I—I just didn't feel safe with Ed Ridgway in the house." She glanced up at her husband, and Frank moved closer to her side. Towering over her, he covered her hand with his.

I stared at the Hendersons. This was the first time I'd ever seen Frank act this way with his wife. If you didn't know better, you might've thought he really did care about her after all.

Maybe hearing about Ed's advances had been a wake-up call for old Frank.

Reed asked, "When you left, then, there was nobody here but Ed Ridgway and Kimberly Metcalf?"

Adrienne nodded. "Miss Metcalf had a friend, I think,

drop her off in the first place, but the friend was long gone."

Reed was scribbling fast now. "Do you know who the friend was?"

Adrienne shook her head. "No, the car just pulled into the driveway and let Kimberly out. Whoever it was didn't hang around. They'd already pulled away by the time I got to the front door and let her in. And then Ed showed up right after Miss Metcalf got here."

I glanced sharply at Adrienne. This was not what Ed had told me. He'd said he'd arrived just minutes before me. So why would he have lied?

My stomach wrenched. The answer to that last question was obvious. Ed had lied because he'd wanted me to believe that he hadn't had enough time to do this terrible thing to Kimberly.

Lord. Could Ed really be guilty?

Right after that, Reed seemed suddenly in a hurry to hustle Adrienne off all by herself to the dining room. I suspected the reason he hadn't tried to hustle her off earlier was that he'd wanted to see my and Frank's reactions to everything Adrienne was saying. "We'll be needing a statement from everybody," Reed said. "Ma'am, if you'll come with me?" Reed took Adrienne's elbow, starting more or less to steer her toward the dining room on my right; evidently, he didn't get her moving quite fast enough. Before Adrienne disappeared through the door, I heard her say again, "The way those two quarreled, why, I am not a bit surprised that he did what he did to her!"

Reed closed the dining room door after them, and I just stared at it for a long moment. Good Lord. Had Ed and Kimberly quarreled that much around Adrienne? Once again I couldn't help recalling Ed's temper tantrums when we were first married. He'd actually kicked a hole in the wall once, he'd been so furious. To this day I couldn't remember what he'd been so mad about, I could only remember how shocked I'd been that the living room wall in our apartment had been so flimsy. The toe of Ed's size-twelve shoe had gone right through the wallboard. Ed had covered up the hole with an electric outlet plate, and you couldn't tell unless you really looked that this outlet had to be at least two inches higher than all the others in the room.

All that had been a very long time ago, though. Was it possible that Ed could have lost his temper like that in front of Adrienne?

I glanced toward the dining room again. The woman did seem to be assuming a lot. Nobody had told her anything about the circumstances of Kimberly's death, and yet she seemed to be taking it for granted that Ed had been responsible.

If Ed really had indulged in a temper tantrum in front of Adrienne Henderson, it must've been a beaut.

I wondered if maybe I should start checking the walls around here for size-twelve holes.

I believe Constello originally intended to follow Reed and Adrienne into the dining room, after settling me and Frank somewhere, but that didn't happen. Constello had just turned to me and Frank, saying, "Y'all wait in the living room until we call you, okay? We'll—" when he was interrupted by a knock on the front door.

Constello hurried to answer the door, and after that, the foyer seemed to fill up with people milling around, doing whatever official types do at the scene of a homicide.

Constello seemed to be in the thick of it, directing people here and there. I didn't hang around to watch, though. Lord knows, I'd seen all this before. I was quite content to meekly do as I'd been told and go wait in the living room—as far away from Kimberly and the others as possible.

Frank didn't exactly look content—in fact, he was still looking more pale than anything else—but he followed me into the living room, taking a seat in one of the pale blue Queen Anne chairs flanking the fireplace. I sat down in the other one. To tell you the truth, after a few minutes I barely knew Frank was there. I was still mulling over Adrienne and the things she'd said. Here was a woman who, for all intents and purposes, was a total stranger to Ed. And yet apparently, in the very short time she'd known him, she'd observed things about his behavior that led her to believe that Ed could actually be capable of taking the life of another human being.

Ed. Adrienne really thought these things of *Ed.*

I shifted position, fingering the armrest of the Queen Anne chair. Could Adrienne be right about him? In my mind's eye I could still see Ed, so clearly, as he had been on the very first day we'd met. It had been the first day of fall semester classes at the University of Louisville, one of those magically clear autumn days that Louisville always gets at least a few times a year. The air was cold and brisk, and the smoggy haze of the summer seemed banished forever. All around me, everything seemed to be in ultrasharp focus.

I'd focused on Ed not five minutes after I'd arrived on campus. It hadn't been hard to spot him—he'd been the only guy on campus that day wearing a suit and tie. Today I realize that Ed had to have been very well aware back then just how strikingly good-looking he was in that navy blue pinstripe suit that made his sandy hair look almost gold. He'd also known, no doubt, that by being the only guy dressed up that day, he'd have the eyes of just about every female on Belknap campus following his every move.

Ed had sat across from me in a social science class called Problems of Modern Society, and when the instructor wasn't looking, Ed had silently mimicked everything the man did. I'd almost choked trying not to laugh out loud.

Later I'd actually felt a little giddy when Ed had waited for me after class and asked me out. I'd walked away with him that afternoon, and I'd felt the eyes of every other girl in that social studies class following us. And, yes, envying me.

Back then, can you believe it, I'd actually thought that Ed was close to perfect. I'd thought him handsome, and witty, and sophisticated. And, of course, if I ever doubted it for even a split second, Ed was always right there to remind me just exactly how handsome, witty, and sophisticated he was.

He also constantly reminded me how extremely lucky I

was that someone like him would want someone like me. Ed had grown up in Louisville's prestigious East End, whereas I, on the other hand, had grown up in the South End—"Blue Collar Country," as Ed always called it. If, in the years that followed, I'd had a penny for every time Ed mentioned how he'd married "beneath him," I'd have been able to afford to divorce him a whole lot sooner. Ironically enough.

Even now I couldn't quite believe that I'd let Ed say things like that to me, again and again, without once arguing with him. And yet, if you've grown up in Louisville, Kentucky, what Ed had to say was something some people around here are eager to tell you. These people seem quite happy to remind you that Louisville's East End is the place to be, and any of the other Ends— the South End and the West End—are not. The North End would probably not be any too desirable, either, except that Louisville doesn't have a North End. The only thing north of Louisville is the Ohio River—and Indiana.

Back when I was in high school, I actually spent some time puzzling over all this. I wondered exactly how one piece of land got designated as the best and another piece of land got designated as the worst. When all of it was just ground, wasn't it? Trees in Louisville's South End looked pretty much the same as trees in the East End. So how did it get decided that the trees in the East End would be a lot more valuable than the trees anywhere else? Who made these decisions, anyway? Did all the residents of Louisville get together and vote?

Naturally, once I became a real estate agent, I understood all this stuff a little better. I remember being told in one real estate class that the value of any given piece of real estate was determined by just three things: location, location, and location.

Of course, once I understood that location dictated the ultimate value of a piece of land, there was still something I didn't quite get. Didn't the location rule just apply to *property*? I asked Ed this, too, not long ago, after hearing him make yet another crack about my coming from the wrong end of town. Oh, yes, can you believe he still did this, even now, even after we've been divorced all this time? As I recall, what he'd said on this particular occasion was: *You can take a girl out of the South End, but you can't take the South End out of the girl.* Whatever that meant.

I'd pointed out to Ed that it was my understanding that location determined the value of *land,* not the value of the people living on the land. Ed had looked at me as if I were speaking in a foreign language.

So, okay, the results were in, and Ed was indeed shallow, and vain, and materialistic, and pompous, and silly. He was also sneaky, and devious, and probably incapable of fidelity. And yet, given that Ed was all these things, did it still necessarily follow that he could actually kill a person?

I shifted around in the Queen Anne chair, feeling more and more uneasy. When I'd divorced Ed, I'd felt so guilty, I'd actually wanted to believe that he was a loathsome human being, capable of almost anything. Sort of like Hitler in World War II—a clear and present danger. A destroyer of dreams. And, yes, perhaps worst of all, a bad influence on the kids.

I'd wanted to believe that Ed was all these things because right after we split up, I hadn't been all that sure that divorcing Ed for being unfaithful to me was fair to Nathan and Daniel. I mean, just because I didn't want to live with somebody who ran around on me, did that mean it was okay to make two little boys stop living with their dad? I'd felt so guilty about what certainly looked like putting my own needs before those of my sons that I'd actually spent quite a lot of time trying to convince myself that Ed was despicable. I had, in fact, called him many terrible things. As I recalled, however, I'd never once called him a murderer.

Now, as I sat in that Queen Anne chair in the Henderson living room, I had the strangest feeling of unreality. Lord. What the hell was going on? How had I gotten from spotting a handsome young man in a suit on campus one day to doing this—sitting in the living room of a two-story frame on Willow Avenue, wondering if he could be a murderer? How in hell had that happened?

"You know, I think this is the longest time I've ever spent in this room."

I was so absorbed in what I'd been thinking that when Frank Henderson spoke, I actually jumped.

Chapter 7

Frank Henderson was smiling at me, but his smile looked a little lopsided. It was as if his face couldn't quite make up its mind whether a smile was appropriate under the circumstances. "Oh, I'm terribly sorry," he said, shifting position in the Queen Anne chair opposite mine. "I didn't mean to scare you."

I just looked at him. I had jumped when he spoke mainly because I'd been miles away. Thinking about Ed, I'd almost forgotten Frank was sitting there. And, to be honest, I'd have to admit my nerves were on edge. After seeing Kimberly in her present condition—and then hearing Adrienne expound on the subject of how my ex-husband had probably *put* Kimberly in that condition—I was most definitely what my son Nathan at the age of nine had called "a rervous neck."

It was pretty clear to me that Frank really had very little to do with my jumping at the sound of his voice. I'd have jumped if a pin had dropped. And yet here Frank was, actually *apologizing* to me. In fact, he acted like a man who had become accustomed over the years to taking the blame. Whether he was actually at fault or not. It sort of made you wonder if Adrienne had been all that easy to live with.

Of course, maybe I wasn't feeling all that kind toward the woman because I knew at that very moment she was telling Reed all the reasons he and Constello should consider Ed homicidal. I took a deep breath and tried to put that little scene out of my mind. "Frank," I said, "don't worry about it." I gave him a quick, possibly lopsided, smile of my own and changed the subject. "So what were you saying?"

Frank himself looked more than a little relieved to be discussing something other than what was going on outside this room. He returned my smile, and this time his smile looked considerably steadier. With a shrug of his broad shoulders, he said, "Oh, well, I was just saying that I think this might be the longest time I've ever spent in this room."

"Oh?" I tried not to sound it, but the truth was, I was eager to discuss just about anything to divert my mind. "Why is that?" I asked. The large living room certainly seemed inviting enough. With gleaming hardwood floors and pale peach walls picking up the exact shade of peach that appeared in the large peach, gray, and blue Aubusson India rug beneath our feet, it was a room that could've been featured in *House Beautiful*.

The room might've been a little too busy for my own personal taste, but from a realtor's point of view, it showed very well. It projected what we in the real estate trade call "an ambiance of opulence." In fact, I believe I'd shamelessly used those very words in the newspaper ad in last Sunday's classified section. The sofa opposite Frank and me was covered in a peach-and-blue print chintz, the floor-to-ceiling draperies were made of a coordinating peach-and-blue print fabric, and there were several throw pillows on the sofa covered in still other coordinating peach-and-blue patterns.

On the down side, the coffee table directly in front of me did have a feature that I hated—a glass top. So that you could see right through to the bottom shelf. In my house, that would've meant that you could clearly see, as soon as you walked into my living room, the huge mound of magazines under there. You could also see that these magazines were in such disarray that mice could've been nesting in them and you wouldn't have been able to tell. In Adrienne's house it didn't matter whether her coffee table was see-through or not. She only had two magazines lying on the pristine bottom shelf—the latest issues of

Atlantic Monthly and *Vogue.* Neither magazine looked as if it had ever been opened.

Frank had apparently followed my gaze, and he was now looking at the glass coffee table top, too. "Adrienne said she was sure I'd be putting fingerprints all over that tabletop, or I'd be tracking mud in on the rug, or I'd be putting my feet on the furniture." At this point he shrugged. "Or something like that. So I was forbidden to ever come in here."

I just looked at him again. He was forbidden to go into a room in his own house? A house on which he himself happened to be paying the mortgage? I could just imagine, back when we were married, my ever telling Ed not to go into our living room. Ed would have been in there, *spitting* on the coffee table, before I'd even finished the sentence. God knows what he would've done to the rug.

My total amazement must've shown on my face because Frank shifted in his chair again, ran a hand through his thinning brown hair, and then said, his tone a little defensive, "That is, Adrienne *used* to tell me not to come in here. Now, of course, she doesn't do that anymore."

Of course. I wasn't about to say anything, but I was pretty sure why Adrienne had decided to lift her living room ban. Adrienne was probably so anxious to keep Frank from going through with their divorce, Frank could finger paint on the coffee table and Adrienne would applaud his creativity.

I think Frank had a pretty good idea what was going through my mind this time, too. He glanced over at me and smiled a little, a knowing look in his eyes. For a brief moment he looked more like a mischievous little boy than a middle-aged man. I returned his smile.

After that, I think both of us relaxed a bit. We actually started chatting about movies and books and whether or not the University of Kentucky would win the NCAA basketball championship again this year. For a little while, listening to us, you might have thought we were two old friends making small talk. That illusion, however, was pretty much shattered a few minutes later when Frank and I both heard heavy footsteps going right past the living room door. Right after that there was the creaking sound heavy plastic makes when it's being unfolded, and shortly after that, the sound of a zipper being unzipped.

I took another deep breath. I could be wrong, but it sounded to me as if the body bag had arrived.

That zipping sound seemed to go on forever. I glanced over at Frank to see if he understood the significance of what we were hearing. His face had paled again, and he seemed to slump a little against the upholstered back of his Queen Anne chair. Oh, yes, I'd say he understood, all right.

Frank noticed my look and sat up a little straighter. "Boy. I am so glad I came back here with Adrienne," he said. He ran his hand through his hair once again. "I thought Adrienne was just exaggerating, you know. I had no idea how dangerous that man was."

I just stared at him. The feeling of unreality was back.

"You know," I said quietly, "Ed might not have done this."

Frank didn't say one word in reply, but his glance looked pitying. He sort of leaned in my direction, and I thought he was about to say something more. The living room door opened right then, though, and Adrienne walked in, followed by Reed—and Constello. Apparently, Constello had finished doing whatever he'd been doing with the people from the crime lab, and he'd joined his partner interviewing Adrienne.

I wasn't sure if the detectives had instructed Adrienne to keep her mouth shut about what she'd just discussed with them or not, but if they had, she certainly had not listened. Adrienne started talking the second she came through the door. "Well," she said, "I'm not one to talk bad about somebody who's not here to defend himself." She fussed with her blond hair, and then gave a little shrug of her shoulders. "But let's face it, Ed Ridgway is one scary human being."

I just looked at her. For a woman who didn't want to

talk bad about somebody, she was doing a remarkable job of it.

I had every intention of making a rebuttal to Adrienne's little pronouncement, but the salt-and-pepper shakers didn't give me the chance. They hustled me out of the living room before I'd barely opened my mouth.

I wasn't sure what the significance of all this was. Maybe Reed and Constello were just trying to get me out of there so that Adrienne and I didn't get into a heated discussion regarding the likelihood of Ed being a cold-blooded killer. Or maybe the shakers just didn't want me to grill Adrienne on what all she'd just told them.

Whatever the reason, I followed the detectives dutifully across the hall, making it a point not to even glance toward where Kimberly had been lying. I could tell, out of the corner of my eye, that the body bag was still lying there, so I knew I didn't want to see whatever was going on. I resolutely looked straight ahead as I headed toward the dining room.

Once inside, I sat down at the dining room table and waited while Reed carefully closed the door. I also waited while both detectives once again got out their matching notebooks and identical Bics. And then I started in answering their questions. There wasn't a whole lot I could add to what I'd already said. I did, of course, mention what Kimberly had told me when she phoned me at Arndoerfer Realty earlier. "Kimberly said Mrs. Henderson had already left."

Constello's dark head had been bent over his little notebook when I got to this part, but after I repeated what Kimberly had said, Constello's head sort of jerked in my direction. "The victim told you that she was the only one in the house at that time?"

I just stared at him for a moment. *The victim.* That's what Kimberly was now. My stomach wrenched.

"Ma'am, you're saying that Miss Metcalf told you that there was nobody else in the house but her?" Reed said.

I did hate to admit it, but it was the truth. I nodded. "She said Adrienne had left, and that she was all by herself." I took a deep, deep breath. It didn't exactly take a genius to figure out that if Kimberly had been alone in the house, then suspicion naturally fell on the next person to arrive. I could feel my stomach tightening. There was no way to get around it. Things did not look good for Ed.

After I repeated everything at least two more times, Constello finally closed his damn notebook and drawled, "Well, I reckon that's all."

I didn't have to be told twice. I stood up.

Reed held up his hand. "Just a second, ma'am. Do you have any idea where your husband could be?"

I cleared my throat. "Ex," I corrected again. "Ed is my *ex*-husband."

Reed looked irritated. "Do you have any idea where your ex-husband could be?"

I looked him straight in the eye. "I could not begin to guess."

Constello tapped his Bic on the tabletop so loudly that I glanced over at him. "You don't have even an inklin' where he might have gone?"

I looked Constello straight in the eye this time. "No, I don't."

"Ma'am," Reed put in, "do you think your ex-husband might try to get in touch with your sons?"

I blinked, then took a quick breath before I answered. "Well, no. No, I don't. My sons have been angry with their dad ever since he left us when they were little." I looked straight at Reed this time. "They haven't even spoken to Ed in years." I reached down and picked up my purse. "I've tried to patch things up between them, but it doesn't seem to do any good. In fact, I'd say that my two sons are the last people Ed would call. Because they wouldn't help him. They'd turn him in."

Reed and Constello were just sitting there, staring at me. I wasn't sure if they believed me or not. I opened my purse and pulled out a ballpoint pen. Hey, it wasn't a Bic, but it would do. "You know," I said, "I can give you a few names of women who've dated Ed. Maybe he's staying with one of them."

Constello looked interested. "Now that would be real helpful, if you'd do that," he said.

It took me a while. In fact, at one point, I was tempted to just hand the salt-and-pepper shakers a copy of the Louisville phone book and have it done with. Instead, I wrote down ten or twelve names from Ed's past. I was surprised; several times I could even recall where the woman lived. A couple times I even remembered a phone number. I must've paid more attention to Ed's love life than I'd thought. Finally finished, I got to my feet. "I don't expect to hear from Ed," I said, "but if I do, I'll be sure to give you a call right away."

I must've been losing my touch. Reed and Constello both looked skeptical. "You'd do that?" Constello asked. His tone was doubtful.

I ignored his tone. "Look, Ed and I are divorced. I may have been showing houses to him and his fiancée, but that was only because I'd have done just about anything to make sure he became someone else's problem. And he totally ignores his sons. If you don't mind my saying so, I'd *love* to see the man behind bars."

That touching sentiment seemed to convince Reed and Constello of my sincerity. They exchanged another one of their looks, but this time after they looked at each other, they both nodded. I still had no idea what any of this meant, but their nods actually looked sort of approving. Evidently, the urge to be nasty and vindictive must've been something the salt-and-pepper shakers could understand, because right after that they let me go.

I intended to say good-bye to Adrienne and Frank before I left, but the Hendersons were no longer in the living room. I had no idea where they'd gone, and I was not about to wander around the house looking for them. Besides, I was pretty sure before I got far, somebody from the crime lab or the coroner's office or whatever would stop me. I decided that, in this one instance, I could be forgiven for a lapse in manners. I made a beeline for my Tercel parked at the curb.

Unfortunately, as soon as I went through the front door, I realized that there were now quite a few vehicles, in addition to my Tercel, parked at the curb. There was a van with WHAS-TV painted on the side, a station wagon with

WLKY-TV painted on its side, and two cars—one with the WAVE-3 TV logo and the other with the *Courier-Journal* logo painted on their driver's doors. There were several other vehicles, too, parked on both sides of the street, that had not been there when I'd arrived.

I supposed all these cars belonged to the small throng of reporters and cameramen who all moved in my direction the instant I set foot outside. Lord. I would've wondered how on earth all these people could have heard about this so fast, but I'd recently sold a house to a cameraman who worked for WHAS. He'd told me that reporters regularly monitor police scanners in an effort to be the first on the scene of a fast-breaking story.

A couple of the faces in the crowd I remembered seeing on local television news broadcasts, but I couldn't have told you what their names were. I also couldn't have told you what any of them said to me as I tried to push past them and get to my car. They were all shouting so many questions at me, all at the same time, it seemed to blend into one loud roar.

I tried to sidestep everybody and just keep going, but one enterprising blond woman moved right in front of me. It was either come to a screeching halt or mow the woman down. On camera. I stopped.

The woman actually smiled, a triumphant gleam in her eyes. Sticking a microphone under my nose, as if it were smelling salts, she screamed, literally, right in my face, "MA'AM! Just a minute, ma'am! Can you answer a few questions?"

She was a very pretty woman, with a perfect oval face, perfect teeth, and perfectly coifed chin-length blond hair. I stared at her, amazed at how rude a perfect woman could be. Was this what it took to get a story? I knew this kind of behavior was often defended with words like "the public has a right to know."

I apparently had not responded fast enough. "Ma'am! MA'AM! Will you answer a few questions, PLEASE!" the blond screamed. Again, right in my face. In back of the blond, a guy with a camcorder balanced on his shoulder moved in closer to me, focusing on my face.

My God. If the public needed to know this bad, the public needed to have its collective face slapped.

I reached for the blond woman's microphone. "Yes, indeed!" I yelled back at the blond, giving her a wide smile. "I'd LOVE to answer some questions!" I looked at the rest of the reporters clustered around us, and tried to smile in the direction of every one of the cameras. "This *is* going to be on TV, isn't it?"

The blond was now looking a little uncertain. "Well, yes, it—" she started to say, looking around at the others as if checking to see if they noticed anything strange about my behavior.

"Great!" I said, interrupting her. I now looked straight at the camera the blond's cameraman was pointing at me. "Hi! I'm Schuyler Ridgway, that's *Schuyler Ridgway,* I'm a real estate agent, and I work for Arndoerfer Realty, that's *Arndoerfer Realty,* located at 4910 Taylorsville Road, phone 502-555-SALE, that's area code 5-0-2-5-5-5-S-A-L-E. Our office is open nine to five weekdays, but we're always on call. At your service. We specialize in—"

"Ma'am? *Ma'am!*" Blondie said, interrupting me this time. "What is happening inside? Have they made an arrest yet?"

"I don't know about that," I said. I stared at the camera again. "I was just here, showing this house. I work for Arndoerfer Realty, located at 4910 Taylorsville Road, phone 502-555-7253, that's 555-SALE. Because we always make a sale! Our motto is . . ."

The blonde was now trying to get her microphone back. And, oddly enough, the other reporters no longer seemed all that interested in what I had to say. They began to wander away. I, however, held on to the microphone, repeating everything I could remember from the one and only television commercial Arndoerfer Realty had ever run, until Blondie began to look a little worried that she might never get her microphone back. Then I let her wrench it out of my grasp. Glaring at me, Blondie immediately put some distance between us, taking her cameraman with her.

I, of course, couldn't help but smile. Maybe the salt-and-pepper shakers were right. I *am* nasty and vindictive.

I hurried toward my Tercel, and this time, oddly enough, nobody tried to stop me. In no time at all, I was heading away from the Henderson house as fast as I could without exceeding the speed limit. I had no intention of giving any policemen I might pass on the way a reason to pull me over.

I drove for several miles in what I knew was the wrong direction, checking my rearview mirror again and again. Then, certain that no reporters and no police cars, marked or unmarked, were following me, I turned around.

And I headed for the place that I was almost certain I'd find Ed.

Chapter 8

At the turn of the century the stately Victorian homes on Third Street near the University of Louisville housed some of the wealthiest families in Louisville. Today this neighborhood is part of an area named—cleverly enough—Old Louisville, and these antique brick-and-stone buildings, with their elegant stained-glass windows and intricate stonework, mainly just house college students.

My sons are notable exceptions. Nathan and Daniel, as a matter of fact, moved into the third-floor apartment that they now occupy on Third Street a few days after they became ex-students at the University of Louisville.

Without my knowledge, my sons had apparently been competing all semester in a Who-Can-Flunk-Out-of-U-of-L-First contest. Nathan is a year younger than Daniel, so he'd started out an entire year behind. Evidently, though, gutsy young man that he is, Nathan had met the challenge and quickly made up for lost time. Within mere months the boys' flunk-out contest had ended in a tie—with both my sons getting identical letters of dismissal on the very same day.

It's things like this that make a mother proud.

Evidently, the boys were afraid that it might also make me furious. Almost immediately both Nathan and Daniel decided that it would probably be in their best interests to live just about anywhere in the United States other than under the same roof with me. Oddly enough.

Considering that their father—in a rare moment of real

wisdom—had steadfastly refused to pay anything toward their college expenses, so that every single penny of their tuition money had come out of my own pocket, I couldn't fault the boys' logic. In fact, I've always been convinced that the main reason my sons moved out so suddenly was that, from the moment those dismissal letters arrived in my mailbox, Nathan and Daniel were afraid to eat anything that I prepared.

Good thinking, I might add.

Once I'd stopped wandering around the Highlands, making sure that I had not inadvertently picked up a police escort after leaving the Henderson home, it took me only ten minutes or so to make my way downtown to Third Street. On the block of Third that Daniel and Nathan live on, there are five houses in a row that look a lot alike. All five houses are red brick, all have stained-glass insets above the door and wide front windows facing the street, and all have cupolas with cone-shaped roofs, looking just like huge witches' hats perched on top.

These houses may have looked alike, but from the very first day I have never had any trouble picking out which one Nathan and Daniel lived in. I wish I could say that I knew because of some strong, mysterious mother-son bond, or maybe because I've got an abundant supply of mother's intuition, or some such. Unfortunately, it's a lot simpler than that. I know which house my sons live in because I know my sons. I can also recall with appalling clarity the exact state of their bedrooms the day the two of them moved out.

That's why I knew from the get-go that the boys' apartment would have to be in whichever building on their block had the most garbage littering the sidewalk out front. Today, as I got out of my Tercel and hurried up the walk, I stepped around three crushed Mountain Dew cans, a crumpled sack from McDonald's with the words BE KIND, DON'T LITTER printed on the side, and a wadded-up Twinkies package.

Still more things that make a mom proud.

On another day, I might've stopped for a moment to pick up the trash and maybe reflect on just how gratifying it was that both my sons had obviously learned what it took to make a house a home. Today, however, I was in a hurry. Not to mention, there was the distinct possibility that if either Daniel or Nathan happened to look out the window and spot me doing trash duty in front of their apartment building, they might decide to scurry out the back as fast as their Reeboks could carry them. That's why, in the interest of maintaining an element of surprise, I sprinted up the walk, took the narrow front steps two at a time, crossed the porch in quick, long strides, and reached for the buzzer—all in a matter of seconds.

The main entrance to Nathan and Daniel's apartment building has a heavy oak double door with an automatic lock. The entire building, according to Nathan, is supposed to be so burglarproof that nobody can possibly get inside unless you call one of the tenants over the intercom and have them buzz you in. I had intended to buzz every tenant's apartment except 3C—the boys' apartment—so that I could still surprise them, but a quick glance at the door told me that going on a buzzing frenzy would not be necessary after all. The heavy double doors were standing ajar. Mainly because somebody—no doubt weary of listening to buzzers going off—had wedged a brick between the two doors.

I stared at the brick. Oh, yes, this place was burglarproof, all right. A regular Fort Knox.

I pulled open the entrance door on the right, stepped into the cool shadows of the center hallway, and immediately started climbing stairs. Shortly after I did this, I came to a not terribly surprising conclusion.

I needed to get more exercise.

By the time I got to the third floor, I sounded like the big bad wolf outside the three little pigs' house. Which was sort of appropriate, considering that when I finally made it to the top landing, staggered over to the apartment marked with a tarnished brass C, and knocked weakly on the door, the only thing I had air enough left to say was a weak, "Let me in. Let me in." If I really had been the wolf, the part of the little pig story where the wolf goes on and on about blowing the house in would never have happened. The only thing there would've been to report was a lot more huffing and puffing.

"Who's there?" This was either Nathan or Daniel on the other side of the door. Nathan and Daniel both have deep, similar-sounding voices, and my own breathing was so loud, I couldn't quite make out the voice well enough to tell whose it was.

"Let me in," I said again. I still sounded as if someone had tied a knot in my air hose, but I do think that this time my voice came across a little stronger. In fact, I believe I was recovering nicely, because I even had wind enough to gasp, "Please."

This time I had no trouble telling who it was who answered me. Daniel yelled, "Yo?" Which is, of course, Danielese for *Who is it?*

Daniel's voice was immediately followed by Nathan's saying in a stage whisper, "Shut UP! If Mom doesn't hear us, she might go away!"

What a sweet child. I hated to break it to Nathan, but the possibility of my leaving anytime soon was pretty much nil. To more or less emphasize this, I gave the bottom of the boys' apartment door a little kick. It didn't hurt the wood or anything, but the sharp sound seemed to reverberate in the silent hallway. "Open up, you guys, right this minute!" I would've liked to scream those words, but in the absence of an oxygen tank, I had to be satisfied with wheezing them. "Daniel. Nathan. I can hear you in there, so you'd better let me in."

I was answered by silence. If you don't count, of course, the continuing noise of my own breathing—and my heart still sounding like soldiers on the march. I stood there for a long moment, considering my options. I hated to do it, but it looked as if I was going to have to haul out the heavy artillery.

"All right, guys," I said. "I've had it." I took as deep a breath as I could, and I said very fast before I ran out of air, "If you don't open this door right this minute, you two can forget about my ever letting you borrow my Block-buster card. Ever again." I huffed and puffed a couple times, and then added, "I mean it, *no more video rentals.*"

Hey, I knew it was cruel, but as they say, desperate times call for desperate measures.

There was no sound on the opposite side of the door. Either Nathan and Daniel were so stunned by what I'd said, they were rendered immobile, or they hadn't heard me. "I mean it," I said again, this time raising my voice as much as I could, "you'll *never rent movies in this town again*!"

I was, you see, well aware that neither of my sons could get a video rental card on his own these days. Over a period of years, stretching back to their freshman years in high school, the two of them had—to put it delicately, as we Southern ladies always do—pissed off every rental place in the Highlands and Old Louisville neighborhoods. It had been tough, but by consistently forgetting to return videos on time—and then by consistently trying to sneak the videos in without paying the late fee—my sons had eventually been refused service by Video Arcade, Video Shelf, Movie World, Movie Place, and not one, but *two* Minute Marts. The only video place left who'd deal with them was Blockbuster, and there they could no longer get a rental card. This last, of course, was because both Nathan and Daniel had recently tied in yet another contest much like their flunk-out competition: the How-Fast-Can-You-Have-Your-MasterCard-Revoked? contest.

That they had done so well in this last contest had not exactly been a shock after the little conversation I'd had with Nathan not too long ago. Nathan had told me, with a totally straight face, that MasterCard was no longer one of his monthly bills. I'd been amazed. Mostly because I could remember with no trouble at all how a couple of months earlier Daniel had let it slip that both he and Nathan had maxed out their MasterCards.

Naturally, when Nathan had announced that he didn't have a MasterCard bill anymore, I'd not only been amazed, I'd been impressed. My very own youngest son had been able to pay off what had to have been a pretty big balance. That he'd accomplished such a feat on the salary of a delivery boy at Poppa's Pizza was awe-inspiring. In fact, right after he'd told me this, I'd been almost afraid to ask, "How did you pay them off?"

Having posed the question, I'd stared at Nathan, my heart in my throat, hoping against hope that he was not about to say anything that included the phrases *pints of blood* or *kidney donation.*

Nathan, however, had looked at me as if I'd suddenly started speaking gibberish. "Oh, Mom," he'd said. His tone, as I recalled, had been scornful. "I didn't pay them off. I'm just not making payments. *That's* all."

I'd stared at him some more. Oh. Well. That explained it. No wonder. MasterCard was not one of his bills. Because he wasn't paying them. Sure. Uh-huh. Right.

On second thought, maybe the kidney story would've been preferable.

Of course, I didn't waste any time whatsoever feeling bad for MasterCard. Let me tell you, MasterCard deserved Nathan and Daniel. This was, after all, the very same company that had wantonly mailed each of my sons a credit card virtually the instant that they had set foot on U of L's campus.

When I'd heard about the cards, I'd been horrified. Unfortunately, I'd heard about it right away, too. Nathan was so elated to have his very own piece of colorful plastic with his very own name emblazoned on it in raised gold letters that he'd started dialing people up with the exciting news right after he opened the envelope. He probably would've told the paperboy if the kid had given him a chance. After I'd gotten off the phone with the happy spender that day, I'd felt like making a call myself. I wanted to phone MasterCard and ask them, *What the hell were you all thinking?*

I—Nathan and Daniel's very own personal mother— would not have felt comfortable loaning either of them twenty dollars, and yet MasterCard—who obviously did not know either of these kids from Adam—had decided to give Nathan and Daniel a credit limit of *five hundred* smackers. Each.

What MasterCard should've done—in the interest of

saving time—was just hand Nathan and Daniel the cash and two matches.

Or, even better, MasterCard should have consulted me. In fact, I do believe if credit card companies would just regularly consult the moms of potential cardholders, it would no doubt save countless man-hours spent trying to squeeze blood from turnips.

All of this goes to explain why my two turnips could not get a Blockbuster Video card. You have to have a major credit card to get one, so that Blockbuster—a company that could, no doubt, give MasterCard lessons—could make damn sure that it collected every red cent of its late fees.

"Do you hear me?" I was now yelling at Nathan and Daniel's door. *"No more Blockbuster! Ever!"*

I was about to give the door another little kick for emphasis when the knob started to turn, and what do you know, the door actually opened. I was suddenly looking directly at my oldest son. "Yo," Daniel said. He was wearing his usual—a black Grateful Dead T-shirt with skulls all over it, faded blue jeans that looked as if they had suffered shotgun blasts to both knees, and a tarnished silver earring in the shape of a cross dangling from his right ear.

"Yo yourself," I said, moving quickly past Daniel into the room.

I was immediately confronted by my younger son. "Mom!" Nathan said, stepping right in front of me, blocking my way. Like Daniel, he too was wearing his usual—designer dress shirt, designer socks, designer casual shoes, and designer shorts.

That's right. *Shorts.* It could be ten degrees outside, icicles could be forming on your eyelashes, and Nathan would be wearing shorts. The boy does have very nice, muscular legs, but I have always wondered why he didn't confine himself to showing them off on days when they wouldn't be turning blue.

Nathan's grin could not have gotten any bigger. "Hey, it's you!" Nathan actually had the nerve to try to sound surprised to see me. "We had no idea! Really." He ran his hand through his sandy hair and looked over at his brother. "Daniel and I thought maybe it was somebody selling something."

I just looked at him. Somebody was selling something, all right, but it wasn't me.

"I am *so* sorry, Mom," Nathan was going on. "I really am. If I'd had any idea that it was you out there, I'd have opened the door right away. Honest."

Uh-huh. It would appear the kid had a lot more in common with his father than a muscular build and sandy hair.

"Really, Mom," Nathan was going on. "It is so good to see you—"

"Nathan," I said, "give it up, okay?" I stepped around him, moved across the living room, and plopped down on the threadbare sofa that the boys bought at a Salvation Army thrift store. This sofa is covered in a truly hideous navy blue-and-gold-striped velvet, and the fabric has gotten so thin in places, you feel as if you're perched on bare springs. Sitting on this thing for any length of time, you begin to identify with a Jack in the Box.

Usually, on those rare occasions when I actually do sit on this thing, I put something between me and the sofa— like a towel or a handkerchief. The boys seem to think that I do this to cushion against the bare springs, and I have let them continue to think so. In reality, after taking one look at this particular piece of furniture, I was afraid that there still lurked within its moldy interior the spores of the mutant virus that had, no doubt, claimed the life of its former owner and resulted in its immediate donation to the Salvation Army.

Today, however, I was so winded I didn't care. Not to mention, considering the way things were going, succumbing to a mutant virus might be a step up. I even leaned back against the thinly upholstered back. As I moved, springs groaned, sounding like the percussion section of an orchestra tuning up.

Nathan's grin had faded a little. "Now, Mom," he began, his eyes very wide, "I don't know how you could possibly get the idea that—"

He was doing the hurt tone so well, I almost hated to

interrupt. "Look, Nathan," I said, "I may be a little winded from climbing the stairs, but I think there's enough remaining oxygen going to my brain that I can still smell something fishy."

Nathan blinked at that one. Then, with a shrug of his shoulders that reminded me of his father, Nathan began to talk very fast. "Mom, really, I'm telling you the truth, we didn't know that it was you out there, or else we would've, without a doubt, unlocked the door and—"

"Where is he?" I said, cutting him off again.

Nathan, amazingly enough, now tried to look as if he had no idea what I was talking about. "Where is who?" he said.

I gave him another look. "Who do you think?" I said. I was getting my wind back. I shifted position on the couch, sending springs once again into a cacophony of sound, and started looking around the room. "Jimmy Hoffa, of course."

Nathan folded his arms across his chest. "Mom, I don't know what—"

I cupped my hands around my mouth. "Ed!" I called to the apartment at large. "Ed, get out here, you coward, you!" My thinking here was that maybe appealing to Ed's sense of pride would do the trick.

Nothing moved.

Except, of course, Nathan. He stepped directly in front of me again. "Okay, now are you satisfied? As you can plainly see, Daniel and I are the only ones here." In back of Nathan, Daniel backed up his brother by nodding his dark head until his earring danced.

I took a deep breath. "Guys," I said, "you don't understand. I'm not leaving until I talk to him." Turning away from the boys and tilting my head back, I yelled again, "Ed! I mean it, Ed, get out here!"

This time Nathan tried to look sorry for me. "No, Mom," he said, shaking his head, "it's you who doesn't understand." In back of him, Daniel continued to nod his head. "I just don't know where you get these crazy ideas," Nathan said, "but, Mom, believe me, Dad is *not* here." In back of him, Daniel stopped nodding his head yes, and began shaking his head no.

Nathan had said that last sentence in a tone of infinite patience, as if he were having to explain to me some tedious fact that virtually everyone else on the planet pretty much took for granted. He could just as easily have been saying, "Mom, believe me, things do not fall *up*."

I cleared my throat. "Right. Your dad's not here." I stared at Nathan. "And you're not here." I glanced over at Daniel. Thank God he'd stopped nodding and shaking. "And Daniel's not here. And I'm not here, either." As I said this, I got to my feet and started to move toward the door leading to their bedrooms.

"Hey!" Nathan said, stepping in front of me.

Daniel moved toward me, too, holding up both his hands like a traffic guard signalling me to stop. For once, he didn't let Nathan do the talking. "Yo, Mom, we're telling you the truth. Dad is not here. Understand? He really isn't here."

I gave him the same look I'd given Nathan. Ever since kindergarten, I've been able to tell when Daniel was lying. It's not exactly a stretch. Shortly after he'd turned five, Daniel made up his mind that the way to be most convincing was to yell. Apparently, nothing had happened in the ensuing sixteen years to make him change that decision.

I didn't even blink. If Daniel was yelling, I suppose I could, too. "Ed! Ed! Where are you?"

"Dad is not here," Daniel yelled even louder. "Nathan and I have not seen him!"

I was now standing almost in the middle of their living room. Even if I hadn't already known that Ed was here, I'd have known it the second I stopped to take a good look around.

The boys' apartment is done in a style that Nathan calls eclectic. He tells me that means that the decor of his and Daniel's apartment is a mix of styles. It's a mix, that's for sure. The sofa was most definitely Danish—in fact, from where I was now standing, I could see a partially eaten Danish wedged under the blue velvet seat cushion on the far left. The battered purple velvet chair in the corner was clearly Taco—half of a taco shell was lying on the seat. And unless I missed my guess, I'd say that the end table on the right was Pepsi. Or maybe it was Coca-Cola. The brown stains marring its wood surface had dried, so it was hard to tell which beverage had pooled there.

It wasn't the furniture, though, that convinced me that Ed had to be here. Not at all. It was the magazines. There was a neat stack of them on top of the left end table. And a stack of three on the floor next to the couch. And yet another neat stack on top of the television. To my knowledge, neither Nathan nor Daniel had stacked anything that neatly since the alphabet blocks they'd had in their playpen.

Daniel had now moved to stand on the other side of Nathan, closer to the door. Unlike his brother, though, Daniel was not standing still. In fact, he was sort of dancing around, moving first one way, and then the other. Either he was trying to anticipate which way I was about to go, so that he could block me, or he was trying to do an impression of Louisville's own Muhammad Ali in the boxing ring. I stopped trying to get around either one of my sons, took as deep a breath as I could, and yelled again. "Ed, I'm not leaving until you get out here!"

Again there was silence. That is, if you didn't count the noise Daniel's shoes were making as he continued to float like a butterfly in front of me. Let me tell you, Ali was not worried. I took another deep breath. "Okay, Ed," I said, "I've changed my mind. If you don't get out here this minute, I *am* going to leave." As I said this, I noticed that Daniel glanced over at Nathan. Can you believe it, the two of them seemed to be exchanging a look of relief. It lasted right up until I hurried on. "I'm going to go around to the back of this building, and I'm going to look in the garage back there. I am pretty sure I'll find Ed's Toy inside. And if I do, I'm going to *key* the side!"

Nathan and Daniel now exchanged a look of alarm. *Keying,* in fact, was a term I'd learned from them. I'd learned it firsthand the day Nathan had come home from high school with a huge scratch all down the side of the old VW bug he'd driven back then. According to Daniel and Nathan, some kid who was mad at Nathan for flirting with his girlfriend had keyed Nathan's car. Meaning, of course, that this kid had scraped off paint all along the side with his car keys. Digging into the surface so deep in some places that bare metal had shone through.

At the time I hadn't realized that hearing about what this kid had done might one day come in handy. I now held up my key ring and rattled the keys as loudly as I could. "I mean it, Ed!" I rattled the keys again. "I am going downstairs right now and—"

I was interrupted by a sound out in the hall—that of a closet door opening.

And, oh, yes, by Ed himself walking into the living room.

Chapter 9

Ed was no longer wearing the navy blue suit he'd been wearing at the Henderson house earlier. Instead, he'd apparently borrowed a few items from Daniel. Ed now had on a pair of stonewashed blue jeans with jagged holes in both knees, an assortment of tears and rips in the front and back, and the left front pocket completely torn away so that what was left was just a flap dangling by a few threads. I've always thought that Daniel's clothes looked as if he'd just been caught in a gun battle. Right this minute, as I stared at Ed, the thought was sobering.

Ed was also wearing one of Daniel's T-shirts—a black, misshapen one with a color portrait of something that looked a lot like a smiling Moby Dick on the front. Under smiling Moby the caption read: NUKE THE WHALES. This was Daniel's idea of humor.

From a distance you might have mistaken Ed for a young friend of Nathan's and Daniel's. Which, I was pretty sure, was the whole idea behind the wardrobe change. If somebody happened to spot Ed through the apartment windows, they'd just think he was one of the boys' friends, visiting.

Of course, the main reason you'd think Ed had to be one of the boys' young friends was that it was hard to believe that anybody over twenty-one would be caught dead in that particular getup. Up close, Ed wouldn't fool anybody. If nothing else, I believe you'd notice right off that Ed was wearing—with ragged jeans and a whale

T-shirt—a pair of black dress shoes polished to a high sheen and black dress socks.

Oh, my, yes, I'd say Ed was making a fashion statement, all right. Particularly if that statement happened to be "Yuck."

He must've been making this statement for quite some time, because neither Nathan nor Daniel seemed the least bit surprised to see Ed in this outfit. It might've been the first time they'd noticed the dress shoes and socks, though. Both boys did seem to be staring in stunned silence in the direction of Ed's feet.

For a man who'd been hiding in a closet—and who'd come out looking as if maybe he should've spent even more time in there—Ed still managed to look indignant. "For heaven's sake, Schuyler," he said. "Do you have any idea how much a Lexus LS 400 is worth?"

I shrugged. "With or without a big scratch down the side?"

Ed ran his hand through his sandy hair—immediately reminding me of Nathan. "I cannot believe you threatened to key my car. Really, Schuyler, you shouldn't even *joke* about doing something like that!"

I shrugged again. "Oh, don't worry, Ed," I said. "I wasn't joking." I gave my key ring another rattle—making Ed actually flinch—and then I turned toward the boys' front door. "Come on, Ed, let's get out of here."

Ed's response was somewhat less than what I'd hoped for. "Schuyler, I'm not going anywhere." Ed was now using the smug tone he used to use with me all the time when we were married—the I-know-more-than-you'll-ever-learn tone. Hearing it again did not make for a warm, nostalgic moment.

"Well, you're not staying here." I said this quite clearly.

The problem was, though, at the same time that I was saying this, Nathan was also saying, "Dad is staying right here, Mom."

And Daniel was also saying, in his own inimitable way, "Yo, Mom, Dad stays."

And Ed himself was repeating, "I am not leaving, and

that's that. They're looking for me, Schuyler. The boys and I heard it on the six o'clock news—on all four local TV stations and WHAS." This last was one of the largest radio stations in Louisville.

Faced with three men all bigger than me, all talking at once, I believe I reacted the way any proper Southern lady would have under similar circumstances. I tried to out-yell them. *"Have you all gone nuts?"* I glared at Ed. "I know they're looking for you. That's why I don't want you staying here!" Next I turned to Daniel and Nathan. "Haven't you two ever heard of *harboring a fugitive*? Are you crazy? Do you want to end up in jail?"

Nathan was the only one of the three to look distressed at such a prospect. "Mom," he said. "We really don't have a choice. We *have* to hide Dad. Because he can *not* get arrested." Nathan actually sounded a little emotional. He ran his hand through his sandy hair, mimicking his dad. "We just can't let Dad go to jail. We *can't*." His voice broke a little on that last sentence.

I stared at Nathan, genuinely touched. This kid really cared about his father. Reaching out to pat Nathan's arm, I said, "Nathan, hon"—my tone was now a lot gentler—"I really don't want you to worry—"

Nathan cut me off. "Mom, if Dad got arrested, it would be *majorly* humiliating!"

I blinked at that one. Evidently Nathan's concern for his dad was not quite as profound as I thought.

"For crying out loud, Mom," Nathan was going on, "what would my friends think?"

Having met some of Nathan's friends, I was not at all sure that thinking was an activity any of them engaged in on a regular basis. However, it did seem to me as if Nathan was overlooking a little something. "Nathan, if your friends have a problem with your dad getting arrested, what do you suppose they'll think when you yourself get hauled off to jail?"

Daniel's response to what I'd just said was disappointing. *"Yo,"* he said, ducking his dark head in much the same way as Keanu Reeves kept doing in *Bill and Ted's*

Excellent Adventure. He combined this motion with a sort of Fonzie thumbs-up sign. "Cool," he added.

I stared at him. Daniel was actually grinning, his dark eyes excited. As if getting arrested would be the adventure of a lifetime. Have I mentioned that I worry about this boy?

Nathan did not quite match his brother's grin, but he didn't look all that concerned, either. "Mom, you've got to be kidding. Nobody's going to arrest me for standing by my own father," Nathan said. He was actually rolling his eyes. "I mean, Mom, *really.* What would it look like, arresting a guy for trying to help his dad?"

"What would it look like? A felony indictment, that's what it would look like," I said.

Nathan's response was a little smile and an indulgent shake of the head. He glanced over at Daniel, and at that moment, what my two sons were both thinking was so obvious, it might as well have been written on their foreheads. *Silly woman, she is totally out to lunch.*

This silly woman, let me tell you, was struck speechless. Because now I had one more thing to add to what has turned out to be a very long list: Things I Never Thought I'd Have To Tell My Child.

Thing Number One on this particular list is, believe it or not: Don't carry fire through the house. I had to mention this to Daniel one wintry day when he stuck a pencil through the grate into the glowing coals in the fireplace and managed to catch the end of the pencil on fire. Daniel was about nine at the time, and he was so tickled to have his pencil blazing away that he immediately headed upstairs with the thing to show it to his brother. Even as I was running after him, yelling Thing Number One, I was thinking, I can *not* believe I'm actually having to say this out loud to an offspring of mine.

I had the same feeling now as I'd had back then. I couldn't believe I was actually having to say to an offspring of mine: "Look, it's against the law to harbor a fugitive! Even if the fugitive is your father!"

Ed, at this point, gave me a look. Apparently, I was not

being as supportive under the circumstances as he thought I ought to be.

Since I already had his attention, I said, "Ed, for God's sake, *tell* them. Tell Nathan and Daniel how the police will probably be watching this place, looking for you. If they're not doing it already, they probably will very soon," I said. "Then tell them that the police might actually tap their phone, and bug this whole place, and pretty much make their lives a living hell. Go ahead, *tell* them."

After I said this, Ed did start talking, but the person he was talking to was not Daniel or Nathan. "Now, Schuyler," he said, "I don't intend to stay here all that long, anyway." He then went into how he really couldn't think of anyplace else to go, and how wonderful it was to have his sons on his side during such a stressful time, and how much he truly appreciated his family standing by him in his hour of need.

Really. Ed actually used those very words. *Hour of need.*

By the time Ed finally finished, I was beginning to feel a little nauseated.

It didn't help to have Nathan jump in, right after Ed had finally shut up, with a rambling, convoluted speech about how he just couldn't stand idly by and let Big Brother come in and take his own father away for a crime he didn't commit. This was, after all, America, the land of the free, home of the brave, and we should stand up and be counted, or else there would be hellfire and brimstone and a plague upon all our houses—or one thing or another bad would happen. To tell the truth, after a while I'd completely lost the thread.

Fortunately, Daniel stepped in immediately after Nathan had finally shut up, and gave a brief summation of both Ed's and Nathan's arguments. "Yo," Daniel said.

Which, I felt, was about as compelling an argument as any the other two had come up with.

Unfortunately, as it turned out, it didn't matter whether their arguments were compelling or not. The three of them kept at me for the next half hour or so, going on and on and on. Until finally, wouldn't you know, I found myself agreeing to still one more thing I knew I'd regret.

Once I'd done it, I could hardly believe it, but I actually agreed to let Ed stay in the boys' apartment for the next forty-eight hours. While he tried to find out who was framing him.

"Forty-eight hours is it, though," I said, glaring first at Ed and then at Nathan and Daniel.

"Not a second more," Ed assured me. "Forty-eight hours from now, I'll be walking into the police station and turning myself in."

Let's face it, I would've been willing to agree to almost anything to get Ed to agree to vacate the boys' apartment. I wanted him out of there, and I wanted him out ASAP. I really didn't relish going to visit either Nathan or Daniel in jail. If that should happen, there was no telling how many things I'd be adding to my Things-I-Never-Thought-I'd-Have-To-Tell-My-Child list. It could become a book.

I didn't particularly want to see Ed behind bars, either. I really didn't. On the other hand, if I had to pick somebody to Go To Jail Without Passing Go, I'd pick Ed over the boys in a heartbeat.

"You'll be gone by the day after tomorrow?" I asked.

Ed looked straight at me without blinking. "I promise," he said.

With my eyes on Ed's, I did have a moment of uneasiness. Lord knows, I'd heard promises out of this man before—promises delivered with the same unblinking sincerity. But then Daniel jumped in. "Yo, then it's settled." He was doing Keanu and Fonzie again.

Ed actually put his arm around my shoulders. "Thanks, Sugar Pie," he said, tightening his arm.

In front of Nathan and Daniel, I tried not to stiffen. It took some real concentration, though. Sugar Pie had been what Ed had called me when we were first married. Lord. He hadn't called me that in years. I can't say I was glad to hear it. Ed's arm suddenly felt far too heavy across my shoulders. I stood there for a long moment, suddenly recalling other unwelcome advances Ed was supposed to have made.

"Oh, by the way," I said, trying to sound almost conversational as I moved away from Ed. "Guess what Adrienne Henderson told the police?"

I was watching Ed closely. He seemed to look simply curious. Nothing more. Certainly he didn't look like someone who felt guilty about making a pass at another woman practically under the nose of his now-deceased fiancée. But, then again, he had never looked like someone who played around on his wife, either. "What did Adrienne tell them?" Ed asked. His blue eyes were perfectly clear.

I took a deep breath, my own eyes never leaving his face. "That this morning you tried to kiss her. And that Kimberly walked in on you."

Oh, brother. For a second there, I thought the top of Ed's head was going to lift off. If Ed was faking, and just *acting* upset, the man had clearly made a poor career choice.

"WHA-A-AT?" Ed's voice was a croak, and to be coldly honest, he looked significantly less handsome with his eyes bulging out like that.

I must have a sadistic streak where Ed is concerned. I slowed down, carefully enunciating every word. "Adrienne Henderson said that you grabbed her when you two were out in the kitchen, and that you tried to plant one on—"

Ed didn't let me finish. "I did no such thing!" He looked over at Nathan and Daniel. "That Henderson woman is lying!" Ed said. "She is making every bit of this up!"

Nathan and Daniel now looked every bit as indignant as their father. "Why, that damn liar!" Nathan said. "What the hell does she think she's doing?"

Even Daniel was positively verbose in his outrage. "This is awful!" he said.

I stood there, staring at my two sons. Neither one of them could possibly know the truth for certain, and yet they didn't hesitate for a moment to take Ed's word for what had happened. I wished I could do the same. The fact was, however, I'd heard these exact same words out of Ed before. I'd heard them quite a few times, and every single one of those times, they'd been lies.

Ed, no surprise, didn't seem to make the connection himself. He went right on, saying even more familiar words. "Schuyler, I cannot believe you'd take the word of this woman—somebody you hardly know—over *me*!"

They were lines from a script that I'd memorized years ago. "But, Ed," I said right on cue, "why would she lie? What earthly reason would this woman have to tell these lies about you?"

And, right on cue again, Ed began to pace in front of me, waving his arms excitedly. "Well, now, how would I know?" he said. "Maybe she's sick. Or deranged. Or maybe she's just got it in for me. I tell you, Schuyler, I hardly know the woman. So why she'd be trying to get me in trouble, I have no idea!"

I stared at him. The words were so familiar, they almost seemed to echo in my head. God. Could it be that Ed really was lying? *Again*?

My stomach burned.

"Hell, maybe she's just a man-hater! Out to get every man she sees!" Ed was now on a roll. "I mean, she *is* getting a divorce, isn't she? Maybe she's so angry about her husband dumping her that she's taking it out on me! Hell, how would I know why this Henderson woman would tell these lies about me?"

Nathan jumped in at this point. "Really, Mom, how *would* Dad know why this—this—" Nathan paused here, obviously searching for the right word. "—this *witch* would make this stuff up?"

I was pretty sure *witch* was not the word that had first come to Nathan's mind.

"Did you ever think that maybe it was Adrienne?" Ed was now saying.

I turned to look at Ed. He did look plenty upset. His hair was now sticking up in little tufts on each side of his head where he'd run his hands through it. "What do you mean," I asked, "it was *Adrienne*?" I thought maybe Ed was now about to tell me that Adrienne had made the first move on him, or something of that ilk, but that wasn't what he meant at all.

"Maybe Adrienne Henderson killed Kimberly," Ed said, "and now she's trying to frame me for it."

I blinked. At the risk of repeating myself, I started to ask, "Now why on earth would Adrienne—?"

That's all I got out. Ed was so eager to answer that one that he interrupted me. "I'll tell you why," he said. "Adrienne could have killed Kimberly because she didn't want to sell her house."

As Ed spoke, both Daniel and Nathan backed him up by nodding, their heads moving in perfect unison. Ed seemed to be doing Gladys Knight, and our sons were doing the Pips.

I stared at all three of them. "Don't you think it's a bit far-fetched to suggest that somebody might commit murder just to avoid selling her house? After all," I said, now looking directly at Ed, "it's not as if you and Kimberly were the only buyers in the world. There *are* always others. Do you really believe that Adrienne Henderson intends to kill everyone who signs a contract on her house?"

After a while, that could amount to quite a body count. It would also be unbelievably easy to figure out who was committing the crimes. I was pretty sure Adrienne was neither homicidal nor stupid. Both of which she'd have to be to do what Ed suggested.

"Besides," I hurried to add, "if Adrienne *had* been eliminating potential buyers, why didn't she kill you, too?"

Ed's response to that was a shrug. Immediately echoed, once again in unison, by the Pips.

I hurried on. "Besides, you forget, I talked to Kimberly myself. Just before I left to meet her at the Henderson place. Kimberly told me then that Adrienne was not there—that, in fact, Adrienne had already left."

Ed's face fell. The faces of the Pips fell even further.

"You're right about one thing," I said, and was rewarded by all three faces swiveling in my direction. "You're right that we should be looking for somebody who might've had a motive to want Kimberly out of the way." I pointed at Ed. "Like, for example, was there anybody who now stands to inherit Kimberly's portion of the Metcalf fortune?"

Ed began pacing again. "Well, there's a brother, Paul Metcalf. He's a year younger than Kimberly, and I suppose he'll inherit Kimberly's portion now." Ed stopped and turned to face me. He tried to put both hands into the pockets of his jeans, but with that one front pocket hanging by a thread, he could only get his right hand in. It took him a moment to realize this, and then he gave up and just crossed his arms across his chest. "He and Kimberly were sharing an apartment. I only met him once," Ed said. "He was leaving Kimberly's apartment one day just as I was getting there, and Kimberly introduced us. He seemed like a nice enough guy."

Seeming like a nice enough guy did not necessarily disqualify you as a murderer. According to everything I'd read, Ted Bundy had seemed like a nice enough guy.

Something else Ed had just said also bothered me. "Kimberly and her brother were living together, but you only met him *once*?"

Ed shrugged again. "The guy was always out when I was there. Besides," he added, "I got the impression that Kimberly and her brother were not particularly close. She hardly ever mentioned him."

I took a second to think about that one. This brother and sister weren't particularly close, and yet they lived together? This didn't exactly make sense.

"You know," Ed said, uncrossing his arms and pointing at me, "it was Paul who drove Kimberly over to the Hendersons' house earlier today. He drove her because he knew that I was supposed to come by and pick her up after she'd finished with her measuring. We were supposed to go to lunch, and Kimberly said there was no use having her car and my car at the Henderson house. The thing is, if Paul drove her there, he'd certainly know where she was and at what time."

I nodded. "So, what you're telling me is that Paul had motive. And opportunity."

Ed returned my nod. "That's right," he said. "And, as far as I know, Paul is the only one who stood to inherit if anything happened to Kimberly." According to Ed, Kimberly had no immediate family other than Paul. The elder Metcalfs were already middle-aged when Kimberly was born, and both her parents had died when she was still in college. From what Ed understood, they'd left a trust fund for Kimberly, which was intended to support her until, at the age of twenty-eight, she would come into the bulk of her inheritance. "Her share was worth," Ed said quietly, "almost a million dollars."

Both Pips whistled when they heard that one. "A million smackers! Oh, my God!" Nathan said.

"YO!" Daniel said.

I was staring at Ed. This certainly explained why Ed didn't care if Kimberly cost him a deposit on a house. By keeping her happy, he stood to gain far more. This was also, believe it or not, the best evidence I'd heard so far indicating that Ed was innocent. From what I knew of him, Ed might—and I just say, *might,* mind you—be capable of snuffing out the life of an actual human being, but there was no way on God's green earth that he'd kill off a million dollars. I took another deep breath. No wonder Ed had looked so devastated when I'd met him at the Henderson house earlier today. He'd just lost a lot more than a fiancée. "So," I said, "does that mean that Paul would inherit a million dollars more with Kimberly out of the picture?"

Ed cocked his sandy head to one side, and then tried to shove both hands into the front pockets of his jeans again. I believe I've already established that this little maneuver was doomed to failure. Once again, Ed ended up crossing his arms. "Well," Ed said, "now that you mention it, I guess Paul *could* be a million dollars richer."

"I'd love to hear what old Paul's got to say for himself," I said.

I was just thinking out loud. That's all. Ed and the boys, however, apparently read a lot more into those words than I meant. "Then you're going to go talk to Paul?" Ed asked.

"That's a great idea!" Nathan said. "Why don't you go

talk to this Paul guy and, you know, see if he acts guilty?"
Nathan asked.

I guess I don't have to mention what Daniel said.

"It shouldn't be difficult to get Paul to talk to you," Ed
said. "You could act as if you'd just heard what happened
and wanted to pay your respects."

I just looked at him. Then I looked over at Nathan and
Daniel. My stomach hurt all over again.

Surely I was not about to agree *again* to do something I
really didn't want to do.

Surely not.

Gladys and the Pips were now all nodding in unison.

Oh, for God's sake.

Chapter 10

There was no doubt about it, I was going to have to change my name to Patsy.

As I headed down Watterson Expressway toward the address Ed had given me, I could not believe I'd actually agreed to go have a little chat with Paul Metcalf, Kimberly's brother. I also couldn't believe I'd actually agreed to take Nathan with me. Was I out of my mind?

Sitting beside me in the passenger seat of my Tercel, Nathan was now saying, "Mom, watch out for that blue Mercury up ahead. It's got its turn signal on, and you're coming up on it awful fast. Better slow down. And that red BMW two cars up—it's changing lanes, so you'd better . . ."

I gritted my teeth and tried to tune him out. Nathan had flunked his driver's test three times. I'd gotten mine on the first try. And yet, every time Nathan was a passenger in my car, I got driving lessons. I also got to watch him stomp on an imaginary brake pedal on the floor in front of him. He was doing it now, his right leg jerking as if it were racked with some kind of terrible spasm.

Unfortunately, Nathan's leg spasms were not something I could exactly ignore. Mainly because—even though it was now beginning to get dark, and it was already so cold, I was wishing I'd worn gloves—Nathan was still wearing shorts. What a surprise. If he'd had on slacks, his leg could spasm and I might not even see it. But in shorts? How could I *not* notice?

"Mom!" Nathan's voice was suddenly shrill with alarm.

"That truck three cars ahead of us is slowing down! *See*? He's probably taking the next exit. So you'd better brake! NOW!"

I was braking already. I was also, in my humble opinion, demonstrating remarkable restraint by not saying one word as I did so. Especially since it crossed my mind that somebody twenty years my junior—with legs rapidly turning blue, for God's sake—had a lot of nerve telling *me* what to do.

I had no intention of getting into it with Nathan, however. I'd gone down that road, no pun intended, too many times before. Harsh experience had taught me that, unless I was feeling particularly argumentative, it was a lot easier to just let Nathan go on and on. If I started barking at him, he invariably barked back. In no time at all, I could find myself in a truly ugly discussion in which the details of every single car accident that I'd ever had were pretty much thrown in my face.

Hey, my plate was full. I'd already had enough to deal with for one day.

As a case in point, before I'd left my sons' apartment, I'd called my office to check my messages. I usually check in with my office every few hours during the day, but today it had completely slipped my mind, oddly enough.

I did, of course, have a great excuse. Running into a murder and having to take time out to chat with the police can definitely cut into a person's efficiency. Unfortunately, I didn't want to tell anybody at my office this particular great excuse. Not today, anyway. It was going to be bad enough when the news about Kimberly appeared in the *Courier-Journal* tomorrow.

Today I wanted to put off answering questions as long as I could. That's why when Arlene, Jarvis's wife and co-owner of Arndoerfer Realty, said something snippy on the phone about professionalism, I couldn't even defend myself. Arlene wasn't about to let it go, either. She went on about how "people in our industry"—meaning *me*—really needed to be super-conscientious about checking in with "the home team"—meaning *her*—because otherwise things could "degenerate into chaos"—meaning, *I've been pulling my hair out, answering your damn phone.*

Arlene did eventually give me my phone messages, her tone getting snippier by the minute. Wouldn't you know, none of the calls were urgent. All were either from clients wanting to make an appointment to see this or that listing of mine in the next week or so, or they were from clients wanting to let me know they'd decided against a property I'd already shown them.

To hear Arlene talk, however, every one of these people was on life support, breathing their last, only hoping to hang on long enough to hear a few words from me before the end. "Thanks, Arlene," I said, "I'll get back to them right away."

"Well, I certainly hope so," she said.

Oh, yes, I'd say my plate was full, all right.

"Mom, get over to your right," Nathan was now saying. "This lane's moving too slow. Get into the other lane as soon as you can. All right, you're doing fine."

It's times like these that I think fondly of the little button that Agent 007 had in his car in all those James Bond movies I used to watch when I was a teenager. If I remember correctly, the little button was located right next to the gearshift, and by pressing it, you could jettison any passenger sitting beside you right through the car roof. Now *there* was an option worth paying extra for.

"Do you see the green Neon in your rearview mirror?" Nathan's voice had gotten shrill again. "It's about to pass us on your side. Watch it! Give it some room, Mom. You never know who's behind the wheel."

I gave him a quick sideways glance. Now that he mentioned it, I did know who was behind the wheel. At least, in *this* car, anyway. It was *Nathan* who seemed to be unclear on the subject.

I turned to look back at the road, gripping the steering wheel a little tighter. I was well aware what a joy Nathan always was to drive with, so why on earth had I agreed to do this? I would have had to say that this was the dumbest thing I'd ever done, but fortunately, I had my marriage to Ed to look back on. That one would, no doubt, continue to beat out all comers in the Dumbest Thing I've Ever Done competition. Still, this had to be up there. Among the top ten, for sure.

In my defense, I would like to point out that Ed and both boys had all ganged up on me. Three against one was hardly fair. And yet, fairness aside, even *I* had to admit that some of the points that Ed, Nathan, and Daniel had made when they were badgering me were certainly valid. Like, for example, Ed had argued that, under the circumstances, he really could not go himself to talk to Paul Metcalf. As a wanted man, Ed had said, he couldn't move around as freely as I could.

I'd known, of course, that Ed was right. It really would be difficult for Ed to talk to Paul without somebody spotting him. If he wasn't seen at Paul's apartment, he could easily be spotted on the trips there and back. "For all I know," Ed had said, "the police could be watching Kimberly's brother right now, so going over there would be the same as turning myself in."

I'd just looked at him, fighting the urge to say, "And your *point*?" Because, let me tell you, given the choice between Ed turning himself in and his continuing to hide out in Nathan and Daniel's closet, I'd choose the first option every time. And not because the closet was cramped, either.

I hadn't said a word, though. I'd already agreed to give the man forty-eight hours before he turned himself in, and I had not wanted to get into a huge argument with Ed any more than I wanted to argue with his son now.

Ed had also made another good point. He'd mentioned that it was probably more likely that Paul would let his guard down with a woman—and perhaps reveal more than he meant to—than with another man. I believe Ed's exact words on this particular subject were: "Guys don't tell other guys squat."

The clincher, however, had come when Ed had suggested an alternative plan. "You know, Schuyler," Ed said, fiddling with the flap of his torn pocket, not meeting my eyes, "if you really don't feel comfortable meeting with Paul Metcalf yourself, Nathan could go."

I'd turned to stare at Ed, actually feeling the blood drain from my face. *Nathan*? Was Ed serious? Or was he talking about some other Nathan, not our mutual son? Surely Ed could not possibly be talking about *our* Nathan, the one standing right next to us, the one whose face had lit up the second Ed had mentioned his name. Surely Ed had to realize, didn't he, that the interview with Kimberly's brother would at least call for *some* tact and diplomacy?

Once again I had no intention of discussing this with either Ed or Nathan—but tact and diplomacy did seem to be two things that Nathan lacked in abundance. If I'd had to prove this in court, Nathan's behavior this past Thanksgiving would've been Exhibit A.

It had been on this lovely, traditional, family holiday that Nathan had evidently decided that a discussion on the wide variety of condoms currently available over the counter would be appropriate conversation for the dinner table. I am still not sure what the hell Nathan had been thinking. Had he brought up this little topic to amuse those present, or had he thought he was conveying a news flash? Have I mentioned that those present at the ill-fated dinner included my parents and several of my aunts and uncles on my mother's side? All of whom were over the age of seventy? As luck would have it, Nathan had opened the floor for condom discussion at the exact moment my seventy-six-year-old father had started carving the turkey. Dad had nearly sliced his thumb off.

With all this going through my mind, I folded my arms across my chest and pinned Ed with a look. "Wait a minute—I thought you just said that guys don't tell other guys squat."

Ed shrugged and looked at his shoes. "Well, yes, that *is* true, all right. There's not a doubt in my mind that the interview would be a lot more productive if you did it, but—" At this point, Ed evidently lost interest in his shoes. Opening his eyes very wide, he looked directly at me. "Well, I am sure that Nathan will do just fine."

I'd known then. When Ed starts using words like *interview* and *productive,* he's shoveling it big-time. He didn't think Nathan would do fine. On the contrary. What he was counting on was that I would never stand idly by and let Nathan, of all people, go in my place.

About that time, I noticed that Nathan was literally bouncing on his heels, in perpetual motion, as if waiting for the sound of a starter pistol to take off. Nathan's eyes were dancing with excitement as they darted from my face to Ed's and back again. I couldn't believe it. My simpleton son actually looked *eager* to talk to a man who might've committed a murder earlier today— a man who just might be in the mood to commit a murder once again. In fact, I'd say that Kimberly's brother Paul might be in a particularly homicidal mood if he got the impression that somebody like, oh, say, *Nathan,* suspected that he was guilty. And, given Nathan's track record in the tact and diplomacy department, I'd say that Paul stood a good chance of getting that impression about five seconds after Nathan opened his mouth and started grilling him.

Like I said, all of these things flashed through my mind immediately after Ed threw Nathan's hat, so to speak, into the ring. Unfortunately, none of these things seemed to occur to Nathan.

"Wow," Nathan said, "that's a great idea." He'd apparently decided, since I had not immediately seconded his father's nomination, that I might've been waiting for his own endorsement. "Now, Mom, don't you worry," Nathan said, "I can handle it. It'll be a piece of cake."

I just looked at him. Thank God this kid had missed the draft. There was not a doubt in my mind that if some army officer had come up to Nathan and said, "Son, as we march into battle, I'd like *you* to lead us, carrying this very large, brightly colored United States flag," Nathan would've responded in much the same way. Beginning with, "Wow, that's a great idea!" And ending with, "It'll be a piece of cake."

I was relieved to notice that Daniel, on the other hand, had started to frown. "Yo, wait a minute," Daniel said. Standing on my right, he shifted his weight from one foot to the other as he thoughtfully fingered one of the largest holes in his T-shirt. I glanced over at him expectantly. *Thank God*, I actually thought. *At least I've got one sane son. At least Daniel realizes how dangerous this little assignment could be.*

Daniel folded his arms across his chest and went through the same look-first-at-Ed-and-then-over-at-me routine that his brother had. "If Nathan gets to talk to this guy, I think I should get to talk to him, too," Daniel said, his tone petulant. "After all, I am the oldest."

It was all I could do to keep my mouth from dropping open. *Gets to*? Did Daniel say, *gets to*? Up till then, I'd apparently been woefully misinformed. Thank heavens, though, Daniel had straightened me out. Getting the chance to spend a few moments, up close and personal, with a possible murderer was a privilege.

Sure it was. What was wrong with me that I'd think otherwise?

I peered at my older son a little closer. Daniel—who, the last time I'd checked, was all of twenty-two years old—now looked as if he were *pouting*. Oh, my, yes, his lower lip could've made a pretty decent bird perch. I shook my head. Was it me, or were my two sons the youngest young adults on the planet?

Ed met Daniel's frown with a frown of his own. "Oh, for God's sake, there's no sense in all three of you going. I mean, what is this—some kind of family outing?"

It was right after that golden moment, amazingly enough, that I found myself actually volunteering to go talk to Paul Metcalf. I knew I was letting Ed pull a fast one, but I didn't even care. Anything was better than having Daniel go up to Kimberly's brother and say, *YO, my mom and dad think you killed your sister with an over-sized flashlight. So, did you*?

Even more amazing, shortly after I volunteered to talk to Kimberly's brother, I also agreed to take Nathan with me. As far as this last was concerned, I didn't have a whole lot of choice. Ed—who for once in his life had actually acted as if he were concerned about me—had insisted. "Don't be an idiot, Schuyler. You can't go over there alone. That would be moronic." Ed always did have the most endearing way of putting things. "I mean, *think* about it. There's no telling what this guy might do."

After hearing that stirring testimonial on the relative safety of this little mission, Nathan and Daniel had both immediately stepped forward. "Mom, we'll both come with you," Nathan said. Beside him, Daniel punctuated Nathan's words by nodding his head. "We'll make sure nothing happens," Nathan went on. "You don't have anything to worry about."

I'd just looked at my sons for a moment. My two bodyguards. How cute. I'd say between the two of them they could definitely get me killed.

"Look, you guys," I said, "I don't think I need either one of you to—"

That's about as far as I got before Ed, Nathan, and Daniel all started talking at once. Several minutes later I gave up and chose the lesser of two evils—one bodyguard instead of two, and Nathan in shorts instead of Daniel in bullet-riddled clothes. My reason for passing on the bullet holes, I believe, was pretty obvious: There was no use putting ideas into anybody's head.

I did make it abundantly clear, however, that I was only agreeing if Nathan stayed in the car and acted solely as a backup. Meaning that, unless he heard me scream, or the sound of gunfire, or something along that line, he was to remain in the car. When I told him this, I did not add, *where no one can see your legs turning blue.* I did think it, however.

"Okay," Nathan said, nodding. "Sounds good to me."

Apparently, it did not sound all that good to Daniel. In fact, as soon as it was definitely decided that Nathan would be the one to tag along with me, Daniel started doing his bird perch all over again. "Yo, I don't see why Nathan gets to—"

I didn't let him go any further. "Daniel," I said, "somebody has to stay here with your dad." My thinking on this subject was that if anybody outside happened to see or hear Ed moving around in their apartment, Daniel would be needed. To explain to people that the person they'd seen was really him. Or to tell them that it had been a friend of his from school. Or, if these explanations didn't work, to point out to the police exactly which closet Ed was hiding in.

Oddly enough, I only mentioned the first two possibilities to Daniel. I tried to make it sound, however, as if what we needed him to do was far more important than tagging along with me. I must've done even better than I expected, because by the time I finished, Daniel's "Yo" sounded positively triumphant. And Nathan was actually looking a little envious of his brother.

I'd decided at that point that I probably ought to quit while I was ahead, and not even try to convince Nathan that his job was the one that was the better of the two. No doubt, Daniel would've started pouting all over again.

"Mom! Watch out for the yellow Volvo!" Nathan's voice was now suddenly so shrill, I jumped. "It's coming up fast on my side!"

I took a quick look over my right shoulder. There was a yellow Volvo at least two car lengths back. "Nathan," I said through my teeth, "I see the Volvo, okay? Don't scream when I'm driving."

Inwardly, I sighed. *Don't scream when I'm driving.* One more thing to add to my Things I Never Thought . . . list.

Nathan had turned around in his seat, looking at the Volvo over his own right shoulder. "It's coming fast, Mom. Really fast! Don't worry, though. I'm watching it."

This is something that Dr. Spock never once mentioned in his best-seller on child-rearing. Believe me, I read the entire book over and over when the boys were small, making sure I was doing everything the way I was supposed to. I know I would've remembered such a thing if it had been in there. Take my word for it, the good doctor never once even hinted that there would come a day, as surely as the sun comes up in the morning, when your baby will actually start telling *you* what to do. When he'll begin sitting in judgment of every move you make, and start bossing you around as if *you* were the baby.

This little omission was a major oversight on Dr. Spock's part, in my opinion. Warning parents about this certainly seemed a tad more significant than telling them how many drawstring gowns they were going to need for the layette.

"Mom, MOM!" Nathan's voice was a shriek. "Slow down! The exit's coming up. Get over to your right. Careful now, easy, easy . . . okay, you're doing fine."

I tightened my grip on the steering wheel once again. What I obviously needed to do was just focus on the road ahead. I needed to concentrate on finding the address Ed had given me, and pretend that Nathan was nothing more than background static.

According to Ed, the apartment Paul and Kimberly had shared was a luxury two-bedroom townhouse in a complex called La Fenetre Garden Apartments. This complex must've been new, because it didn't sound familiar. Ed had said that it was located on La Fenetre Way, just off Shelbyville Road on my left, a little past Oxmoor Shopping Center.

I increased my speed a little, and Nathan's right leg immediately started doing its Saint Vitus's dance. I ignored it, took the Shelbyville Road exit, and in no time at all, I was turning onto La Fenetre Way, going past a large green marble sign in which the name LA FENETRE had been etched in large gold script letters.

Oh, my, yes, Ed was right about La Fenetre being a *luxury* apartment complex. Of course, I'd already reached that conclusion when Ed was still giving me directions. La Fenetre Garden Apartments was located in what is known in the real estate biz as a prestige area. If you weren't sure just how prestigious this area was, the fact that the apartment's name was French was a major tip-off. In Louisville's East End, having a French apartment name was probably worth an extra hundred dollars a month. Mentioning the word *Garden* in the name added another fifty.

A mention seemed to be just about all you were going to get in the way of a garden in this place, however. As Nathan and I pulled up in front of La Fenetre Garden Apartment #A-4—the number Ed had given me—I couldn't see anything that even came close to a garden.

The place did look sort of French in a New Orleans kind of way, with brick facades painted white and black fili-gree wrought iron decorating windows, porches, and bal-conies. All the doors were painted a green so dark it was almost black, and every apartment building seemed to have a hanging basket near its entrance. It being October, most of these baskets were either empty or held some-thing that was now straggly and brown. Even if all the baskets had been in full bloom, however, I don't think they would've fooled anybody. I hated to break it to the La Fenetre folks, but come on now, plastic pots dangling on ropes? These were gardens?

I left Nathan in the car with firm instructions to come only in the event of calamity—and loud calamity, at that. I really didn't expect to have a problem; I was just more or less placating Ed and the boys to even have brought Nathan with me. Still, just to be on the safe side, I told him to roll down the window on his side of the car so he'd be sure to hear if anything went wrong.

And, as I trotted up the sidewalk toward A-4, I felt in my purse for my little canister of pepper spray. I found it, got it out, and then I started to put it in the front pocket of my jacket where I could get to it in a hurry if I had to.

Not that I really was scared of Paul Metcalf or any-thing. Lately I've been carrying something like this on my person, ever since the day it dawned on me that my job— meeting total strangers in vacant houses, often after dark—could possibly be dangerous. This dawned on me, strangely enough, a few months ago when a real estate agent that I worked with turned up dead in the basement of one of my own listings. Hey, I may be slow, but even-tually I get the message.

Now, before I dropped the pepper spray in my front pocket, I paused long enough to check to make sure that the canister's top was secure. I always try to remember to do this. Mainly because I've also discovered that these little canisters of pepper spray can be dangerous to their user, too. I discovered this the day I was showing a tri-level way out in Shelby County. The young couple I was showing the place to had started talking about making an offer, so naturally I'd started rummaging around in my blazer pocket for a pen. Instead of the pen, I'd grabbed the pepper spray and somehow managed to set the thing off.

Can you believe, the tri-level had to be fumigated? At my expense.

My blazer—which was an Anne Klein that I'd gotten on sale at seventy-five percent off, meaning, of course, that the thing was irreplaceable—had to be thrown away. Goodwill wouldn't even take it.

And, last but not least, the young couple had decided against making an offer, after all.

Like I said, I may be slow, but I do finally get the message. I didn't give up on carrying pepper spray around with me, but I did get a lot more careful with it. Now, as I walked toward the garden-apartment-without-a-garden, I found myself giving the canister in my front pocket a little pat.

Ed may have been right about how luxurious the apartment was, but he was most certainly wrong about something else. Paul and Kimberly must've been a lot closer than Ed had thought. When I rang the doorbell, it took forever before the door was finally opened. I could hear somebody shuffling around in there, too, but whoever it was didn't seem to be making much progress getting to the door.

I had to ring the doorbell two more times before the door was finally opened. Peeping around the edge of the door, his dark hair disheveled, his eyes red-rimmed, and his face covered with a dark stubble, was a guy who looked more than just grief-stricken. He looked as if his world had ended.

What's more, he smelled as if he'd been bathing in bourbon.

I put my hand in my front pocket, tightened my hold around the pepper spray, and took a step forward.

"Hi there," I said. I tried for the subdued, soothing tone usually employed by the director of a funeral home. "Are you Mr. Paul Metcalf?"

The guy seemed to be having a little trouble focusing,

but when his eyes cleared, he started to nod his head. "Yeah, I'm—"

That was all he got out. Behind me I heard a car door slam. And then Paul Metcalf and I both turned to see Nathan hurrying up the sidewalk directly toward us.

I was so surprised, it was all I could do to keep my mouth from dropping open.

If my car wasn't on fire, Nathan was in big trouble.

Chapter 11

Nathan didn't seem to notice until he was about halfway up the sidewalk that Paul Metcalf and I were staring at him. When Nathan finally realized it, he shot his hand into the air. In a wave, I might add, far too cheery for a condolence visit. "Hi there!" Nathan said, looking past me, directly at Paul. "I'm with *her*!" Nathan punctuated this last statement by giving his head a little jerk in my direction.

I was standing right in front of Paul, but I turned around so that all Paul could see was the back of my head. Then I gave Nathan a look that could've been registered as a lethal weapon.

What the hell do you think you're doing? Didn't we have an agreement? Weren't you supposed to stay in the car? My lethal look said all these things. Nathan, however, chose to miss my look entirely. He kept his eyes glued to Paul's face. Oddly enough.

"Look, if you two are selling something . . ." Paul's voice was slurred, and he didn't quite finish his sentence, letting that last word just trail off. I got the gist, however, when he started to shut the door.

I immediately stopped trying to convey to Nathan just how thrilled I was to have him join us. Instead, I quickly turned back around, faced Paul once again, and utilized a time-honored technique that I'd mastered years ago, shortly after I'd gotten my real estate license.

Back then I'd been working for a real estate firm that insisted that all its agents spend at least ten hours a week canvassing. Meaning you were expected to go door-to-door, begging for business. As I recall, I'd mastered the aforementioned time-honored technique inside of a week. Now I realized it must be like riding a bicycle—once you learn it, you never forget it. I had my foot in Paul's doorway, preventing him from closing the door all the way, before I even realized what I was doing.

It was at this point, of course, that it occurred to me that this was a time-honored technique best employed by men in work boots. The black suede pumps I was wearing didn't do much in the way of cushioning the impact of wood against flesh. I swallowed a pained yelp, and then hurried on to say, "Oh, my goodness, no, we are certainly not selling anything." I was still going for the soothing, sepulchral tones of a funeral home director. "The truth is, Mr. Metcalf, we heard what happened, and we wanted to come by to pay our respects. We were good friends of Kimberly's."

Paul had been staring blearily at my foot—the one wedged painfully in his doorway—as if he couldn't quite decide what it was doing there. When I mentioned Kimberly's name, though, his head sort of bobbled in my direction. He squinted first at me, and then over at Nathan, who had by that time reached my side. In fact, Nathan was now standing shoulder to shoulder with me, as if we were partners or something. Like Bonnie and Clyde. Or, maybe more appropriately, Lucy and Little Ricky.

"You two were friends of Kimmie's?" As Paul said this, his tone clearly doubtful, his bloodshot eyes strayed in the direction of Nathan's bare legs. Apparently, even in his present inebriated state, Paul strongly questioned whether Kimberly would have ever befriended somebody who obviously didn't have the sense to wear slacks on an evening already so cold you could see your breath.

Nathan must've felt that, since Paul was looking steadily in his direction, albeit below the knees, it was a lot like being called on in class. He cleared his throat. "Oh, yeah," Nathan said, nodding his sandy head emphatically, "Kimberly was a good friend, all right. A good,

good friend. Why, when I heard about her being murdered"—at the mention of this word, Paul grimaced—
"you could've knocked me over with a feather."

I felt like giving Nathan a knock of my own—only with
something a little more substantial than a feather. A brick,
maybe.

"Oh, yeah, it was quite a shock," Nathan was now
saying. "Because Kimberly was such a good, good friend
and all."

I stared at Nathan. To the best of my knowledge, he'd
barely known Kimberly. She had been just one more
woman in a long line of women that his father had been
engaged to. It appeared then that Nathan was attempting
to follow in his dad's illustrious footsteps. He was lying
his head off.

I can't say I was proud.

"I mean," Nathan was going on, "I was totally shocked
when I heard—"

It looked as if Nathan might be prepared to babble on
for the rest of the night on the topic of "Shock and Friend-
ship." Before Paul nodded off—or worse, tried to shut his
door again—I interrupted. "I'd gotten to know Kimberly
quite well myself," I said, "when—"

I had intended to actually finish this sentence,
explaining how I'd been helping Kimberly and her fiancé
house hunt. Nathan, however, interrupted my interrup-
tion. "Oh, yeah, we were all real good friends," Nathan
said. "Why, I always thought of Kimberly as a sister, you
know?"

I just looked at Nathan. I'd say Kimberly's brother
knew, for God's sake.

"Yeah," Nathan blathered on, "we were darn close, that
was for sure—"

There was hope, after all. Nathan obviously did not
have his father's natural gifts in the lying department. It
could very well be that Nathan would not be capable of
following his father's bad example.

What a shame.

Once again, I tried to cut Nathan off. "As a matter of
fact," I said, "I talked to Kimberly just this morning. I

believe I might've been the last person she talked to before—before . . ." Unlike Nathan, I was reluctant to put what had happened to poor Kimberly into words. Instead, I followed Paul's earlier example and just let that last sentence trail off.

I'd apparently said enough, anyway. Paul's eyes darted to my face and stayed there. "You talked to Kimmie? Today?" He opened the door a little wider and peered out at me blearily.

With the door open a little more, I got a much better look at Kimberly's brother. Unlike Kimberly, Paul had dark brown eyes and dark brown, curly hair. I usually don't like curly hair on men, but on Paul Metcalf, it was sort of endearing. In his distress, he obviously hadn't combed his hair in quite some time, and his tousled curls made him look boyishly appealing. He was about Nathan's height and build, only more muscular.

There was one other thing that I noticed which, in the interest of accuracy, I should probably mention. Paul Metcalf, no doubt about it, was *extremely* good-looking. He had obviously seen better days, but even in his present condition, he could make female hearts beat a little faster just by walking into the room. A cross between Brad Pitt and Mel Gibson, Paul Metcalf could easily have been a male model.

He was not exactly dressed for the part, however. He was wearing a badly wrinkled white dress shirt rolled up at the elbows, tan chinos that had lost their crease hours ago, and black socks with no shoes.

Wearing socks sans shoes on a hardwood floor was not one of Paul's better ideas. He kept sliding a little. Fortunately, he was still sober enough to realize just how unsteady he was on his feet. He didn't let go of the doorknob even after he'd opened the door wide enough for me to get my own foot out. Instead, Paul leaned heavily on the knob, as if it were the top of a cane.

I stared at him. *This* was the guy that Nathan, Daniel, Ed, and I had all thought might've actually killed Kimberly? That possibility was looking more and more remote by the minute. If Paul Metcalf really had killed his sister, he was now regretting it to the extreme. It seemed far more likely, though, that this guy was exactly what he seemed to be—devastated by grief.

"When did you talk to Kimmie?" Paul's eyes had not left my face. "The police told me that they think it—it happened around noon."

I didn't want to tell him that I thought I might've actually been on the phone with Kimberly when she was attacked. Just the thought made my stomach wrench. "I talked to her this morning," I told Paul. "She and I didn't really discuss anything important; it was just chitchat."

Chitchat regarding her being afraid. That was all.

Paul nodded, his eyes getting unfocused again. "How—how did you say you knew Kimmie?" he asked.

"I'm a real estate agent," I said. "I've been helping Kimberly and her fiancé find their new home—"

You could tell that it was taking all of Paul's concentration to follow what I was saying. When I said the word *fiancé,* he sort of winced, frowning. He looked as if there was something about that word that was supposed to bother him, but in his alcoholic haze, he couldn't quite remember what it was. He blinked a couple times and ran a shaky hand over his face as if trying to wipe away the cobwebs. Finally, he pointed a trembling finger in my direction. "Wha—what did you say your name was again?"

I hadn't mentioned my name yet, so it was not going to be *again.* I decided, however, that it wasn't necessary to point this out to Paul. He seemed to be having enough trouble following the conversation as it was. "My name is Schuyler—"

I'd been intending to give Paul my maiden name, Koenig. For good reason. If Paul was looking strange when I mentioned the word *fiancé,* then he'd probably already heard on the TV or the radio that the police were looking for Ed Ridgway. If I could possibly avoid it, I didn't want Paul connecting me with Ed. That would, no doubt, be the fastest way to get him to clam up on me.

There was a chance, of course, that Kimberly had already mentioned to Paul that her real estate agent happened to be her fiancé's first wife, but she might not have. And even if she had, in his present condition, Paul might not remember.

I would've liked to have told all of this to Nathan—so that he, too, would pretty much omit the name Ridgway from his conversation—but I couldn't exactly fill Nathan in with Paul standing right there. There was nothing to do except hope that Nathan would know enough to follow my lead.

Before I could even get out my last name, Nathan jumped in with his two cents. "Ridgway!" he finished for me. "She's Schuyler *Ridgway*." That last name seemed to echo off hills in the distance. "And I'm her son, Nathan Ridgway!" As Nathan said this last, he took a step forward and stuck out his hand, as if to shake Paul's.

I held my breath, waiting for Paul's reaction.

He didn't disappoint me. Paul leaned forward, still holding on to the doorknob for support, and squinted at me and Nathan.

"Ridgway?" he mumbled. "*Ridgway?*" For a second, he looked a little confused, and he even started to shake Nathan's hand. Then he must've made the connection. "Wait a minute," Paul said, snatching back his own hand as if Nathan's were on fire. Paul blinked a couple times, looked more confused than ever, and then apparently decided that a scowl was called for. "You're not related to Ed Ridgway, are you?" Paul's scowl deepened.

About that time it must've dawned on Nathan that he was looking a little strange, standing there with his hand sticking out and nobody responding in kind. Nathan immediately ran the offending hand through his hair, as if that had been his intention in the first place. Oh, my, yes, this kid was smooth, all right. Once Nathan had gotten his hair all smoothed down, his blurted, "Yeah, we're related to Ed Ridgway." Unbelievably, Nathan now sounded more than a little belligerent. "Ed Ridgway's my dad." He didn't say it out loud, but his tone implied, *So? What of it?*

It occurred to me then, as I stared at my younger son, that I still had the canister of pepper spray in my pocket.

What's more, at that particular moment I was only inches from Nathan. At this distance there wasn't a chance in the world that I could miss him.

· Of course, if I were going to pepper spray Nathan, I should've done it when he'd first walked up. Now it would not be prevention, it would just be punishment.

Which, I must confess, was not an altogether bad idea.

"Your *dad*?" Paul was now saying to Nathan. "Ed Ridgway is your *Dad*?"

"Paul?" I wasn't sure what I was going to say, but I thought I'd try to divert his attention. He did seem to be staring rather bug-eyed at Nathan. "Paul? PAUL?"

Paul's eyes finally moved in my direction. "Then, uh, Ed Ridgway is your husband?"

"Ex," I corrected. "He's my ex-husband."

Paul actually drew back as if I'd slapped him. "He's a murderer!" he said. "*That's* what he is!"

I caught my breath. Once again, I had that odd sensation of unreality. Was this guy actually saying such things about *Ed*? Did Paul Metcalf really believe what he was saying? Could he really think that a man I'd lived with for eight years had committed murder?

If Paul didn't believe it, he could've fooled me. "He's scum," Paul said, turning away from me and jabbing his finger in Nathan's direction. "He's an asshole!" Paul's slur had gotten worse, a thing I would not have thought possible. "Ed Ridgway's a funking murderer!"

Paul obviously meant an entirely different word, but what he said quite clearly was "funking."

Of course, judging from the way Nathan reacted, Paul's mispronunciation didn't matter. Nathan seemed to get Paul's drift, regardless. "You take that back! My dad is not a murderer!" Nathan shouted even louder than Paul. "He's being framed! He never killed anybody in his whole life!"

I glanced around us. Had Nathan forgotten? We were standing in the middle of a luxury apartment complex, for God's sake. I could see a few heads appearing in windows already, all of them looking this way. My guess was that these people probably didn't hear the word *murderer* shouted around here any too often. If Nathan didn't shut his mouth soon, we'd be lucky if somebody didn't call the cops.

What's more, I knew without even thinking about it exactly which two cops would respond to the call.

I reached for Nathan's arm. "Nathan," I said, tightening my grip. "Nathan?"

He didn't even glance at me. He was too busy glaring at Paul. "Dad has never killed anybody in his whole life!"

Paul did not appear to be the least bit willing to take Nathan's word for Ed's innocence. Oddly enough. "The hell he didn't kill anybody!" Paul said. "He killed my beautiful, sweet Kimmie!" Paul's eyes were now wandering around the room, as if he'd just realized that he was lost. Lost, in his own apartment. "Oh, God, I can't believe she's gone. My beautiful Kimmie!" Paul's voice was almost a wail. "Kimmie didn't deserve to die so young!"

My throat tightened up as I flashed on Kimberly as I'd seen her last. "No," I said sincerely, "she certainly didn't."

When I spoke, Paul's head jerked in my direction. The motion of his head must've thrown his balance off some, because he reeled sideways a little and had to grab the doorframe with both hands to keep from falling. "She was a beautiful bride!" he said. "Just beautiful!"

He had to mean that she was *going* to be a beautiful bride, but I let it go. "I know," I said, nodding my head.

"*I* should've known what was going to happen," Paul said, his lower lip quivering. "I should've known." For a moment, I was sure he was going to start sobbing right there in front of us, but instead, he blinked a couple of times and took a ragged breath. "Ed Ridgway always was a weird wolf."

I blinked at that one. Ed was a wolf, all right. But weird? "What do you mean?" I asked.

At my elbow, Nathan echoed, "Yeah, what exactly do you mean by that?"

Paul was shaking his tousled head. "He—he was just odd."

"What do you mean, odd?"

But Paul had apparently said all he intended to on the subject. He cleared his throat, rubbed his eyes, and then mumbled, "Kimberly loved him, though. She really did, you know." He directed a bleary look in my direction, as if he half expected me to argue with him.

And yet, how could I argue? Kimberly had certainly never confided in me. I supposed that she really had loved Ed. After all, that *was* usually the main reason you got married to somebody.

When I didn't say anything, Paul went on, his face pale. "Damn right, she loved him. That was all I really needed to know about the guy." He glanced my way again, his eyes moist. "Kimberly loved the guy. She did. She really loved him."

I stared at him. Paul did seem to be going on a bit much regarding the depth of Kimberly's feelings. Was it me, or was he overdoing it a little? Of course, knowing Ed the way I did probably prejudiced me a little. It was hard for me to conceive of any woman actually believing that she was in love with Ed, of all people. Hell, I even found it hard to believe that I myself had ever thought I was in love with him. But that's the way it always is, isn't it? Falling out of love with somebody is pretty much retro-active. You're not only no longer in love in the present, you can't even remember what it was like to have ever been in love with the guy in the past.

"Kimmie loved him, and look what he did to her," Paul was now saying, his voice shaking with fury. "Well, I just hope the son of a bitch gets the electric chair!"

Nathan took that last comment well. "*What*?" Nathan asked. "What was that you just said?"

I could not believe it. My son was clenching his fists. As if he were actually considering taking a punch at a guy in mourning. Lord. I couldn't actually recall ever telling Nathan that it was not good manners to pick a fight with the recently bereaved, but I believe I'd always assumed that this was one of those self-evident truths that went without saying.

As far as manners went, Paul didn't seem to have an

overabundance himself. "*I said,* I'd love to be there when they strap your dad in the chair, because I'd like to personally throw the switch!"

I blinked this time. Now wait a minute. I'd heard what Paul had just said, and that was definitely not it. Nathan, however, didn't seem to care whether Paul was repeating himself or saying this for the first time. Either way, Nathan was furious. He doubled up both fists and started to move forward. I reached out and grabbed Nathan's arm again, digging my fingers in this time, trying to hold him back.

There was no way, of course, that I'd really be able to hold Nathan back if he made up his mind to take Paul on. I was hoping, though, that the thought of having to drag his mom along with him as he waded into a fight might be enough to put a damper on the entire idea.

Evidently I was right. With me hanging on to him like some kind of extra-large barnacle, Nathan did stop moving forward. "You're wrong about my dad," Nathan said glaring at Paul.

Paul was now doubling up his own fists. "Your dad had better hope that the police find him before I do, because if I see him, I'll kill him with—with—" Paul paused then, looked completely confused for a moment or so, and then apparently recalled where he'd been going with this. "I mean it," he said, "I'll kill Ed Ridgway with my bare hands!"

"Oh, yeah?" Nathan said. "You and who else? The way I see it, maybe *you're* the one who killed Kimberly. Maybe that's why you're so anxious for Dad to be arrested! *You're* the one trying to frame him!"

That went over big. Paul's cheeks suddenly got as red as the whites of his eyes. "You—you—you—" He was so angry, he was sputtering.

Nathan apparently took this reaction as encouragement. "Yeah," he said, pointing an index finger at Paul. "You heard me right—maybe you didn't like Kimberly as much as you say you did! Maybe she wasn't quite so wonderful as you'd have everybody believe, huh?"

I stared at Nathan. Now he was talking ill of the dead. If

this kept up, I was going to have to start a whole new list. Things I Never Told My Children—But Should Have.

"You asshole!" This was Paul. Not exactly Emily Post himself. "You funking asshole!"

I know. I know. He obviously meant that other word again, but clearly, what Paul said this time, too, was *funking*. It could very well be that he was just too drunk to enunciate properly. One thing for sure, I wasn't about to point out his error.

"Everybody loved Kimberly! *Everybody*!" Paul added.

Nathan made a scoffing noise. "She didn't have any enemies?"

Paul's reaction to Nathan's question was something of a surprise. His dark head went up, and his bleary eyes actually seemed to clear for a second as he stared directly at Nathan. "Now," he said, "what would make you say something like that?"

Nathan shrugged. "Because everybody's got enemies. *Everybody*."

Paul shook his head so hard, his curls bounced. "Not Kimmie. *Not* Kimmie. Got it?" He was doubling up his fists again. "She didn't have any enemies because she was wonderful. *Wonderful*, understand?"

His voice was slurring so bad that he pronounced the word *wonderful* the way Lawrence Welk used to pronounce it—*wunnerful*. As Paul continued to speak, his face got redder and redder. As if maybe he were working himself up into something. Like, oh, say, beating Nathan to a pulp right in front of his mother.

While that last idea did have a certain appeal—particularly in light of Nathan's recent decision to join me and Paul—it seemed to me that Nathan and I should be on our way. Pronto. We had learned just about all we were going to under the circumstances. Now that Paul knew our connection to the chief suspect in this case, it was hardly likely that he'd willingly do anything that might help us exonerate Ed.

"Everybody loved Kimmie," Paul was now sort of mumbling as he stood there, leaning on the doorknob once again. *"Everybody."* He ran his hand over the stubble on his chin. "Because she was so sweet, that's why they loved her. My Kimmie was a truly good person. Truly good. In all the years I've known her, I've never once seen her do anything bad to anybody. Unless, of course, they deserved it."

Unless they deserved it? What on earth did that mean?

I stared at Paul as something else he'd just said hit me. *All the years he'd known her.* What an odd way to put that. Wasn't he Kimberly's younger brother? So, correct me if I'm wrong, but "all the years he'd known her" would've been his entire life, wouldn't it? So why didn't he say it that way?

Of course, Paul did have several sheets to the wind. Maybe asking him to make sense was asking too much. Hell, there was every chance he didn't even realize he was talking out loud.

"She was just a wonderful, wonderful person," Paul was now saying. "Wunnerful, wunnerful, wunnerful."

I took a step backward, pulling Nathan along with me. "We really ought to be going now," I told Paul. "We just wanted to stop by and let you know how truly sorry we were about"—what was it that he had called her?—"poor *Kimmie.*"

Paul was obviously moved by the sentiment. "Yeah, yeah, yeah," he said. He directed a final glare at Nathan, and this time he finally succeeded in doing what he'd failed to do earlier.

He slammed the door.

Nathan stiffened. "Man," he said, *"what* a jerk!"

As the saying goes, it takes one to know one. I was still gripping Nathan's arm, but I turned to give him a pointed stare. "Speaking of jerks," I said, "weren't *you* supposed to wait in the car?"

Nathan extricated his arm from my grasp and put a few feet between us. A wise move, believe me. "Now, Mom, don't tell me you're mad."

Okay. I wouldn't tell him. Besides, I shouldn't have to. The smoke coming out of my nostrils ought to be a big enough hint. I turned and started walking toward the car.

"Nathan," I said over my shoulder, "I thought we had an agreement—"

Nathan followed me, still keeping his distance. "But, Mom," he said, interrupting me, "it was a dumb agreement. I mean, how in the world was I supposed to hear you scream, or a gun going off, or something like that, if I was sitting out in the car?" Nathan was now wearing that contemptuous How-Dumb-Can-You-Be look that I'd seen far too many times on his dad's face. "I mean, think about it, Mom, how could I have heard anything?"

"As I recall," I said, trying to keep my voice even, "I told you to roll down the window." I gave him a look. Nathan had better not try to tell me that he would've been bothered by the cold. Not when he was wearing shorts, for God's sake.

"Oh, Mom," Nathan said. His tone was ridiculing, and the How-Dumb look was back. Apparently, rolling down a window was such an outlandish concept that nobody should be expected to think of it.

"Nathan," I said, "if you had problems with what we'd both agreed to do, you should've brought them up and talked about them long before we got here."

Nathan had been keeping pace with me, but now he slowed down a little. So that, apparently, he could shrug his shoulders without missing a step.

I stopped dead in my tracks, and turned to face him. *This* was the best he could do in his own defense? A shrug? This was it? The sum total of his argument?

I was suddenly so angry with him, I could hardly get my breath.

Fortunately for Nathan, we were still within viewing and hearing range of the La Fenetre complex. And getting into a screamer with my son in this particular neighborhood would, no doubt, be an excellent way to ensure another fun-filled chat with the salt-and-pepper shakers.

I turned on my heel, picked up speed again, and headed straight for my Tercel as fast as I could go, without looking back even once to see if Nathan was still with me. In fact, there was a moment there when I first took off toward the car that I was more than a little tempted to leave Nathan behind, eating my dust in a manner of speaking. I think he realized that the thought crossed my mind, too, because he actually began to run to keep up with me. I have power door locks, which means when I unlock one door, all unlock. Nathan had his door open and was in the passenger seat before I'd even slipped behind the wheel.

I didn't even look at him. I just started the car and pulled into traffic. Nathan immediately twisted around in his seat, looking over his right shoulder. "Okay, Mom, you'd better get over to the far lane, there's a—"

I didn't take my eyes off the road. "Nathan," I said, "you'd better shut up."

My tone could've cut through solid steel, but Nathan was either unbelievably courageous—or a total fool. "For crying out loud, Mom," he said, "I'm just trying to help. I don't understand why I can't help you out—"

It was at this point that I interrupted him, saying the familiar words I'd heard so many times myself when I was little. They were, of course, words that back then I'd sworn that I'd never say to my own children. Staring straight ahead, I said, "Because I said so."

This time Nathan evidently picked up on the cold fury in my tone. He didn't say another word until I was pulling up in front of his and Daniel's apartment. "So," he said cheerily as he opened the car door on his side, "do you want to come in and have dinner with us?"

I couldn't believe what I was hearing. Oh, yes, the votes were in, all right. Nathan was indeed a total fool.

"We're probably going to order pizza," Nathan smoothly went on. "With mushrooms, sausage, and extra cheese."

Nathan knew very well that this particular combination was my favorite. Did he really think I could be bought off with a pizza?

I shook my head. "Not interested," I said through my teeth. I reached across the passenger side, pulled the door shut, put my Tercel in gear, and drove away without a backward glance.

On the way home I found myself going over what had

just happened. Lord. Nathan was getting more and more like his dad with each passing day.

Not a cheery thought, believe me.

And yet, what was I supposed to do about it? How exactly do you discipline a grown child when he misbehaves? This was yet another topic not covered in Dr. Spock's book—yet another instance of *Where are you, Doctor, when I really need you*? Exactly what was I supposed to do now? *Ground* Nathan? I was pretty sure that in order to enforce that one, I'd need handcuffs. And maybe a gun.

So what was left? Was I supposed to give Nathan the silent treatment? Or maybe light into him in front of witnesses? Those two alternatives seemed pretty childish. I mean, why didn't I just have a tantrum and be done with it?

I was still mulling all this over in my mind when I pulled into my driveway. I had every intention of phoning either Reed or Constello the second I got inside. I wanted to check out Paul Metcalf's story, and find out for sure if the police really had notified him of Kimberly's death like he'd told me and Nathan. Was that really how Paul had found out that Kimberly had been murdered?

Or could it be that Paul had known because he himself was the one who killed her?

As it happened, however, I couldn't call anybody right away. My phone started ringing off the hook as soon as I opened my front door.

Chapter 12

It was Matthias. After everything that had happened today, I felt better just hearing his voice. Not to mention, he usually phoned just before he came over, so maybe he was on his way? I would definitely be glad to see the man. I wanted to tell him all about this terrible day. I was badly in need of a hug. And yes, anything else he could think up to do for little old me would certainly be most welcome.

Matthias immediately repeated what Barbara had already told me. "Barb decided to take an earlier plane."

"Yes," I said, "I know." I tried for a light tone.

I guess I succeeded. Matthias went right on. "Oh, yeah, that's right. Barb told me that you two had talked. Can you believe she'd just hop on another flight without telling anybody? Can you believe that?"

Considering that Barb had actually done this, I didn't have any trouble at all believing it. "Hmm," I said.

"I guess I should've expected it. Because, believe me, Sky, this is just like Barbara—changing her plans at the last minute, with no regard for anybody else. She is always doing things like this. *Always*."

I couldn't help it—I winced. I knew, of course, that I was just being silly. That, no doubt, this god-awful day had taken its toll, and I was just feeling ultrasensitive. Matthias was now going on about something else that Barbara had done, but I wasn't really following it. He sounded irritated, so it certainly wasn't as if he were recounting some cute thing that he remembered Barbara doing. Matthias was obviously *complaining* about his ex-wife's behavior. And yet, it seemed to me as if everything he was saying only underscored how intimately he and Barbara knew each other.

Hell, Matthias knew Barbara so well, he could even predict exactly what things she *always* did.

Like I said before, I knew I was being an idiot. After all, Matthias and Barbara *had* been married. That would seem to imply that there had been some intimacy involved. Moreover, it wasn't as if I myself had never been intimate with anybody other than Matthias.

When you came right down to it, there were undoubtedly people in the world who at this very moment were under the impression that Ed and I knew each other intimately, too. What's more, these people were probably right. And, off the top of my head, I could name any number of things that could be listed under the general topic of Things That Were Just Like Ed.

Like, for example, when we were married, it was just like Ed to eat in front of the TV in the living room and leave his dishes on the coffee table, blithely assuming that *I* would gather them all up and put them in the dishwasher. It was just like Ed to go through the *Courier-Journal,* cutting out articles that interested him, without bothering to check if I'd gotten a chance to read the newspaper yet. So that when I picked up the paper, it resembled Swiss cheese. And, it was just like Ed to keep track of every single penny I spent on books and magazines—and totally ignore how much he himself spent playing golf.

Hell, I'd barely scratched the surface of Things That Were Just Like Ed. I could easily go on and on. And yet, what would be the point? Comparing Ed to Barbara was clearly like comparing apples to oranges. For one thing, to know Ed was definitely *not* to love him. For another, I could never imagine Ed and me getting back together. Actually, now that I thought of it, I *could* imagine Ed and me getting back together, and the thought was scary.

Unfortunately, I could also imagine Barbara and Matthias getting back together. That thought was scary, too, in an entirely different way. My stomach was beginning to feel as if I'd just swallowed a few razor blades.

"Barbara has always acted as if the entire world revolved around her," Matthias was now saying. "She seems to think that all she has to do is pick up the phone and everybody should come running."

"Hmm," I said.

That was all I said. Really. I'd just made the exact same sound minutes earlier, and Matthias hadn't missed a beat. This time, though, there must've been something in the way I said it. Matthias stopped abruptly. There was a long moment of silence during which I wasn't sure what was going through Matthias's head. And then, finally, he said, "Sky? Is everything okay with you?"

"Oh, my goodness, yes," I said. No hesitation whatsoever. "Everything is just great." Hey, other than the murder, and the fact that at this very moment your ex is no doubt plotting her strategy on how to reel you back in, I'd say that everything was peachy-keen.

"What I mean is," Matthias went on, lowering his voice as if he were sharing a confidence, "are you okay with Barbara being here?"

Now what was I supposed to say to that? Silly boy, can't you tell that I'm just *delighted* that your ex-wife has showed up to try to win you back? It tickles me pink that you two are toasting each other over her favorite wine? I'm pleased as punch that practically the minute Barb gets back in town you immediately run out to the store in order to satisfy her every whim? What was there not to like? "Of course I'm okay with it, Matthias," I lied. "I've got no problem at all with Barbara being here. None whatsoever. In fact, after all this time, I'm really looking forward to finally meeting her."

Okay, so maybe I overdid it a little. There was an even longer silence on the other end of the line this time. "Are you telling me the truth?"

Oddly enough, Matthias's tone seemed to indicate that he didn't believe a word I was saying. The nerve of the man. If I had not happened to have been lying, I would have been insulted. "Of *course*, I'm telling you the truth."

I lied again. I even managed to sound a little indignant that Matthias would even hint that I was not being entirely honest.

There was another long moment of silence, during which I could almost hear the wheels in Matthias's head turning, and then he said hesitantly, "Well, if you're sure everything is okay—"

"Everything's okay," I assured him.

"Well, then," Matthias went on, "there *is* something I wanted to run by you."

Uh-oh.

"My mother has asked me to put Barbara up."

The razor blades in my stomach twisted and turned.

Put Barbara up? What a quaint way to say that. In my family, the only thing we ever talked about *putting up* was preserves. Somehow, I was pretty sure that Matthias's mom was not suggesting that he cook Barbara on the stove for a few hours, and then pour her into a jar.

Although, if this did turn out to be what Mother Harriet meant, I believe I was all for it.

Matthias's mouth was going about a mile a minute now. "Barbara was supposed to be staying with my mother. But, as it turns out, my mother is right in the middle of having her carpets cleaned, and her house is going to be a mess. Not really fit for guests. So Mother has asked me to do her this little favor."

Another *little* favor. "I see," I said. I did see, too. In fact, I saw exactly what Harriet was up to. What's more, I'd bet my next commission that this sudden carpet-cleaning project was planned right after Harriet had found out about Barbara's upcoming visit. In the months Matthias and I have been seeing each other, his mother has made no secret of how much she totally disapproved of Matthias's continuing relationship with me.

Not to mention, I could not quite forget that Harriet at one time had seen fit to stand in this very living room and call me names, all of which appeared to be synonyms for the word *prostitute*. For someone without a thesaurus at her disposal, Harriet had managed to come up with quite a few. The woman should do crosswords.

Of course, I could understand Harriet's hostility. Sort of. Harriet and I—and Matthias, too, for that matter—had met under difficult circumstances. It had been in an attorney's office on the occasion of the reading of the will of Ephraim Benjamin Cross, Matthias's father and Harriet's husband of forty-plus years.

The poor man had been found shot to death in Cherokee Park, a municipal park not far from my own house. This was the guy who, if you'll recall, had been kind enough to leave me over one hundred thousand dollars—in spite of the fact that I'd never even met him. As a matter of fact, as I recall, there had been considerable evidence that I had not only known the elder Mr. Cross, I'd known him in the biblical sense. And, because I suddenly had over one hundred thousand reasons to have wanted the man dead, I had even been suspected of his murder for a while. When you considered all this, I suppose it wasn't exactly a stretch to understand why Harriet might not have warmed to me right off the bat.

That was then, though. This was now. Excuse me, but may I point out that these days Ephraim Cross's murderer was in jail, and the entire sordid mess had been cleared up. Hell, even the salt-and-pepper shakers no longer believed that I'd had anything to do with the elder Mr. Cross's death. For that matter, I was pretty sure the shakers didn't even think I'd ever had anything to do with Ephraim Cross himself. The case was closed. Finished. A done deal. Harriet, in fact, appeared to be the only person in the English-speaking world who still harbored any suspicion that I might've actually had something to do with her late husband's death—or, at the very least, that I really had been having an affair with the old man.

And now, of course, tramp/harlot/trollop/hooker/slut that I was, I had taken up with Harriet's son. Like I said earlier, I could understand her attitude at the beginning. But *now*? Every time I saw her, I felt like handing her the latest *Roget's* and telling her, "Look, lady, after you get finished looking up *prostitute,* how's about looking up *innocent*?"

Harriet's attitude being what it was, I certainly wouldn't

put it past her to be trying her best to get Matthias and Barbara back together again. I believe if you had a choice between an ex-daughter-in-law who was the mother of your grandchild and a woman you believe pumped a few bullets into your late husband, you'd probably lean toward the ex-daughter-in-law.

In all honesty, I admit I even felt a little guilty myself for not wanting Matthias to get back with Barbara. After all, they did have a daughter together, who—even though Emily was nineteen and attending college—would no doubt love to have her parents back together again. Before now I'd never thought of myself as a home-wrecker, but in this instance, the shoe might actually fit.

"Sky, I mean it," Matthias was now saying, "if you have any problem whatsoever with Barbara staying with me while she's in town, I'll just put her up in a motel somewhere, okay?"

I tightened my grip on the phone. Wasn't this just like a man? Acting as if there was actually a question regarding the obvious. Once again, I mentally ran through possible responses. Of course, Matthias, I think it's terrific that you and your ex are going to spend time in your apartment alone. Oh, boy. What a good idea. And while you're at it, next week why don't you invite whoever's the current *Playboy* centerfold for a little sleep-over?

"I mean it," Matthias said. "You say the word, and Barb is gone."

My mouth felt as if I'd just swallowed a spoonful of sand. Let me see now. If I told Matthias that I had a problem with him and his ex sleeping under the same roof, I was just as good as telling him flat out that I didn't trust him.

Which wasn't so. I trusted Matthias. It was Barbara I didn't trust.

Then, too, if I objected to the sleeping arrangements, I was also more or less conceding that I felt as if I couldn't possibly compete with Matthias's ex. Barbara was filet mignon—and I was chopped liver. Not to mention, if Matthias was asking for my permission, it meant that he himself didn't mind having Barbara stay with him. Which was pretty much the crux of the matter.

My throat was beginning to hurt pretty bad. If Matthias really could not spend some time alone with his ex without being tempted to hop in the sack with her, wasn't this a little something I ought to find out? And *soon*?

I hate myself when I'm being sensible. I cleared my throat so that my voice didn't come out as a pathetic squeak. "Nonsense," I said. "Of course Barbara should stay with you. A motel room would be a needless expense." Lord. Once again I sounded sincere. This was getting frightening. "I have absolutely no problem with your ex-wife staying with you. None in the least."

In all modesty, I was good. Broadway beckoned. Matthias actually sounded relieved. "Sky," he said, "you are one in a million."

I did not smile. One in a million what? *Fools*?

"You know, a lot of women would have trouble with this—"

Yes, a lot of woman are sane.

"—but not you."

Yeah, yeah, I know. I'm not well.

"You really are—"

Matthias paused here, as if hunting for the right words. And I, like a total idiot, all but held my breath, waiting.

Usually, I don't go in for flowery, romantic little speeches. I guess that's one of the differences between me in my twenties and me in my forties. When I was twenty, if some guy had come up to me and said, "You're the most beautiful woman I've ever seen," I'd have fallen all over myself saying thank you. Now, in my forties, if a guy tells me, "You're the most beautiful woman I've ever seen," the first thing that pops into my mind is: *Where have you been*? *Prison*?

Up until now, in fact, I'd always thought that I really didn't need to hear outrageous compliments from the man in my life. Now I knew I'd been wrong. I may not have *needed* to hear them, but I sure did *want* to. Right this minute, as a matter of fact, I wanted to hear Matthias tell me the most outrageous lie he could think up. How I was

the sexiest woman he knew, how I was his idea of femi-
nine perfection, how I light up his life. Hey, any suitable
song lyric would do.

"—well, what can I say?" Matthias finished. "You're
great."

I stopped holding my breath. *Great?* I was great? Not to
look a gift compliment in the mouth—to mix a few
metaphors—but great didn't exactly cut it. I mean,
Frosted Flakes were gr-reat! Ask Tony the Tiger.

"I mean it," Matthias added.

"Hmm," I said.

Apparently, that was not quite the response he had been
hoping for, because Matthias said, "Sky?"

"Uh-huh."

I believe any moron could tell by my tone that I was
now not in my best mood, but Matthias didn't seem to
pick up on it. Instead, he said, his voice very low and very
husky, "I love you, Sky."

For a split second, my heart actually gave a little leap.

Which shows you that I probably really am one in a
million fools. Because my heart was in midleap when
something occurred to me. Matthias had *lowered* his
voice when he'd said this last. He'd lowered his voice so
much that it was almost a whisper. It could actually give
you the idea that Barbara might be in the same room with
him right this minute, eavesdropping.

*Obviously, Matthias had not wanted his ex-wife to hear
him tell me he loved me.*

Now why exactly would he not want her to hear? I
mean, if the two of them were split up, what difference
did it make? I gripped the receiver a little tighter and tried
not to grit my teeth.

"Hmm," I said again. "Me, too."

It was the best I could do under the circumstances.
Matthias sounded a little uncertain again. "Uh, Sky?" he
said. "There *is* one more thing I wanted to run by you—"

Good Lord. What was it this time? Would it be okay if
he and Barbara slept in the same bed because his mother
had sent every other piece of furniture out to be cleaned?

"Oh? What would that be?" I said. I sounded curious. Nothing more. God, I was good.

"My mother is having a little dinner thing tomorrow night, and I would consider it a colossal favor if you'd come with me."

Still another favor. And this time it wasn't even a little one. It was colossal.

"I mean, I know it's going to be a royal pain, but if you were there, it would make things so much easier."

So much easier for whom? I was white-knuckling the phone again.

"It's not going to be anything big, just a few of Mother's closest friends."

It sounded about as much fun as sitting down to a steak dinner with a pack of ravenous pit bulls. Only not as safe.

"So what do you think?" Matthias asked.

What I thought was, how in the world could Mother Harriet have a little dinner thing if her house was in such a shambles she couldn't even have overnight guests? Riddle me *that,* Batman.

I took a deep breath. "I'd love to come with you," I said. I was sounding sincere again. If this kept up, I should think about running for Congress.

I started to add, "I'm really looking forward to it," but I wasn't sure I could pull that one off without sounding sarcastic. I decided not to push my luck, and instead, I asked, "Should I meet you there, or will you pick me up?"

"I'll be at your house around seven."

Oh, goody. Another appointment to dread.

"Okeydoke." I'm ashamed to admit, I actually said this. Out loud. I wanted to ask if Mother Harriet had any idea that he was inviting me, but considering that it might open up a topic I really wasn't in the mood to discuss, I let it go. Besides, surely Matthias wouldn't invite me to his mother's without her consent. Or would he?

"Well, then," Matthias said.

I wasn't sure what he meant by this, so I said nothing.

"Well, then," Matthias repeated. Apparently, it had worked so well the first time, he'd decided to go with it again. "I, uh, guess that's about it."

It was at this point that something else occurred to me. Like I mentioned before, I may be slow, but eventually, I do get it. *Matthias was actually getting ready to hang up.* He really was, and he hadn't said a thing about coming over. In fact, it actually looked as if he had no intention of dropping by tonight. I glanced down at my watch. It was not even seven-thirty.

Well, hell. Also, damn. Not to mention, *shit.*

Of course, it wasn't as if Matthias and I got together every single night of the week. We certainly didn't. We didn't even have a regular set day we always saw each other. Bearing all that in mind, however, wouldn't you think, in the interest of calming any possible insecurities that I might have regarding his ex-wife, Matthias would make it a point to come by on this particular night?

"Well," Matthias was now saying, "I guess I'll see you tomorrow night around seven."

The man had the gall to sound as if nothing whatever was wrong. My throat tightened up. "Sure," I said, "see you then."

"Bye," Matthias said. And then there was a soft click as he actually hung up.

I, on the other hand, just stood there, staring at the receiver in my hand, while a single thought reverberated in my head. *Matthias has decided to spend the evening with Barbara.*

Of course, she *was* a guest. From out of state. And there was such a thing as Southern hospitality. Uh-huh. Right.

On the other hand, if Matthias did happen to be incredibly rude—and left Barbara all by her lonesome to, oh, say, come visit *me,* for instance—what difference would it make? I mean, if he made her mad, what did he think she'd do—*divorce* him? Why should he care what Barbara thought?

Unless, of course, Matthias still cared about Barbara.

My stomach felt as if I'd just poured boiling oil over the razor blades.

I hung up the phone and headed into the kitchen to get the bottle of Maalox I kept in the refrigerator door for just such emergencies. Like the refined Southern lady that I am, I took a big swig straight from the bottle.

Good old liquid chalk. My stomach immediately felt better. My mouth, however, immediately tasted much, much worse. To get rid of the peppermint-chalk taste, I followed the Maalox with several huge gulps of milk. And yes, I admit it, I drank the milk straight from the bottle again. Or, to be more accurate, the plastic jug.

This is one of the less publicized advantages of living alone. You can eat and drink right out of whatever container you pull out of your refrigerator, and there's nobody around to see you do it. Out of deference to my mother, who would've been horrified to hear that I ever did such a thing, I'd like to note that I did wipe off all traces of lipstick on the top of the jug before I put it back in the refrigerator.

Hey, I've got class.

With my stomach no longer on fire, I seemed to be thinking a little clearer. As far as Matthias and Barbara were concerned, maybe I was jumping to conclusions a little fast. After all, Matthias's own mother had asked him to play host to Barbara. He couldn't exactly refuse, could he?

As I closed the refrigerator door, however, I couldn't help wondering what exactly Matthias's plans were for tonight. Was he going to open another bottle of wine with his ex?

To put that little scenario out of my mind as much as anything else, I hurried back into the living room and started dialing the telephone number Constello had given me. I intended to find out if what Paul had told me was correct, and if the police had indeed contacted him regarding Kimberly's death. I also intended to put all thoughts of Matthias and his ex right out of my mind.

I finished dialing the last number. Of course, it could be that Matthias didn't head right over here because he just didn't want to leave Barbara alone in his apartment. Maybe it wasn't that he didn't want to be rude. Maybe he just didn't want Barbara to go through his stuff.

Hell, maybe he thought she'd steal his silverware.

Uh-huh. Right. That *had* to be why he had decided to spend the entire evening with the woman who was no longer his wife. Yessiree. I'd hit the nail on the head, all right.

"This here is Tony Constello." The detective must've been standing close to the phone, because he answered after just two rings.

I told him who I was, and then I guess I was still mainly thinking about Matthias and Barbara, because I couldn't decide exactly how to begin. "Well, I thought I ought to tell you, that is, I believe that you should know, that is—" Good Lord, I was babbling. I took a breath, and began again. "I talked with Kimberly Metcalf's brother today, and—"

Constello immediately interrupted me. "Her brother?"

"That's right," I said. "I spoke to her brother today—"

Constello interrupted me again. "Mrs. Ridgway, I don't know who you've been talking to, but it couldn't have been Miss Metcalf's brother. Kimberly Metcalf was an only child."

I was so surprised, I almost dropped the phone.

Chapter 13

As a real estate agent, you get accustomed to surprises. One day you find out that the couple who insisted that they could afford a house in the hundred-and-fifty-thousand-dollar range can barely afford one in the seventy-thousand-dollar range. The next day you discover the lovely scented candles that your newest client placed in every room of her house was really an effort to mask the unlovely scent of five cats using the wall-to-wall carpet as a litter box. And the day after that happy discovery, you find out that another listing of yours that supposedly never had any leaks whatsoever in its basement has enough water down there to make prospective buyers consider building an ark. In the real estate business, surprises are par for the course.

What Constello had just told me, however, went beyond mere surprise, all the way to shock. I was so shocked, in fact, that I blurted out the first thing that came to my mind. "Detective Constello," I said, "are you *sure* that Kimberly Metcalf didn't have a brother?"

Okay, so the first thing that came to my mind was a pretty dumb thing to ask a police detective. If you didn't know better, you might actually have gotten the idea that I was questioning Constello's investigative ability. I certainly didn't mean to, but I suppose I did sound as if I didn't trust Constello to have checked something like this out.

Constello apparently agreed. In fact, he seemed to think my question was not only dumb, but insulting. Even over the phone I could hear his exasperated sigh. "Miz Ridgway," he said, "the victim's parents drove here all the way from Lexington to identify her."

I almost dropped the phone again. The victim's *parents*? Hadn't Ed told me that Kimberly's parents were dead?

"It wasn't all that many hours ago," Constello went on, "so I remember real clear that Mr. and Mrs. Metcalf both remarked on how she'd been their only child." He cleared his throat and added, "I reckon if Miz Metcalf had had a brother, her parents would've known about it."

I certainly couldn't argue with Constello's reasoning. Although I could have done without the sarcastic tone.

I started to open my mouth to try to somehow smooth things over, but Constello had evidently only paused for dramatic effect. "Or," he said, "are you suggesting that the Metcalfs could be lying about how many kids they had?"

Oh, my, yes, Constello was working himself into a snit.

"Detective Constello, I'm not suggesting anything of the kind." I said this in the ultrasoothing, ultrasympathetic tone I usually reserve for telling clients that their loan application has been turned down. "I'm sure if the Metcalfs said that Kimberly was their only child, then she was their only child. No doubt about it. None whatsoever. They just had one daughter, and that was Kimberly."

I might as well admit it, especially since I believe it's obvious—I was babbling again. I was trying to act normal, but my mouth seemed to be operating of its own accord. I couldn't seem to concentrate very long on what I was saying. Mainly because what kept going through my head over and over again, pretty much blotting everything else out, was this: *If Paul Metcalf was not Kimberly's brother, who the hell was he?* And if Kimberly's parents were alive, what the hell had Ed been talking about?

I quickly decided that I'd said all there was to say on the subject of only children. I also decided, given what I'd just discovered regarding Kimberly's parents and "brother," that I needed to find out just how much of what Ed had told me about Kimberly was really true. I took a deep breath. "Detective Constello," I said, "did I understand you right? Did you say that the Metcalfs are from Lexington?"

"They gave us a Lexington address, yes." The detective's tone was clipped.

I found myself nodding like an idiot, even though I was on the phone, for God's sake, and Constello could not possibly see me. "Then Kimberly was one of *the* Metcalfs?"

"*The* Metcalfs?" Constello now not only sounded irritated, he sounded confused. "Well, she was a Metcalf, that was for sure. At least, that's what her parents' last name was. Herb and Ethel Metcalf. They both work at the Wal-Mart on Nicholasville Road."

I didn't realize how tightly I'd suddenly gripped the phone until my hand started to hurt. "Wal-Mart?" I repeated weakly.

Good Lord. Had Kimberly lied to Ed about everything? Now I had something else racing through my head. *Did Ed know that Kimberly had lied to him?*

"That's right," Constello said. "Mr. and Mrs. Metcalf are both salesclerks at Wal-Mart." Constello paused, and I could practically hear his brain spinning as he put it all together.

This seemed to me to be an excellent time to get off the phone, before Constello had a chance to grill me. "Well, thanks for your help, Detective—"

Constello, however, wasn't about to let me go that easy. "Uh, Miz Ridgway," he said, cutting me off, his eastern Kentucky accent thicker than ever, "what in the world gave you the notion that Kimberly was one of *the* Metcalfs? Of horse farm fame and all?"

Evidently, Constello wasn't so confused after all. I took another deep breath. One good thing about being in real estate and dealing with surprises day in and day out, it teaches you to think fast on your feet. I certainly didn't want to tell Constello that it had been Ed who'd given me the "notion"—as the detective so quaintly put it—that Kimberly had been related to the wealthy Lexington Metcalfs. If Constello found out that Kimberly had lied to Ed regarding her family, it would only give the detective one more reason to believe that Ed had killed her.

"Why, you know, I don't remember who told me about Kimberly's family," I said. I tried to sound genuinely surprised to realize this. "I guess somebody must've told me, of course, but offhand, I can't recall who. Whoever it was, they must've gotten the story wrong."

"Yep," Constello said. He sounded grim. "I reckon they got it wrong, that's for sure."

I could tell by his tone that he didn't believe for an instant that I'd forgotten who told me. He didn't press it, though. Mainly, I suppose, because he had something else he wanted to ask me even more. "Miz Ridgway, being as how you seem to have a memory problem"—his voice was heavy with sarcasm—"do you think you could try real hard to recall who it was you've been talking to here lately? You know who I mean—the guy you thought was Miz Metcalf's brother?"

Maybe I don't think so fast on my feet, after all. My mind suddenly became a total blank. I couldn't think of a thing to tell Constello. Other than the truth. "Actually," I said, "I was under the impression that the guy presently living in Kimberly's apartment was her brother."

"Paul Hettinger?"

"Hettinger?" I repeated.

"Yeah, Hettinger," Constello said. "At least, that's the name he gave us. What name did he give you?"

I thought back. "You know, I don't think he ever did exactly tell me his name." He might not have mentioned it, but I was pretty sure that sometime during our conversation at La Fenetre Apartments, I'd called the guy Mr. Metcalf right to his face—and he hadn't said a word. Of course, maybe he was so drunk, it just hadn't registered. "I guess I just assumed that his name was Metcalf," I went on, "since I thought he was Kimberly's brother."

There was a long moment of silence, during which I guess Constello was digesting what I'd just told him. Then he hurried on. "Hettinger's name was on the Who To Contact In Case of Emergency card that we found in Miz Metcalf's purse. That's how come we knew to get in touch with Mr. Hettinger in the first place. That card had Mr. Hettinger's name, address, and phone. Which also happened to be Miz Metcalf's address and phone." Constello paused again and then asked, "So what exactly gave you the idea that Paul Hettinger was Miz Metcalf's brother? He told us that he was her *roommate.*"

From the way Constello said that last word, I could tell he didn't believe for an instant that Paul had been merely a roommate of Kimberly's. And yet, just because Constello didn't believe Paul was Kimberly's roommate didn't necessarily mean that it wasn't true. Constello *was* a cop—a profession not exactly known for its boundless optimism and willingness to assume the best about people.

Not to mention, this was, after all, the nineties. Men and women could actually be roommates these days. I suppose Paul and Kimberly really could've had a sort of *Three's Company* roommate situation, totally platonic, much like that old TV show starring John Ritter and Suzanne Sommers. Kimberly and Paul could have simply shared an apartment, and nothing more.

Although, even as the thought crossed my mind, I couldn't help mentally adding: Uh-huh, *right,* and they felt compelled to lie about being brother and sister because nothing whatsoever was going on between them. *That* made sense.

Not to mention, as I recalled, even in that TV show, *Three's Company,* John Ritter and Suzanne Sommers had not lived alone. They'd had a constant chaperone in the form of this little brunette who'd also lived with them.

"Miz Ridgway?" Constello prodded. "It wasn't your ex-husband, by any chance, who told you that Hettinger was Miz Metcalf's brother?"

The answer, of course, was, Yes, it was, but once again, I certainly didn't want to tell Constello that. This whole thing was beginning to sound too much like a commercial for H & R Block. Reason Number 846 Why Ed Must've Murdered His Fiancée: *He found out that her roommate was not her brother.*

"Oh, my goodness, no." I tried to sound as if the very idea was preposterous. "It wasn't Ed." As soon as I said Ed's name, I felt a wave of uneasiness. Oh, God. This felt familiar. I was doing it all over again—lying for Ed, covering up for him. Just like old times.

I hurried on, as much to blot out my own uneasy thoughts as anything else. "It couldn't have been Ed." At this point I realized that I didn't have any idea why it could not have been Ed, so to avoid having to explain what I'd just said, I added, "As a matter of fact, Detective Constello, I'm not really sure what made me think that Paul was Kimberly's brother. I think I might've just assumed it."

That one went over like the proverbial lead balloon. "You just *assumed* it?" Constello asked. "Like you assumed his name was Metcalf?" He sounded as if he were rapidly running out of patience. "Miz Ridgway, it appears to me that you do an awful lot of assuming."

I cleared my throat. I have always felt that one of the advantages of being a woman is that occasionally you can act like a total ditz, and sure enough, some man will believe that you're not acting. "Why, yes, Detective, I do assume a lot," I said. "In fact, I am *always* assuming things. And, what do you know, sooner or later I find out that whatever it was that I assumed is absolutely wrong. So I really don't know why I keep making these stupid assumptions. Of course, I keep assuming I'll stop—but there I go again. Why, I could just kick myself, I really could."

There was another long moment of silence on the other end, and then Constello made a noise that sounded a whole lot like a grunt.

How articulate.

This seemed to be an excellent time to try to get off the phone again—before Constello could ask me anything else. "Well, thanks so much for your help, Detective Constello," I said. "I really do—"

"Miz Ridgway?" Constello cut me off again. "You called *me,* remember? You said that there was something you wanted to tell me?"

I swallowed. I had indeed told Constello that, but that had been when I'd first started talking to him. I'd been about to tell him what Paul had told me about how he'd been notified by the police. As a matter of fact, I'd been about to tell Constello this, so that the detective could verify Paul's account. Now, though, there was no point. I'd already found out what Paul had told me earlier was true. The police had read the emergency card in Kimberly's wallet, and they'd contacted Paul just like he'd said. So what was there to talk to Constello about?

I cleared my throat once again, and returned to full-ditz mode. "Oh, my goodness, I am *so* glad you reminded me. Really, I'd forget my head if it wasn't attached. What I wanted to tell you, Detective Constello, is how terribly *glad* I am that you and Detective Reed are on this case. I feel *so* much better just knowing that you two are involved in this investigation, because I know without a doubt that you two will come up with the truth. I just know it, I *really* do."

Talk about shoveling it big-time. I could give Ed a serious run for his money.

"You phoned just to tell me that?" Constello said. He sounded more than a little skeptical.

Apparently, I didn't shovel anywhere near as well as Ed did.

"Why, yes—yes, I did," I said. I tried to sound a little hurt that he didn't seem to appreciate my having made the effort. "I wanted you to know that I have no doubt *whatsoever* that you and Detective Reed will see to it that whoever did this terrible thing to poor Kimberly will be punished to the full extent of the law. I have every confidence in you two. I really do. *Really.*"

Lord. Stop me before I ditz again.

"Oh, you can bet on it," Constello said grimly. "And so can your ex," he added.

I suppressed a shiver. I'm not sure exactly what I said after that. I mumbled something or another and quickly said good-bye. If Constello had anything more to say, I didn't hear it. I was hanging up the phone as fast as I could, my mind racing.

The police certainly seemed to be zeroing in on Ed. And yet, how could I blame them? At this very moment I myself was wondering uneasily if Ed could possibly already know everything that Constello had just told me. Could it be that Ed had somehow found out that Kimberly had lied to him? Had he discovered that everything she'd told him about having a trust and inheriting wealth was sheer fabrication? I suppose she'd told him these things so that he'd be that much more anxious to marry her. Hell, maybe Kimberly had heard about all of Ed's previous fiancées and realized that she'd needed some extra icing on the cake. Could Ed have found out about who her parents really were? Could this have been the real reason that Kimberly had expected Ed to be mad earlier today?

Or could it be because Ed had discovered that Kimberly's "brother" wasn't her brother at all? In spite of Ed's own wandering eye, I had no doubt that he would not think that having his bride-to-be share space with a young, handsome, male-model type was a terrific idea. In fact, I was pretty sure that if Ed had found out about it, he'd have been furious.

Which reminded me. I had never come right out and asked Ed himself why Kimberly had thought he'd be mad. I suppose, with everything else going on, I just hadn't thought of it until this minute. Now, however, all of a sudden it seemed terribly important to find out just how Ed would react to such a question.

I picked up the receiver again, and I dialed Nathan and Daniel's apartment. Can you believe, their phone rang five times before anybody answered? By that time I was steeling myself to hear what, over the last year, has become a familiar recording. It's the one that sounds as if the person speaking is holding her nose as she says, "The number you have reached has been temporarily disconnected." Of course, in my sons' case, she should be holding her nose. Certainly, the way they pay their bills stinks. In fact, in the interest of accuracy, the woman on the recording should probably say, "The number you have reached has been temporarily disconnected because the customers haven't paid their telephone bill in months, because they've been throwing away every thin dime playing video arcade games, so we've decided to hold their phone hostage until they cough up what they owe us."

Nathan and Daniel's phone has been taken hostage three times this year. I'd just decided that this was hostage situation number four when the phone was finally answered. "555-2267. Nathan Ridgway speaking."

Nathan didn't have to identify himself. Even if I hadn't recognized his voice, I think I would've known who he was the instant he picked up the phone and said anything other than "Yo." "Nathan," I said. My tone was cool. I was still mad at him for not waiting in the car like we'd agreed, and I was sure Nathan would want to know it. Sure he would. "Where's your dad?"

"Dad?" Nathan asked. "What do you mean, my *dad*?" Nathan actually sounded as if he'd never heard of such a person.

I guess, in a way, I should've been glad that Nathan reacted in this way. It certainly seemed as if all the things I'd told him and Daniel earlier about harboring a fugitive had finally sunk in.

I was not, however, glad. What I was more than anything else was annoyed. I'd just spent far too much time listening to my sons' phone ring, and now Nathan wanted to play Twenty Questions? "Nathan, will you go get your dad right this minute?"

"Mom!" Nathan made the word sound as if it had two syllables. Mah-um. "What are you saying? For God's sake, this phone could be tapped. You said so yourself. So—ix-nay the estions-quay over the own-phay!"

I couldn't believe what I was hearing. Did Nathan actually think that the police didn't know pig latin?

"Okay, Nathan, listen to me. I need to talk to the closet case," I said.

"Huh?" Nathan asked.

I tried not to grit my teeth. "I have to talk to your *end-fray*," I said. "Put him on."

"No can do," Nathan said smoothly. "Mom, there could be bugs everywhere. Isn't that what you said? *Even the walls have ears.*" Nathan lowered his voice as he said this last, dragging out each word. He seemed to be doing his best now to sound like a criminal on the run.

Oh, brother.

I gripped the phone a little tighter, and tried not to think what I was thinking. Which was, of course: I should've pepper-sprayed Nathan a good one when I had the chance. "Look, Nathan," I said, "earlier today Kimberly told me that your dad was going to be mad about something. I want to know what that something was, okay? And I want to know it NOW."

"For God's sake, Mom," Nathan said, "why would you call here to find *that* out? I certainly wouldn't know. Neither would Daniel. And you know very well that neither one of us has seen Dad in a long, long, long time." Nathan said this last sentence quite a bit louder than everything else. Evidently, if there were indeed eavesdroppers in on this conversation, Nathan wanted to make sure they didn't miss a single word he said.

I was getting tired of playing this game. "Nathan, put your dad on the phone. *This minute!*"

"Mom," Nathan said, making the word have two syllables again. "I don't know where you get these crazy ideas. We have not see Dad in years. What's the matter with you, have you been smoking something strange?"

I almost choked on that one. Let me get this straight. Nathan seemed to really believe that the police might've tapped his phone, and yet he was suggesting over the very same line that *I* was doing illegal drugs? It was a good thing that Nathan was not standing anywhere close to me, or I think I would not have been able to resist the temptation. I'd have gotten him with the pepper spray for sure.

"Okay," I said, biting out the word. "Go ask *somebody* why Kimberly thought *somebody* was going to be mad, okay? Ask *somebody* that RIGHT NOW."

If the police really were listening in on this line, referring to Ed as *somebody* would hardly fool them. And yet, would you believe, it did seem to satisfy Nathan. He didn't say anything, but from the sound that rumbled across the phone line, I guessed that he'd put the receiver down on a table and gone off to find Ed.

The closet Ed must've been hiding in this time had to have been nearby, because Nathan was only gone for a couple of minutes. When he returned, he said, "Mom?

Listen up. *Somebody* doesn't know for sure, but *somebody* thinks that maybe Kimberly might've had an objection to the neighbors again. That's what *somebody* thinks."

As Nathan spoke, he gave the word *somebody* a little extra punch every time he said it. Oh, my, yes. There was no way anybody could decipher this. If the police had tapped this line, they would be completely baffled.

I hated to break it to Nathan, but he should've stuck with the pig latin.

I gripped the phone even tighter, and considered what he'd just told me. Having shown the Willow Avenue house several times over the last few months, I knew that the next-door neighbors were two elderly widows, one on each side. One, I believe, was a retired schoolteacher, the other the widow of a Methodist minister. So what objection could Kimberly have possibly had to them? Surely Kimberly couldn't have thought that these women were rednecks, could she?

Of course, now that I thought about it, I'd never agreed with Kimberly's assessment of the neighbors next door to the first house that she and Ed had contracted to buy—the one that Ed had forfeited his deposit on when Kimberly had insisted that they back out of the deal. At the time, I'd gone along with Ed and Kimberly's wishes, but I'd never believed that their prospective neighbors were what Kimberly called rednecks.

Of course, it could've been just me. Occasionally, I have had the sneaking suspicion that quite a few of my own Kentucky relatives might fit into the redneck category. I'd never given it much thought, but it could very well be that I wasn't all that tuned in to the precise hue of a person's neck.

Even so, I still thought the entire episode had been odd. Kimberly, as far as I knew, hadn't even spoken to her potential neighbors, and yet she'd been sufficiently unhappy as to cancel the entire deal. Could she really have been all that put off by the presence of a pickup truck in the driveway next door?

In *Louisville*? There were an awful lot of trucks in an awful lot of driveways around here. Hell, there were trucks in driveways in the most expensive of neighborhoods. In fact, if what you were looking for was a neighborhood completely devoid of trucks, you probably needed to leave the state.

It seemed to me now that I probably should've questioned this at the time. And yet, Ed had forfeited his deposit without batting an eye, so it hadn't been a problem. Now I wondered. "Nathan?" I said. "I need you to go ask *somebody* something else. Ask him if having a redneck next door really was—"

Nathan had the gall to interrupt me. "Mom, we shouldn't be talking any more on this line. Eeple-pay could be listening!" He said this last with the same hushed urgency that, as a preschooler, he'd told me that he had to go to the bathroom. "We have *got* to get off this phone!"

That's right, the kid who, when he lived with me, had talked on the phone for so many hours straight that I feared I might have to get the receiver surgically removed from his ear, this was the kid now rushing *me* to get off the line. I started to repeat what I'd just said, but I was too late. The dial tone sounded in my ear.

I considered calling Nathan back for about a half second. Then it occurred to me that there was someone else I could talk to about Kimberly's decision to cancel that first contract. And there was a good chance we wouldn't even have to speak pig latin. I got my coat, my purse, grabbed a cold can of Coke from the refrigerator so that I could have one for the road, and I headed for the door.

Chapter 14

The first house that Ed and Kimberly had contracted to buy—a charming Dutch colonial located on the corner of Lauderdale Drive and Speed Avenue—wasn't all that far from my own house. In fact, I was there in less than ten minutes. As it turned out, however, it didn't much matter how long it took me to get there. As I slowed down in front of the Dutch colonial, the first thing I noticed was that the brick bungalow next door was dark. There were no lights in either the upstairs or the downstairs. There was also no Ford pickup in the bungalow's driveway, or for that matter, parked along the curb on either side of the street. The bungalow did have a detached single-car garage, the kind with double doors that nobody builds anymore, and one of these doors had been left open. You could plainly see that the garage was empty.

It looked as if the alleged redneck wasn't home.

The next thing I noticed was that there was now a bright red Chevrolet pickup truck parked in the driveway of the Dutch colonial. As I recalled, the house had sold only a couple days after Ed and Kimberly had withdrawn their contract on it. I stared at the pickup as I drove by. Lord, two pickups right next door to each other. No doubt Kimberly would've thought that this was a redneck invasion.

At the thought of her, my throat tightened up. Even seeing her the way she'd been earlier today, it was still hard to believe she was really gone. I hadn't known much about her other than that she intended to marry Ed—

which, of course, made me question her sanity—but I did know this. She was far too young to die.

I circled the block once, making sure that there were no lights on in the back of the bungalow. There weren't. I didn't want to park in the bungalow's driveway, so I pulled over to the curb directly in front of the house, braked, and turned off the ignition.

I sat there for a while, sipping my can of Coke, and hoping that Kimberly's alleged redneck would show up before my can was empty. A half hour or so later, though, the chances of that happening were not looking good. My Coke can had maybe one good sip left, and I'd begun to notice that I was attracting attention. A white-haired woman in the brick duplex across the street, a middle-aged couple in the Tudor on the other side of the bungalow, and a teenage girl in the Dutch colonial kept coming to their front windows, pulling back the curtains, and peering out at me worriedly. All of these people seemed to be trying to decide what the hell I was doing out there, sitting in a car all by myself in the dark. Before any of them decided to pick up the phone and report my suspicious behavior to the police, I took a final sip of my Coke, started up my Tercel, and headed back the way I'd come.

As I drove away, it occurred to me that, if you didn't count Coke, I hadn't put anything in my stomach since this morning. Well before I'd met Ed at the Willow Avenue house. And well before I'd seen what had happened to poor Kimberly.

Oddly enough, I hadn't felt the least bit hungry until now. Of course, if getting a look at a murder scene doesn't ruin your appetite, I suppose nothing would. My appetite, however, now seemed to have returned with a vengeance. My stomach was actually growling.

I wasn't sure if my getting my appetite back was a good sign or not. Either I was a strong person with a healthy constitution who could bounce right back after a terrible shock, or I was a callous jerk without an ounce of empathy who cared more about food than another human being. Oddly enough, I myself tended to lean toward the strong-person scenario. And, since a healthy constitution like my own obviously required sustenance, I decided to stop on my way home for some truly elegant cuisine—a Quarter Pounder, a super-sized fries, and a medium Coke.

Before anybody starts thinking that I was finally approaching my daily Coke limit—and that it was mainly to avoid a Real Thing overdose that I was ordering just a medium-sized one—let me shamelessly confess that this was not the case. No, the truth is, lately McDonald's seems to have followed the lead of several designers of women's clothing. In recent years I've noticed that designers like Liz Claiborne and Anne Klein have resized their clothes so that what used to be a ten has become an eight, and what used to be a large has become a medium. I always figured that designers did this as a sort of favor to their customers—if you were going to pay the outrageous sums these people asked for their clothes, then you deserved to think you were a size smaller than you really were.

What Mickey D's was thinking, however, was beyond me. These days McDonald's offers small, medium, large, and super-sized drinks. The small is the size it's always been—with the Coke-carrying capacity of a thimble—but the medium is now what, I believe, used to be a large. And the large and the super-sized? They're gigantic—so gigantic, in fact, that neither of them can fit into my Tercel's cupholder. My choice then, if I'm going to be in the car for any length of time, comes down to this: Either order the medium, or try to drive holding something super-sized and ice-cold between your knees. Not the sort of thing you want to do when you're wearing a skirt. And most definitely not the sort of thing you want to explain to a traffic cop pulling you over for driving recklessly every time the ice in your drink sloshes to one side or the other.

I went through the McDonald's drive-thru, ordered my medium Coke and the rest of it, and in no time at all, I was pulling away with a McDonald's sack that smelled unbelievably good. It smelled so good, in fact, that I decided that I couldn't wait until I got home. Instead,

I parked next to the side entrance of Mickey D's, and I dug in.

I'd only taken one bite of my Quarter Pounder when I made up my mind that the best time for me to drop in on the alleged redneck would be bright and early tomorrow morning. Before he left for work. And when he was more likely to be caught off guard. Maybe if I caught him off guard, he'd tell me more than he intended. If, indeed, he knew anything to tell.

I was kind of sorry that it hadn't taken me hardly any time to decide to call on the guy early tomorrow, because that pretty much left my mind free to ponder other things. Things that, frankly, I didn't particularly want to ponder. Like, for example, what were the odds that Ed had discovered that Kimberly had lied to him about her family ties and her "brother"? Exactly how likely was it that the father of my two sons had discovered the truth, and had gotten so angry that he'd given Kimberly a shove down the stairs—and then made sure she would never lie to anybody again by hitting her with the flashlight?

I'd like to tell you that I was so distressed by all this that I could not stop worrying about Ed, but to be honest, I could. In fact, if I put my mind to it, I could resolutely push all those awful Ed-and-Kimberly thoughts right out of my head. It was an entirely different set of thoughts that I had the most trouble with. The ones featuring Matthias and Barbara. As I sat there, chain-eating French fries, my mind kept drifting down Bardstown Road to Douglass Boulevard and Matthias's condo.

Where Matthias was, at this very moment, entertaining his ex-wife.

As a favor to his mother.

At least, that's what he wanted me to believe. It was also, of course, precisely what I myself wanted to believe. Which made me wonder: Was I being a total fool or what?

Every time I find myself wondering if I've got an accurate view of a particular situation, I give it the *Oprah* test. I imagine myself standing up in front of the audience on *Oprah* and telling them all about whatever I'm worrying about. I tell the audience everything I know, and then I picture their reaction. I believe, in this instance, I'd be getting hoots, catcalls, and outright laughter before I finished any sentence that included the word "mother."

Which, let me tell you, was a depressing conclusion to reach. It was also depressing to consider the following: While I was sitting here all by my lonesome, washing down French fries with a medium Coke, what do you suppose Matthias and Barbara were washing down? Another bottle of her favorite wine? Or, perhaps, *each other*?

That last thought I did manage to blink right out of my head. My Quarter Pounder, however, was suddenly tasting not quite so good. Depression, in fact, seemed to be settling around me like a wet blanket.

I read once—in one of those self-help books that always seem to be on the market—that when you fear something, you're supposed to imagine it in vivid detail, as bad as it could possibly be. You're supposed to go over the whole thing in your mind, detail by detail, and according to this book, this is supposed to "demystify" whatever it is that you fear, reducing it to something you can easily deal with.

For instance, if you're afraid of going on a job interview, you're supposed to picture the whole thing, minute by minute, as completely terrible as it could possibly go. Like maybe you could imagine that you threw up on your interviewer right after you introduced yourself, or something like that. Anyway, this demystifying process was supposed to make you realize that nothing could possibly be as bad as you imagine it.

Since I couldn't seem to get Matthias and Barbara out of my mind anyway, I decided I might as well give this little technique a try. I finished my Quarter Pounder, polished off the very last French fry, and then I gathered up all the pieces of paper that said DON'T LITTER. I obediently tossed all this in the nearest garbage can in the Mickey D's parking lot that I could drive up to. Then I headed in the direction of my house, all the while picturing in my mind Matthias-and-Barbara scenes.

This wasn't the easiest thing in the world to do, since I had never met Barbara face-to-face. I had, however, seen two or three snapshots of the woman, so I pictured her as I remembered her in those photographs. A pretty, round-faced, dark-haired woman about my height and at least— I'm being honest here—thirty pounds heavier. I know. I know. I admit it—I *am* the shallow sort who notices such things.

As I drove down Bardstown Road, heading toward Harvard Drive, I pictured Matthias and Barbara kissing. That one almost made me run a red light. After that I pictured them walking hand in hand, smiling into each other's eyes. That one almost made me drift into the next lane. And, finally, just as I was turning off Bardstown Road onto Harvard at Douglass Loop, I pictured the two of them in bed. That one made me almost rear-end the car in front of me. It also made my stomach hurt so bad I immediately decided that picturing it once was enough. After that, in the interest of surviving the rest of the trip home, I confined myself to just visualizing Matthias and Barbara talking. Or watching TV. Or listening to music together.

Oddly enough, these innocent little vignettes were almost as painful to imagine as the others.

Having visualized Matthias and Barbara together as vividly as I could, I was surprised, just about the time I was pulling into my driveway, to realize something totally unexpected. Whoever wrote that self-help book was an idiot.

Far from demystifying anything, visualizing Matthias and Barbara together just made it all seem more real. And far more likely.

My God. What if Matthias really did decide to go back to Barbara? Obviously, thirty pounds didn't mean anything at all to him. He'd still been married to Barbara when the snapshots I'd seen of her had been taken. And she had left *him*, not the other way around.

Frankly, I'd always been of the opinion that Barbara must've been out of her mind to have ever let Matthias go. Matthias, after all, not only cooks, he cleans. He's not only great in the bedroom, he's great in the kitchen. Can you believe he actually loads the dishwasher without being asked? And he wipes down the table and countertops as if it were the most natural thing in the world. For God's sake, what more could any woman want?

That, of course, was what worried me. What if Barbara had finally had a moment of lucidity and realized that she really didn't want anybody but Matthias? And what if Matthias had decided that he and the mother of his only child really ought to be married? My throat tightened up. Lord. What if Matthias's recent invitation to me had been the only chance I'd ever have to move in with him?

And I'd blown it?

The thought made my stomach hurt even worse. It also gave me nightmares. All night long, in fact, I tossed and turned, dreaming again and again that I was attending Matthias and Barbara's second wedding. In one particularly awful version, Barbara was at least two hundred pounds bigger than me, and still Matthias preferred her over me. In that one, I had a little fit, screaming at both of them from the back of the church. It was a lot like that scene toward the end of *The Graduate,* in which Dustin Hoffman tries to stop his girlfriend from marrying someone else. Only, I believe, Dustin came off positively subtle compared to me. After the scream-dream, I was giddily relieved to wake up and find out that none of it had really happened. I'd immediately gone back to sleep—and, of course, dreamed the same damn dream all over again.

This sort of thing, let me tell you, does not make for a restful evening.

It also doesn't make for a good disposition the next morning.

I was grumbling the second my alarm went off, even before my feet touched the floor. "I cannot believe Matthias actually expects me to think that he's letting his wife stay with him because his mother said so. Does he think I'm an idiot?"

Realizing almost immediately that I'd referred to Barbara as his wife instead of his ex-wife did not improve my mood. I headed for the shower, and wouldn't you know, I was so distracted that when I stepped in front of the shower head, for a moment I just stood there like a zombie and let the first blast of water hit me full force. This, mind you, is something I never do. Considering that I know very well that the first blast of water is always going to be ice-cold.

The instant the water hit me, I, of course, immediately screamed "Shit!" at the top of my lungs, and jumped out of water range. It was while I was standing there at the very back of the tub, shivering and waiting for the water to warm up, that I resumed my grumbling. Mainly, I suppose, to give me something to do other than listen to my teeth chatter.

"I cannot believe," I said, "that I have to make a cold call this morning."

The irony of being this cold and getting ready to make a cold call was not lost on me.

For the uninitiated, cold calls are calls you make on people who don't know you're coming. You haven't phoned beforehand to make the appointment; you just drop in, unannounced. Needless to say, it is not a fun thing to do. In fact, I believe that the reason these things are called cold calls is because *cold* pretty accurately describes the reception you're almost always going to get.

Before this week, the last time I'd made a cold call was over ten years ago, right after I passed my real estate exam. Back then I'd been under the impression that bigger had to mean better. So, naturally, I'd started working for a huge real estate firm which shall remain nameless. Huge Firm was the one I mentioned earlier— the one that required every one of its realtors to spend at least ten hours per week canvassing.

Today it sounds pretty archaic, but back then we were actually expected to go door-to-door, wearing those dumb burgundy blazers with Huge Firm's logo appliquéd on the pocket, asking total strangers if they wanted to sell their house. Or if they happened to know anybody who wanted to sell their house. Of if they happened to know anybody who knew anybody who—well, you get the idea.

If dazzling them with your burgundy blazer didn't work, Huge Firm had another canvassing technique that was alleged to be surefire. You were supposed to pick a

house—any house at all—march up to the front door, ring
the bell, and when the current occupants came to the door,
you were to gush all over the place. Literally. You were
supposed to tell Mr. and Mrs. Occupant that their house
was so outrageously gorgeous that, even though you were
on your way to have a kidney stone removed, or a heart
murmur corrected, or some such that required your being
in a terrible hurry, you'd felt compelled to stop. You were
so bowled over, in fact, that you just had to park your car,
trot up to their amazingly beautiful front door, and take
just a brief, fleeting moment to tell them how unbelievably impressive their lovely piece of property really and
truly was.

Once you'd gushed sufficiently, you were then supposed to mention that this particular house was so completely perfect that you were sure that, if it were ever to
be put on the market, it would be snapped up immediately
at a price that would leave the present owners gasping in
astonishment. Then, very casually, you also mentioned in
passing that, oh, by the way, if they ever did decide to
unload their staggeringly fantastic house, you were most
certainly willing and able to help. And you just happened
to have all the resources of Huge Firm standing behind
you, ready to serve.

At this point, according to the Huge Firm manual, you
were supposed to press a business card into Mr. and Mrs.
Occupant's eager hands. In reality, it was quite often at
this point that you were ushered unceremoniously off the
fantastically gorgeous property.

On those rare occasions when this ploy actually worked,
it only worked for a short while—and then only with
people who never talked to their neighbors. If Mr. and
Mrs. Occupant didn't happen to be hermits, the word got
out pretty fast that you'd spotted compellingly gorgeous
houses all up and down the entire block. Which meant that
after you spent a day or so in the same neighborhood
knocking on doors, people were waiting for you. All ready
to say, "Drop dead," or worse, and slam the door in your
face.

Huge Firm had also seemed to be under the impression

that there were hordes of people waiting anxiously for their very own truly ugly burgundy refrigerator magnet with the Huge Firm logo and telephone number emblazoned across the front. It hadn't taken long for me to decide that, if given the choice between facing a firing squad or spending another day dodging refrigerator magnets being hurled at my head, I'd pick the firing squad every time. Once I'd decided that, I'd wasted no time at all moving to the firm I still work for today—Arndoerfer Reality. Which doesn't require its agents to do any canvassing whatsoever.

When I finally got out of the shower, I'd warmed up considerably, thank God. I'd just put on my robe and was heading back to my bedroom down the hall when I heard the familiar *thwack* of the morning paper hitting my front door downstairs. I kind of hated to look at it—I knew Kimberly's story would be in there—but I headed downstairs and got the paper anyway. Sure enough, Kimberly was on the front page. I stood there in the middle of my foyer, staring at her photo and skimming the article for any mention of Ed. Oh, God. They'd done a lot more than just mention him. In fact, from the way the article read, you could get the impression that the case against Ed was a done deal.

My stomach started hurting all over again.

The paper also made me a lot more anxious to have a little chat with Kimberly's alleged redneck. I now knew that Kimberly had indeed told several lies, so maybe she'd also lied about the reason she'd insisted that Ed withdraw their contract on the Dutch colonial. I hurriedly dressed in what the saleslady who'd sold it to me had called "a suit that commanded respect." An austere gray pinstripe, it had not only commanded respect, it had commanded a fairly steep price tag. Oddly enough. Then I downed my usual nourishing breakfast, a few handfuls of Fritos and another Coke. I took the Coke with me, along with today's paper, and I all but ran out the door.

Ten minutes later, I was once again parked in front of the bungalow next door to the Dutch colonial on Lauderdale Drive. This time there was a Ford pickup in the

Dutch colonial's driveway. I got out of my car, squared my shoulders, and walked determinedly to the front door.

In the middle of the door, so you couldn't miss it if you tried, was a brightly polished brass door knocker with the name MCGRAW etched in it in an elegant flowing script. I stared at the thing. This was new. When I'd been showing this place, it had not had a door knocker at all, just a doorbell.

Apparently, Kimberly's alleged redneck was named McGraw. I supposed that McGraw could be thought of as a redneck sort of name—maybe. It had been etched in a delicate script, though. Not exactly the sort of lettering you'd expect a redneck to choose.

I reached for the knocker and gave it several sharp raps. The sound seemed to thunder around me, but nobody came to the door. Undaunted, I turned to the doorbell. I must've rung that thing at least five times before I heard the sound of footsteps heading my way, and finally, the clunk of the dead bolt being unlocked.

The front door opened, and I immediately recognized on the face of the man standing there an expression that I remembered well from my canvassing days. It was an expression that said, loud and clear: *Who the hell are you? And what the hell are you doing ringing my doorbell this early in the morning?*

I realized, of course, that this was the part where I was supposed to jump in and start talking very fast, but to tell you the truth, for a moment all I could do was stare.

This was a redneck?

Chapter 15

Mr. McGraw answered his door wearing something that I thought men only wore in black-and-white movies made in the thirties: a smoking jacket and an ascot. At least, I was pretty sure that you'd call the short robe thing that McGraw had on over his slacks a smoking jacket. I was making an educated guess, based pretty much totally on my having spotted a pipe sticking out of McGraw's right breast pocket.

Just looking at McGraw, I believed I could make another educated guess, too, this one regarding his favorite color. His smoking jacket was blue, his ascot was blue, and the sharply creased slacks McGraw was wearing under his smoking jacket were—surprise, surprise—blue.

McGraw's eyes were also blue, which might explain his fondness for the color. Someone had probably told him once that blue-eyed people look good wearing blue. This was true, all right. It was also true, however, that McGraw here would need a lot more than the color blue going for him to get even close to good-looking.

As it was, average-looking would've been a major step up. McGraw looked to be in his early fifties, and yet his round cheeks still bore the scars of what must've been at one time a bad case of acne. In fact, looking at McGraw, I recalled a sentence I'd heard both my sons say more than once. *He looks as if his face caught fire, and they put it out with an ice pick.*

What can I say? It's this kind of warm empathy that once again makes a mother proud.

Actually, McGraw's ice-pick complexion was the least of his problems in the looks department. He was only a little taller than I was, and yet he had to weigh at least two hundred fifty pounds. He had a bulbous nose several sizes too large, bags under the aforementioned blue eyes, and the reddest lips I'd ever seen on a man. I couldn't help staring at his scarlet mouth as McGraw said, "Yes?"

I'd interrupted his breakfast, and he wanted me to know it. He held a white linen napkin in his right hand, and when he finished his one-word question, he dabbed both sides of his mouth with the napkin, looking at me pointedly. "May I help you?" he added.

Before I answered, I couldn't resist giving the napkin a quick glance, half expecting to see a bright smear of red on its snowy surface. But, no, the napkin was still as white as ever. McGraw then was *not* wearing lipstick. That was something of a relief.

I cleared my throat. "Hi," I said. I gave him my standard realtor smile, friendly but not pushy. "I'm Schuyler Ridgway, and I'm looking for a Mr. McGraw?"

McGraw answered me with a brief nod of his head. He had dark brown hair peppered with gray, and when he nodded, not a hair on his head moved. McGraw might not wear lipstick, but it certainly looked as if he moussed his hair. Or used hair spray. Or both.

McGraw was wearing his hair in a style a lot of men wear these days—combed straight back from his face. I'm not quite sure why so many men today seem to be drawn to this look, since the only men it looks good on are those men who would look good no matter how they wore their hair. Everybody else wearing this slicked-back style, however, looks as if they're perpetually standing in front of a powerful invisible fan.

McGraw was no exception. What's more, with his hair combed back from his forehead like that, you couldn't miss the deep frown lines between his eyebrows. They looked like ruts in the scarred road of his face. Unless I missed my guess, I'd say that McGraw had spent a significant portion of his life in a bad mood.

He didn't look as if he were in a terribly good mood

now. Apparently, I hadn't responded to his nod quickly enough, because he added, his tone impatient, "Yes, I am he. I'm Carl McGraw."

"Glad to meet you, Mr. McGraw. I'm Schuyler Ridgway."

I was saying this, and giving him another standard realtor smile, but what was going through my mind was: I am *he*? I knew that this was proper English, of course, but I also knew very few people who ever actually said it this way. It was always *I'm him,* or even *that's me,* but never *I am he.* I stared at McGraw. All this, and an ascot, too? So what was the real reason Kimberly had not wanted to move next door to this guy?

It could be because he was rude. "Do I know you? What is it that you want?" he said.

I'd been about to try to shake his hand, but as he spoke, McGraw crossed his arms. Uh-oh. One thing my canvassing experience taught me—once whoever answers the door crosses his arms, you'd better start talking fast. If you don't, you're going to have a door flattening your nose in about a half second. "Mr. McGraw," I said, continuing to smile, "I-do-apologize-for-bothering-you-so-early-in-the-morning-but-I-need-to-ask-you-a-few-questions." I said all of this so fast, it sounded as if it were just one word.

McGraw dabbed at the corners of his mouth again, and once more gave me a pointed look.

I just stared right back at him. Look, Buster, I got the message, okay? I'm interrupting your breakfast. I have no manners. So sue me.

I started speed-talking again. "Mr.-McGraw-if-I-could-have-just-a-moment-of-your-time."

I don't see how I could possibly have said any of this any faster, but I must not have been moving things along quickly enough to suit McGraw. He cut me off. "What's this all about?" His eyes traveled uncertainly to the copy of the *Courier-Journal* I was holding.

Well, he'd asked, hadn't he? I unfolded the front page and held it up so that McGraw could see the picture of Kimberly. "It's about this woman. I—"

Once again McGraw didn't let me finish. Holding up both hands in a gesture of innocence, he said, "Look here, I have not seen that woman in almost a year. I don't see how I could possibly be of any help whatsoever to you people."

I blinked. *You people?* What in the world did he mean by that?

McGraw was hurrying on. "And yesterday, I'll have you know, I was at work all day. I own a printing company, and day-to-day operations require that I be on the premises at all times from nine to five. So I have plenty of witnesses."

I blinked again. Obviously, there was some mistake. I looked down at the paper I was holding. There was a photograph at the bottom of the page of a woman who'd been arrested for shoplifting. According to the caption, the police were looking for a male accomplice. "No, no, no," I said, smiling and shaking my head. I held the paper up a little higher so that McGraw could get a better view of Kimberly's photo. "I mean, *this* woman." I pointed at the photo.

McGraw looked at me as if questioning my intelligence. "That's correct, Kimberly Metcalf. As I just said, I haven't seen her in months." He dabbed at the corners of his mouth again—although, in my opinion, they'd been dabbed all they needed to be. "As a matter of fact," McGraw went on, "I was just now reading about what happened. I was afraid you police types might be coming around."

Police? Did he say, *police?*

Lord. The saleswoman had said that this suit would command respect, all right, but she hadn't told me people would be mistaking me for the *police*.

I was so surprised at this turn of events that for a second I just looked at McGraw, unsure what to do next. Should I act as if I were a cop? I certainly was tempted. Lord knows, if McGraw thought I was on official police business, I'd certainly learn a lot more.

On the down side, however, wasn't there a law against this sort of thing? A rather unpleasant regulation against impersonating a police officer? I really didn't want to give the salt-and-pepper shakers a reason to put me behind bars. I was pretty sure, after all we'd been through together, the shakers would be more than delighted to direct me to a nice, quiet jail cell.

McGraw evidently interpreted my hesitation as something else. He opened the door a little wider. "Oh, all right," he said, his tone resigned, "if you must, come on in. I don't know how you found me, but I guess it was only a matter of time."

This time I didn't hesitate. I was inside before I even had a chance to think about it.

McGraw gestured toward the living room on my left. "We'll talk in there. Let me get my wife."

I turned to look at him. I wasn't sure why, but up till now, I'd been under the impression that this guy wasn't married. Some cop I'd make. Hell, I didn't even have one of those little spiral notebooks. I wasn't sure anybody could be a convincing cop without one of those.

"Elena!" McGraw was now calling toward the back of the house. "Come here, Elena! Elena, *come*!"

I'd started moving toward the living room, but that last stopped me in my tracks. Was this guy calling his wife? Or his dog?

I heard a door open down the hall, and I turned to see a woman in her late twenties come through a swinging door and head rapidly in our direction. Judging from the smell of frying eggs and bacon that came wafting our way the moment the swinging door opened, I guessed Mrs. McGraw was coming out of the kitchen. The woman actually began to run toward us, wiping her hands on her apron as she came.

I watched her, and to be honest, it was an effort to keep my mouth from dropping open.

She had thick shoulder-length chestnut-brown hair, an oval face so pale it made her large dark brown eyes even darker, and the kind of full, pouty mouth most often seen in lipstick ads. Elena McGraw was, in a word, beautiful. And she was married to a man who was, in a word, *not*. I glanced over at Carl McGraw, and naturally the obvious thought crossed my mind.

Good God, man, you've struck the mother lode.

"Yessir?" Elena was now saying.

The moment she spoke and I heard her heavy accent, I knew that she was not an American. Actually, I suspected it the moment I saw her. I'm not sure what it was exactly that gave it away. Maybe it was because she immediately came running as soon as McGraw called her. Let's face it, how many American women do you know these days who actually *run* when their husbands call? Unless, of course, it's in the opposite direction.

The tip-off might've also been what Elena had on. She was wearing yet another outfit I hadn't seen in years—a bib apron over a blue gingham housedress. A floral print with red rickrack trimming the edge and pocket, the apron looked almost exactly like one I remembered my mother wearing back when I was in elementary school.

McGraw immediately stepped forward. I thought for a second that he was going to introduce us. Instead, he said, "Elena, bring me my coffee in the living room." He spoke very deliberately, enunciating every word. When he said the word *coffee* he made a motion as if drinking from an invisible cup. When he said *living room,* he gestured toward the door that I had been about to go through.

Elena barely gave me a glance. She was too busy watching McGraw's hands, with the intent stare of a deaf person trying to decipher sign language. Finally, with a quick nod of her dark head, she turned to go back the way she'd come.

McGraw's voice stopped her. "Elena!"

The young woman immediately froze. When she turned to face him, her face looked paler, and her eyes looked bigger. The poor woman actually looked a little scared that she might've done something wrong.

McGraw didn't even seem to notice. He was holding up an index finger, in the classic pose of a teacher addressing an errant student. "Elena, when an American lady leaves a room, she always says, 'Excuse me,' before she goes."

I just looked at McGraw. I'd left a lot of rooms in my

lifetime without bothering to excuse myself first. Evidently, I was not an American lady.

Oh, darn.

"Now, Elena, repeat after me," McGraw was saying.

I wasn't at all sure that Elena understood any of this, but she certainly looked as if she were giving it her best effort. Her eyes were riveted on McGraw's red mouth.

"Excuse me." McGraw's tone was now that of an indulgent parent.

To my surprise, Elena actually managed to say something that sounded a great deal like "Excuse me." Her effort was apparently not good enough for McGraw, though, because he held up that index finger again. "No, Elena, NO. Now listen. Ex-cuh-use meee."

This actually went on for several minutes, right in front of me, in the middle of the hall, with McGraw repeating the two words very slowly, and poor Elena trying to imitate the sound.

I couldn't believe it. I felt as if I'd just walked in on a scene from *My Fair Lady*. Funny, it had never occurred to me until now that what had looked rather charming on the big screen could be positively obnoxious in real life.

Finally, Elena Doolittle said a final "Ex-cuh-use mee," and Professor McGraw let her escape to the kitchen. To enjoy a real treat, no doubt—the privilege of fetching McGraw's coffee.

As Elena literally ran for cover, McGraw turned back to me. "Elena is new to this country, but she's a fast learner."

"She's very pretty," I said, smiling.

I'd evidently said the right thing. McGraw returned my smile for the first time since I'd rung his doorbell. "Elena—and I'm not exaggerating in the least, mind you—Elena is the prettiest girl I've ever dated. I mean it. Bar none. She actually surpasses our American girls."

I kept right on smiling. I did wonder, though, exactly how old a woman would have to be for McGraw not to consider her a *girl* anymore.

"Of course, Elena hardly has any competition in her own country." He leaned toward me and lowered his voice. "Most Russian women are *large*. If you get my meaning."

I got his meaning, all right. He was telling me that, in his opinion, most Russian women were overweight.

Like him.

Or, rather, like *he*.

Evidently, McGraw was now on a subject he loved to talk about. Or else he wanted to put off talking about Kimberly for as long as he could. He led the way into the living room, waved me toward the couch, and claimed the black leather La-Z-Boy to the left of the couch for himself. "My Elena is old-fashioned," McGraw said. "That's the great thing about Russian women. They still know how to act like a woman, and how to treat a man like a man. Not like American women these days. Why, you can't even get *them* to clean house anymore. They want to hire someone. None of them want to be a housewife anymore; all of them want to have some ridiculous career—"

Apparently, it dawned on Mr. Sensitive a little late that I could possibly take some of his comments personally, and that it probably wouldn't be in his best interest to get a police officer mad at him. His blue eyes darted anxiously to my face.

I gave him another smile.

McGraw tried to return my smile, but the one he'd just given me must have been his quota for the day. This time what he ended up stretching his mouth into looked a lot more like a grimace than a smile. "No offense," he said.

I didn't even blink. "None taken," I lied.

Elena came galloping back in then, carrying a tray with one steaming coffee cup and a plate piled high with chocolate-covered donuts. Watching her run into the room balancing all that was a lot like watching one of the events held in Louisville the week before Derby every year—the Run for the Rosé. The Run for the Rosé is a footrace in which waiters and waitresses from area restaurants compete while balancing a glass of wine on a tray. The object is to win the race without spilling a drop. It looked to me as if Elena here was a natural.

"Here iss coffee," Elena said, putting her tray down on the maple end table on McGraw's right.

McGraw glanced over at me. "See? Didn't I tell you what a fast learner she is? We've only been married two weeks, and she already knows a lot of English words."

I looked over at Elena. She was now unfolding and placing another linen napkin in McGraw's lap.

It seemed to me as if there were quite a few more words Elena still needed to learn. Complete sentences even. Like, oh, for example: *Get your own coffee, lard ass.*

I smiled at McGraw again. "Two weeks, huh? Well, congratulations to you both."

McGraw gave Elena a fond look and nodded. "Two weeks of wedded bliss," he said.

I was having trouble maintaining my smile. I didn't doubt what he said for a minute. It sounded like bliss, all right. For McGraw.

Elena was now holding the plate of donuts directly in front of McGraw so that he didn't have to reach at all to take one. Or, rather, to take *three,* as that was how many he ended up getting.

It was certainly no mystery how McGraw had gotten to be two hundred and fifty pounds.

Once again it seemed to occur to McGraw a little late that he might possibly be remiss. "Oh," he said, looking over at me, "may I offer you something? Coffee? A donut?"

I shook my head.

While Elena had been treating her man like a man, I'd been taking a quick look around. The living room looked spotless. In fact, unless I missed my guess, I'd say that those looked like fresh vacuum cleaner tracks on the carpet. There was also a faint scent of lemon furniture polish lingering in the room. So, let me get this straight, it was just after eight o'clock in the morning, and already the furniture had been dusted and polished, and the carpet had been vacuumed. I turned to stare at Elena. How long had she been up? Did she get up before Man Mountain here in order to get her cleaning done? Even before she made breakfast?

"Yes," McGraw was now saying, "the smartest thing I ever did was marry my Elena here."

I'll say. I felt inclined to marry Elena myself.

"So," I said, "how did you two come to meet?"

I didn't mean to put anybody on the spot. I just asked this as a sort of lead-in to my next question. Carl McGraw, however, suddenly looked uncomfortable. "Well," he said, clearing his throat, "I certainly don't mind telling you; I don't mind at all."

Clearly, though, he did.

"It's not anything I'm ashamed of. It's just a little unusual, that's all." McGraw glanced over at Elena, who was at that moment still standing at his elbow, holding the plate of rapidly disappearing donuts. She looked back at him, a soft smile playing around her mouth, her eyes a little puzzled. Obviously, she didn't understand most of what was being said. "Elena and I met through an introduction service. Can you believe I picked her picture out of one of their singles magazines?"

Actually, I could. In fact, I remembered reading something about international matchmaking services in the *Courier-Journal* not too long ago. According to the *Courier*, ever since Communism fell and the economic conditions in Russia have deteriorated, introduction services have become a booming business. Single women in Russia—where, if I recalled correctly, the newspaper article had mentioned the average monthly wage these days was a whopping twenty-five dollars a month—were so eager to marry American men and move to this country that they ran advertisements in singles magazines, complete with photo. When I read the article, I'd felt so sorry for all those poor women.

Now, seeing Elena, I felt even sorrier.

McGraw was taking three more chocolate-covered donuts. "A lot of my friends have been making awful predictions," he said. "They've told me that Elena will leave me just as soon as she gets in this country. But"—at this point, he reached out and patted Elena's arm. The motion shook Elena's tray a little, but she immediately regained control of the thing—"Elena and I are going to prove everybody wrong. Elena and I are staying together."

I smiled. "I'm sure you're right," I said. I meant it, too. Elena was not about to leave him.

Not soon, anyway. At least not until she learned a lot more English, and could understand what, no doubt, quite a few of her female neighbors would be only too happy to tell her. Hell, I could just hear them now. *Elena, for God's sake, you don't have to take that crap. Tell that lazy lout to take a hike.*

I stared at McGraw. If I were a friend of his, I'd tell him that he really shouldn't be teaching Elena any English at all. That, in fact, he'd better hope she never learned the language.

I smiled at McGraw yet again. My mouth was beginning to hurt. "Now that I know how you two met," I said, glancing over at Elena, who was still doing her personal impression of a donut dispenser, "I wonder—how did you meet Kimberly Metcalf?"

I thought I'd eased into this new topic, but McGraw stiffened anyway. Elena picked up on the change in his manner right away. She took a step closer to him and put her hand on his arm.

McGraw didn't even acknowledge that Elena had touched him. "I met Kimberly," he said, "during an intermission at Actors' Theatre. They were doing *'night, mother.*" He reached for another donut and pointed the thing at me. "Are you familiar with that play?"

I started to tell him that, yes, I'd seen the movie twice, and the play three times—it's one of my favorites—but McGraw went right on without waiting for me to answer. "It's the play by Marsha Norman, it won the Pulitzer, and in my opinion, it's really quite good."

I stared at him. I was sure that Marsha would be delighted to know that he approved.

"So much of what you see these days is just garbage, you know. Just a rehash of the same tired stories." McGraw looked over at Elena. "My wife and I have season tickets to Actors' Theatre—"

I blinked at that one. The theatre should be a lot of fun for somebody who barely understands English.

"—and, of course," McGraw was going on, waving a donut in the air, "I'll make sure that we'll also attend the symphony and the ballet. I guess I'm old-fashioned myself, but I happen to believe that a lady needs to be educated in the finer things. And my Elena, well, right now she's a diamond in the rough."

I just looked at him. And you're the *polish*?

I needed to get away from this guy fast, before I lost it entirely and taught Elena two brand-new words she might get immediate use out of: *Pompous* and *asshole*. I leaned toward McGraw. "So how long ago was this?" I asked. "When you ran into Kimberly at Actors' Theatre?"

McGraw inhaled still another chocolate donut. You had to admire this guy's endurance. "Well," he said, "it was before I moved here, when I was still living in southern Indiana. I've lived here about six months, more or less. So, I guess it was about thirteen months ago. I'd just gotten divorced from my second wife, and I think I must've been terribly depressed."

I had to look away for a moment while I digested that one. Divorced? Twice? *Him?* What a shock.

"That's no doubt why I was so vulnerable to somebody like Kimberly."

Oh, sure, it didn't have anything to do with your being in your fifties and Kimberly being in her twenties and very pretty with long blond hair. Oh, no, it couldn't have had anything to do with *that*.

McGraw glanced over at Elena, and said, "Cigarettes."

That's all he said, and she was off like a shot. Apparently, she'd mastered that word right away. Of course, it had probably been said to her a lot.

I couldn't help glancing at the pipe in McGraw's breast pocket. It did look new. Evidently it was just a prop, the finishing touch that made a smoking jacket, as Jim Carrey said in *The Mask, smokin'*.

McGraw now leaned toward me and lowered his voice, as if he were sharing a confidence. "Can you believe

Kimberly actually told me that her people were *the* Metcalfs? Do you know the people I'm talking about?"

Once again, he didn't wait for me to answer. "They're
the ones that made all that money in oil, and then moved
to Lexington and started raising thoroughbreds."

"No kidding," I said.

"No kidding," McGraw said, nodding his head. "Kimberly was good, I'll grant you that. She actually had me
considering marriage. So, naturally, I hired a private
detective to check up on her."

Naturally. Everybody knows that's one of the things
that all prospective grooms do. You rent a tux, you buy
the rings, and you investigate the bride.

I guess I looked a little surprised at the private detective
bit, because McGraw got defensive all over again. He sat
up a little straighter in the La-Z-Boy—for him, not an
easy task. "Now look," he said, "you can't be too careful
these days. I learned years ago that if you don't want to
get taken, you can't take anything for granted."

Words to live by, no doubt.

McGraw shrugged. "Why, I even hired a private detective to check out Elena. And you know what I found out?"

I shook my head.

Elena came trotting back in with a pack of Camels and
a Bic lighter then, and McGraw gave her another fond
look. "I found out that Elena here was just exactly what
she said she was—a Russian woman living in one of the
poorest areas of that beleaguered country. Her parents
were long dead, and her husband had been killed in a car
accident two years ago." Having said this last, McGraw
glanced over at me. "That's right, Elena was married once
before, but I decided I could overlook it."

How big of him. Or rather, *large*.

McGraw, by his own admission, had been married
twice himself, and yet he acted as if he were doing Elena
a huge favor by overlooking her previous nuptials? I was
beginning to think I might gag.

Elena had lit his Camel, and now she handed it to him.
As he took the cigarette, McGraw said with a shrug, "The
detective I hired confirmed that my Elena was working as

a maid and selling vegetables on the street just like she'd told me. What's more, the detective told me that she'd often talked to friends about coming to America."

Uh-huh. Let me translate. Poor Elena was so desperate to get out of a country that was currently in economic ruin that she was willing to become McGraw's personal servant to do it.

I looked over at Elena and felt another rush of sympathy for her. I looked at McGraw and felt a rush of contempt. I mean, couldn't the man hear himself? He'd admitted, in so many words, that he'd had so much trouble finding a woman in this country who'd put up with him that he'd finally been reduced to importing one.

McGraw was now shaking his head. "The detective's report on Kimberly, however, was an entirely different story. She'd been married a ton of times."

My head went up at that one. What exactly was a *ton*?

"Nearly everything Kimberly had told me was a lie. *Everything*."

I couldn't help noticing that a muscle had begun to jump in McGraw's jaw, and the ruts between his brows now looked a little deeper. Good Lord. He was still angry. More than a year later, happily married to someone else, and knowing what had happened to Kimberly, Carl McGraw was still angry with her. In fact, he didn't just look angry, he looked furious.

I felt a sudden chill.

"Naturally," McGraw was saying, "after I got that detective report, I told Kimberly that I never wanted to see her again. Or that phony brother of hers."

"Phony?" I echoed. Did McGraw know about Paul, too?

McGraw nodded. "Oh, he was phony, all right. I mean, if he was her brother, I'm Abraham Lincoln."

I nodded. My goodness, yes. I'd testify myself that Carl McGraw could not possibly be Abraham Lincoln. Abe had *freed* the slaves.

I got to my feet. I'd learned all I needed to know. Everything that McGraw had told me about Kimberly fit in with what I already knew.

It had been, no doubt, during one of the visits we'd

made to the Dutch colonial house next door that Kimberly had spotted McGraw. The second she saw him, she must've recognized him and realized instantly that she could not possibly live right next door to a man she'd told the same lies to that she'd told Ed. It would be only a matter of time until McGraw saw her. If that happened, Kimberly would've known that McGraw would waste no time telling Ed everything the detective had discovered about her.

The contract on the house next door must've been already signed by the time Kimberly spotted McGraw. So she'd suddenly started insisting that she couldn't possibly live next door to a "redneck." The contract had been cancelled, Ed had forfeited his deposit, and Kimberly had, no doubt, breathed a huge sigh of relief. She'd made sure that the next house she and Ed decided on would be miles away.

I got to my feet and said my good-byes. First to Elena. Who, looking directly at me for the first time, gave me a shy smile. And then to McGraw. I was already out on the porch when I stopped and turned back to face McGraw. "Oh, by the way, I thought you should know, I'm not a police officer."

I then turned and, as my Kentucky relatives say, high-tailed it out of there.

McGraw was shouting something or another at me when I drove away. Something on the order of, "Who are you? Come back here at once! I demand that you . . ."

Hell, he could demand all he wanted.

It was probably childish of me, but before I left, I did want to irritate the hell out of him. Much like the way he treated Elena had irritated the hell out of me.

I was almost home when something occurred to me that I hadn't yet thought of. If Kimberly had seen McGraw, couldn't McGraw also have seen *her*?

Oh, God. Could Carl McGraw have somehow found out that Kimberly was alone yesterday in the Henderson house? Hell, he admitted he'd used a private detective to investigate her. If he had indeed spotted her next door, much like she'd spotted him, could he have then had a detective tail her? Just because he had witnesses that would place him at his office didn't necessarily mean he was really there. After all, he said he owned the business. Wouldn't his own employees lie for the man upon whom they depended for their paychecks?

Lord. Could McGraw have just been biding his time, waiting for his chance? Yesterday, finding out that she was alone, had he finally paid Kimberly back for what she'd tried to do to him?

He *had* sounded furious when he'd talked about her. Carl McGraw did not seem to be the sort of man whom you could wrong without his wanting to get even.

I wished I'd asked McGraw the name of the detective he'd hired. Although, let's face it, whoever it was probably wouldn't tell me anything. From what I understand, a detective pretty much stays in business by keeping his work confidential.

It seemed to me the only person who could shed a little more light on just how angry Carl McGraw actually was after he'd found out about Kimberly's phony stories would be Kimberly's phony brother.

I went right past the turn onto Harvard Drive, and I picked up speed.

Chapter 16

I headed toward the Watterson again, and the Shelbyville Road exit. Under the driver's seat of my car, I keep one of those phones that, in a weak moment, I'd let a salesclerk at Sears talk me into buying. This thing plugs into my car's cigarette lighter socket, and from the way the salesclerk had talked, it would come in unbelievably handy.

According to this guy, once I bought the thing and signed up for an entire of cellular service, I would be on my car phone all the time, returning client phone calls on the way to open houses. Negotiating contracts while waiting at the drive-up window at my bank. Taking information for loan applications on my way to a closing.

Uh-huh. *Right.*

What the sales guy neglected to mention, oddly enough, is that it costs just about the same to talk on my cellular phone as it does to chat with Hong Kong. And, if you happen to be on the outer edge of one of their calling areas—or if, say, you go under a bridge, or you pass a semi—you'll understand what's being said just about the same as you would if you really were talking to Hong Kong.

Needless to say, I almost never use my car phone. Right this minute, though, I was tempted to give Ed and the boys a ring. I wanted to let them know where I was headed. Just in case. In case of what, I wasn't exactly sure, and the more I thought about it, the more I realized I didn't particularly want to put whatever I was afraid of into words.

Note that I said I was *tempted* to call. I'd already taken the Shelbyville Road exit, and I was still trying to make up my mind. If I did call the boys—and Ed—there wasn't a doubt in my mind that every one of them would badger me unmercifully. Ed would try to talk me out of going altogether, much as he'd done yesterday, by pointing out how idiotic I was to even think of doing such a thing. Ed's strategy, in all the years I've known him, has always been the same: Deride and conquer.

Nathan and Daniel wouldn't be derisive like their dad—not if they ever wanted to borrow my car again. Then, too, I do believe that my Blockbuster card was still hanging in the balance. No, what the boys would do was what they'd also done yesterday. They'd insist that I take at least one of them with me. For protection. As if, should shots ever ring out, both my sons would not try to beat me to the nearest exist.

I was turning into the entrance to the La Fenetre Apartments when I finally made up my mind. I wasn't going to phone anybody. I didn't need the hassle.

Just like yesterday, however, as I got out of my car and started walking toward Paul's gardenless garden apartment, I felt around in my purse for my pepper spray. When I found it, once again I dropped it into the left front pocket of my suit jacket. I had my hand in my pocket, holding the spray canister, all ready to aim and fire, when I rang the doorbell.

Paul took his time getting to the door. When he finally opened up, however, and I got a good look at him, I realized that he had an excellent excuse for moving so slow. The man could barely stand up. In fact, Paul looked as if he'd been drinking nonstop ever since Nathan and I had left him yesterday.

Paul was still wearing what he'd been wearing then—white dress shirt, tan chinos, black socks, no shoes—but he'd made a few changes. Paul's chinos now looked as if he'd slept in them. Which, of course, he probably had. He no longer had black socks on both feet. What had happened to the missing sock was anybody's guess. And his shirt was now not only wrinkled, but unbuttoned. So that you couldn't help but notice that the T-shirt Paul was wearing underneath had several large brown stains down the front. They were either coffee stains or cola stains, I couldn't tell which. Or they might've been something else, a faint odor of which I thought I picked up when Paul opened the door.

Uh-oh. If Paul had spent any of his time in the last twenty-four hours doing what my sons refer to so charmingly as tossing his cookies, I didn't want to know about it. I took a step backward, so that if any odors were headed in my direction, they might dissipate before they got to me.

I ventured a greeting. "Paul? Hello?" I felt like adding, "Anybody in there?" because for a long moment after I spoke, he just stood there and stared at me. Once again he was using the doorknob as a cane.

Apparently, Paul had run his hand through his hair so many times during the night, his dark brown curls were no longer curls. They'd been reduced to limp waves, clinging damply to his neck and forehead. The dark stubble he'd had last night had grown considerably darker. And yet, even with his hair a mess and more than a day's growth darkening his face, Paul Whatever-His-Name-Really-Was still managed to be one of the best-looking men I'd ever seen.

Judging from the blank look on his face, I wasn't sure Paul recognized me at all. "Whuf?" he finally said. That's an exact quote. The man was nothing if not articulate.

"Paul," I said. "I'm Schuyler Ridgway; I came by yesterday? To offer my condolences?"

Paul continued to stare at me blankly.

I cleared my throat. This could possibly be a tiny bit harder than I thought.

"Paul," I said, "I just talked to Carl McGraw."

If the name meant anything at all to him, Paul sure didn't act like it. Of course, in the condition he was now in, his own name might not mean a whole lot.

"I said, I just talked to Carl McGraw," I practically yelled at Paul.

Paul's response this time was to blink at me, over

and over again, as if I'd just shined a flashlight in his eyes. "Yeah?" he finally said. "So?" Saying only those two words must've worn him out, because he slumped a little against the doorframe, his hand tightening on the doorknob.

I myself was tightening my grip on the pepper spray in my pocket. I'm not sure why. Maybe I was afraid that Paul might fall on me or something, and I wanted to make sure I had my defense ready. It did cross my mind, however, that if Paul could stand up under all the chemicals he'd already ingested, hitting him with this spray might not even faze him. It might be just a chaser.

Paul looked as if he really was dozing off. "PAUL!" I said, and was rewarded by his head jerking in my direction. "Mr. McGraw told me a lot of things."

Paul started doing his flashlight-blinking again. He took an unsteady step forward, but he didn't let go of the doorknob. "Like what?" Paul asked. Only it came out sounding more like, *Lack whuf?*

I shrugged. "Well, he said your name isn't Metcalf. It's Hettinger."

Paul just stared at me. "Hettinger," he said, as if the sound of it was a surprise to him, too. Then, straightening up, he began to button the front of his shirt. As if maybe it had just occurred to him that it badly needed buttoning. Some of the buttons ended up in the wrong hole, but I do believe it was the thought that counted. "Hettinger, huh?" Paul repeated, his eyes on his shirtfront. "Who says?"

It was my turn to just stare at him. Correct me if I'm wrong, but hadn't I just given him that information?

"*Carl McGraw* says." I spoke slowly and distinctly. "Carl McGraw says that your last name is Hettinger." Lord. I felt as if we were playing some kind of children's game. *Carl McGraw Says.*

Paul evidently didn't like this particular game. He was still buttoning his shirt, but he was now frowning.

I was beginning to fear that it might dawn on him any minute that all he had to do was take one giant step backward, and then he could slam the door right in my face. If he did such a thing, this little game would be over.

I decided I didn't care if I got a whiff of tossed cookies, after all. I took a step toward him, and began all over again. "Paul, listen to me. I just talked to Carl McGraw, and he said that your name isn't Metcalf. It's Hettinger."

"Who says?" Paul said again, his tone belligerent this time.

I was beginning to tire of this game myself. I mean, was Paul not paying attention, or what? "Paul, Carl McGraw told me your real name, but it wasn't news to me. The police had already told me—"

Paul had the gall to interrupt me. "Who's this Carl McGraw you're talking about? I don't know a Carl McGraw." He had stopped buttoning, and was now pointing at me. Lord, his hand was unsteady. "I have never heard of a Carl McGraw." He looked me straight in the eye. Unwaveringly.

I stared right back at him. Both my sons have used this gambit ever since they were in elementary school. The lie-your-head-off-but-look-her-straight-in-the-eye-when-you-do-it bit. Who did Paul think he was kidding?

"Sure you know him," I said. "Carl McGraw used to be engaged to Kimberly. And I know for a fact that you were introduced to him as her brother. What do you think of that?"

The obvious answer, of course, was that Paul wasn't thinking at all. He seemed to have zoned out again. In fact, judging from the blank look in his eyes as he stared at me, I'd say there was an excellent chance that old Paul here could have a totally flat brain wave.

"I asked you a question, PAUL!"

Paul might've had a little spike in his brain waves when I yelled his name, because he jumped. Then he frowned at me like a man rudely awakened. "Whaa—aaf?"

Another exact quote. The man did have a way with nonwords.

"I'd like to know why Mr. McGraw broke his engagement to Kimberly right after he hired a private detective to investigate her."

Paul shrugged. "Damn prick," he said.

Considering that he had mentioned a body part rarely

found on women, I believe Paul was referring to Carl McGraw, not me. At least, I preferred to think so.

"Paul," I said, and yes, I *was* gritting my teeth. "I want some answers."

"Answers," he repeated, his eyes going blank again.

I'd had it. "Okay, PAUL!" His eyes cleared a little. "Look, either you tell me what Kimberly was up to, or I'm going to head downtown and tell the county prosecutor everything I've learned, and you'll be answering *his* questions instead of mine. How's that grab you?"

This is where watching too much TV comes in handy. I wasn't even sure Louisville had a county prosecutor, for God's sake, let alone whether it was a man or a woman, or where the office was. However, I'd heard the term bandied about on *NYPD Blue* and *Law and Order.*

Paul stared at me for about a second, tops, and then his shoulders slumped. "Okay, okay," he said. He stepped back and held his door open. Standing to one side so that I could go past him, he indicated with a wave of his hand that I should take a seat on the sofa on my right.

When Paul opened the door, the suspicion that I'd had earlier—the one regarding tossed cookies—was pretty much confirmed. Judging from the odor, I'd say that there could very well be tossed cookies all over the place. It was dark in Paul's apartment, too. The drapes had been pulled shut, and there didn't seem to be any lights on. Difficult to tell if you were about to sit on tossed cookies, or if, say, you'd just stepped in them.

Oddly enough, I suddenly decided that it would be a terrific idea to continue our little chat out here on the porch. In the fresh air. "You know, Paul, it's such a nice day, why don't we just talk out here?"

Even in his condition, Paul could tell that nice was not exactly the right word to describe this day. It was overcast, threatening rain, and the wind was getting cooler by the minute. He glanced at the dark storm clouds overhead, and then looked at me. As if trying to decide if I, too, had been drinking.

The nerve.

I took a seat on the porch steps, the second one from the top.

"So, Paul," I said, turning to look over at him, "what were you saying about Kimberly?"

"Kimberly," Paul said. His face crumpled a little, and I thought he might actually cry. Then he mumbled something, turned abruptly, and headed inside.

I just sat there, staring after him. And wondering, of course, if I was going to have to go inside and dodge tossed cookies after all.

I didn't have to wonder long. Paul reappeared almost immediately, carrying an unopened bottle of Jack Daniel's.

Oh, joy. Idly, I wondered which was worse. Trying to avoid stepping in tossed cookies, or carrying on a conversation with a drunk about to get drunker.

Paul let the door close behind him, and he moved unsteadily forward to sit on the step right next to me. "I told her, you know," he said, pointing the Jack Daniel's bottle at me. "I told her that she'd better be careful."

"Careful?"

Paul nodded. Not a good idea in his condition. For a moment there I thought he just might topple right off the steps. He caught himself in time, though, and started tearing off the seal of his bottle. "I told Kimmie one day her luck was going to run out. And she was going to try to scam the wrong guy."

I just looked at him. "Scam? What do you mean, scam?"

Paul shrugged. "It was this thing that she did, that's all. Kimmie really thought it was funny. Pulling a fast one on all the damn climbers."

He'd lost me. "Climbers?" I echoed. "Did you say, *climbers*?"

Paul frowned at me. He had his bottle open by now, and gentleman that he was, he took a long, long swig without even asking if I minded. "Yeah," he said, wiping his mouth on his sleeve, "climbers. That's what I said. You know, people trying to move up the ladder. Trying to keep with the Joneses. Climbers."

Oh. *Social* climbers. I nodded.

Paul shrugged, a motion that almost sent him toppling off the porch again. It took him longer this time to regain his balance, and I was relieved when he finally did. I wasn't sure what I'd do if he fell down the stairs. He looked too heavy for me to pick up alone.

Not to mention, I wasn't sure I particularly wanted to touch him when I wasn't wearing rubber gloves.

Leaning back against the top step, Paul ran his hand through his hair and went on. "You know, if Kimberly's last name hadn't been Metcalf, none of this ever would have happened." Paul rubbed his eyes and leaned toward me. I immediately wished he hadn't, because it was then, of course, that I realized that he had not brushed his teeth anytime lately. A thing I really would recommend after cookie tossing. "I mean, Kimmie might never have thought of doing this."

I was trying to look encouraging, as if I was hanging on his every word, but considering that I was also trying to decide if Paul was too drunk to notice if I started to hold my nose, looking encouraging was a stretch.

"You do know that Kimmie was not one of *the* Metcalfs, you know that, don't you?" Paul punctuated his question by taking another long swig.

I nodded. No, I was pretty sure he'd notice the nose-holding. I mean, how could he miss it? I contented myself with leaning as far away from him as I could.

"That was just something she told people so as to attract wealthy older men. You'd be surprised how many men don't even check up on somebody before they marry her."

I blinked. "*Marry?* She actually married these men?"

Paul grinned. Apparently, he had not seen fit to floss anytime lately, either. He was rapidly looking less and less handsome, oddly enough. "Kimmie's been married twice already this year alone." He lifted his bottle in a mock salute. "Kimmie was very good at what she did."

What could I say? I was happy she'd found such a fulfilling career? "How many times had she been married in all?"

That evidently was a real stumper. Paul scratched his chin, rolled his eyes, took another drink, and then finally said, "I'm not sure. Quite a few."

"A few, like five? Or a few, like twenty?"

Paul shook his head. "Oh, no, no, no. You're not getting it. This is what Kimmie did for a living. So it was for sure more than twenty. Hell, it might've been fifty or a hundred. I don't know. We didn't count."

Paul took another long drink. This time he didn't bother wiping his mouth. It needed wiping, too. Bad.

Instead, Paul sighed and looked over at me, his eyes suddenly misty. "Kimmie made such a beautiful bride."

I just looked at him. Well, of course she did. She'd had a lot of practice.

Paul was hurrying on. "She married me first, you know."

Once again, I was at a loss for what to say. *That must've meant a lot? You never forget your first time?* Or maybe something simple, like, *How nice?*

Fortunately, Paul hurried on so I didn't have to say anything. "Of course, we had to get divorced because of her work. She didn't want to be a bigamist."

Paul, believe it or not, was now grinning again. "Boy, that was the life. Me and Kimmie. We traveled all over, California, Florida, Hawaii, always on the move. Following the wanderlust."

Dodging the police. And angry ex-husbands. Oh, my, it did sound grand.

Paul actually seemed to think so. He kept right on smiling as he told me all about it. According to Paul, once Kimberly got some guy to marry her, she'd reveal all the things she hadn't quite gotten around to telling him before the nuptials. How she'd been married countless times before, and how her roomie, Paul, was not really her brother, but her lover. The most important thing she told her new hubby, though, was how she expected to be paid off handsomely, or she was going to let everybody hubby knew learn all the details of how she'd made a first-class fool of him. Because all the men she targeted were professionals with reputations to protect—and, let's face it, a great deal of pride—they'd all ended up paying exactly what she asked.

"Man," Paul said, shaking his dark head, "you wouldn't believe what some men will pay to avoid being embarrassed."

Actually, I would believe it.

Paul was now rubbing his eyes again. "But I guess this last one figured it out," he said. His voice quavered. "It— it's just like I told her, 'Kimmie, someday you're gonna pick the wrong guy to scam.' I was right."

I shook my head. "Paul, I don't think that Ed knew anything about—"

Paul didn't even let me finish. "Hell, yeah, he knew," Paul said. "In fact, Ed Ridgway called me up, ranting and raving about everything. Calling Kimmie some real ugly names. Names she didn't deserve. Because she was a nice person."

I stared at him, shocked. Ed had called him?

Paul, though, must've thought I was shocked about something else. He sat up a little straighter and glared at me. "Kimmie was too nice a person, she really was." Paul's tone was belligerent. "Kimmie never did anything to anybody who didn't deserve it. She made sure they had it coming."

I just looked at him, feeling a little sick. No wonder Kimberly had kept asking me if Ed had been unfaithful. Kimberly had been making sure that Ed truly deserved what she was about to do to him.

"It was justice, that's what it was," Paul said. "Poetic justice."

I was not about to discuss the concept of justice, poetic or otherwise, with a drunk. Particularly a drunk who was admittedly an accomplice to fraud. Besides, I had a lot more pressing things to discuss. "You said that Ed called you. Are you absolutely sure it was Ed?"

Paul shrugged, and took another drink. He seemed to be taking his sweet time about it, too, first wiping the top of the bottle, then licking his lips, then wiping the top of the bottle again. I was just getting ready to grab that stupid whiskey bottle right out of Paul's hands and hurl it to the sidewalk when he finally answered. "Hell, yes, it was Ed Ridgway. He was yelling his goddamn head off. He knew who I was, too. I mean, my real name. *Hettinger*."

I stared at him, actually feeling sick. Here I'd gone to all this trouble to find out what had really happened, and sure enough, I'd found out an entirely new story. The only problem was, the new story wasn't any better than the old one, as far as Ed was concerned. Both still pointed straight at Ed.

Either Ed had killed Kimberly during a fight over his making a pass at Adrienne Henderson, or Ed had killed Kimberly because he'd discovered that she was making a fool out of him. No matter which story you believed, it still ended up that Ed had killed Kimberly.

My stomach suddenly felt like I'd just struck a match to it. "When did you get this phone call from Ed?" I asked.

Paul shrugged again. "I'm not 'xactly sure. Maybe a week ago." He lifted his bottle to his lips again, this time closing his eyes.

I was shaking my head. A *week* ago? That couldn't be right. Paul had to be remembering wrong. Ed would never have continued to go through with the purchase of the Willow Avenue house if he'd found out all this a week ago. Of course, as intoxicated as Paul seemed to be, I wasn't really surprised that he might've gotten part of his story wrong.

But was it likely that he'd gotten all of it wrong? As much as I would've liked to believe otherwise, I had to admit the chances of Paul making up everything he'd just told me were slim. For one thing, there was really no reason for him to lie at this point. He'd actually admitted to being part of a fraud. And Kimberly was dead. There was nothing anybody could do to her now. In fact, that could very well be why Paul was talking. Kimberly couldn't get into any trouble over what he told me, and he wanted her killer caught.

Paul was waving the whiskey bottle at me now. "But it was funking Ed Ridgway, I know damn well it was!"

I didn't even blink. Somebody needed to tell Paul how to pronounce that word he seemed to like to use so much.

"Ed Ridgway better hope the police find him, 'cause I'm going to kill him dead."

That was generally how that worked.

Paul was wobbling a little on his feet. "I am gonna blow that sumbitch away for what he did to Kimmie. Sure as I'm standing here."

That didn't look any too sure to me.

Paul seemed to expect me to say something in response to his last little announcement, but frankly, I couldn't think of anything. I would've liked to have tried to convince him that Ed was innocent, but I wasn't totally sure myself. If Ed had known about Kimberly, he could have been angry enough to kill her.

There didn't seem to be anything else for me to do except to go back to the boys' apartment and discuss this new story with Ed himself. For one thing, Paul seemed to be fairly preoccupied. Planning Ed's murder and all.

I left Paul on the steps, finishing off the last of the Jack Daniel's, and I hurried to my car. I wasn't sure Paul even noticed when I left.

Damn. I probably could've held my nose, after all.

Chapter 17

I headed straight for Nathan and Daniel's apartment, and once again, I managed to haul myself all the way up their narrow stairs to the third floor. Once again, I also managed to sound like the big bad wolf, huffing and puffing outside my two little pigs' apartment.

While I tried to get my breathing and my heartbeat back to normal, I leaned against the wall next to their doorbell, and pushed the thing again and again.

My heart had settled down considerably by the time it occurred to me that nobody was going to answer. This was particularly irritating because I was sure when I'd finally made it to the third-floor landing, and I'd staggered over to apartment C, I'd heard the sound of a TV inside. It had been playing the theme to *I Dream of Jeannie,* which strangely enough happens to be one of Ed's all-time favorite television programs.

I have always been certain, of course, that Ed's fascination with this show has nothing whatsoever to do with the way it stars a scantily clad, gorgeous blond whose entire existence consists of satisfying every whim of her master. I'm sure Ed doesn't even notice that when her master doesn't happen to have any whims to satisfy, he still always knows just where to find his Jeannie—corked inside of a bottle, waiting for him to come up with a whim.

Oh, no, I can't imagine that any of this would appeal to Ed. No, I'm sure that Ed loves this old TV classic because he's interested in the way it accurately depicts the socio-economic conditions of its era.

Come to think of it, that's exactly why I myself happen to like Antonio Banderas movies. You can never get enough of those socioeconomic conditions.

Strangely enough, the *I Dream of Jeannie* theme had stopped abruptly right after I rang the doorbell the first time. It stopped so abruptly, in fact, that you could get the idea that the second the doorbell sounded, somebody had hurried over to the TV and snapped the thing off. Imagine that. The sound of *Jeannie* was immediately replaced by the sound of feet moving very fast. Away from the front door.

It would appear, then, that Ed the Courageous was home.

Unless, of course, one of our equally courageous offspring had started dreaming of Jeannie since he'd moved out of my house. This last, however, I strongly doubted. These days, if I recalled correctly, Nathan's idea of the ideal woman was Cindy Crawford. And Daniel's idea was, of course, Madonna—or, for that matter, any female with more than three body parts pierced.

No, if the person on the other side of my sons' apartment door had been watching *Jeannie,* my best guess would be that it had to be Ed.

Having reached this conclusion, I was tempted to just start yelling for Ed to get his butt in gear and let me in. I was afraid, however, that the boys' neighbors would hear me. Not that I minded them hearing me yell the word *butt.* I believe I've yelled worse in my lifetime. No, the thing that I minded was that if the neighbors heard me calling Ed's name, and reported what I said to the police, I might someday have to admit that I'd known all along exactly where Ed was hiding. An admission that might very well encourage the salt-and-pepper shakers to arrest me for harboring a fugitive, or aiding and abetting a felon, or some such.

I believe I've already established just how happy I'm sure that the shakers would be to make reservations for me in a nice cell somewhere. So, with yelling eliminated as an option, I went for my second choice. I tried the doorknob. It turned easily.

This was not altogether a surprise. This was, after all, the current residence of the very same two sons of mine who'd never locked the front door when they lived with me. Even after I'd told them again and again and again. The surprise here was that Ed must not have checked himself to make sure the dead bolt was on.

I suppose what I did next could technically be called trespassing. However, since I was pretty sure that my precious sons would not bring charges against their own beloved mother—particularly if they ever wanted to borrow my car again, or let us not forget, my Blockbuster card—I didn't hesitate. I gave the front door a little push, and when it swung open, I strolled on in.

There was a lamp on the side table next to the sofa. It was still lit. I went over to the TV, and I touched the back. It was still warm.

"Nathan? Daniel?" There was no answer.

"Ed?" Still no answer.

I walked directly to the living room closet, opened it, and said to the clothes inside, "Ed, come on out here, I want to talk to you."

I had to hand it to him. Ed stepped out from behind a row of coats and suits, wearing another pair of Daniel's torn jeans, a ragged T-shirt that said I BRAKE FOR BEER, and the black dress socks–black dress shoes combo he'd worn yesterday, and he managed to give *me* a look of contempt. "Schuyler, what do you think you're doing? You can't just walk in here anytime you want," he said. "There are laws, you know. The police do not look any too kindly on breaking and entering."

Can you believe he actually said this to me? The man who was wanted for murder—who was himself so afraid of being arrested that he had actually been hiding in a closet—this was the guy lecturing *me* about laws and police.

To use another phrase I've often heard my sons say: Did Ed have big brass ones, or what?

"Ed," I said, "I need to talk to you—"

Ed wasn't through. "I mean, Schuyler, I don't think you realize what you've done here. Breaking and entering is a serious crime. You could—"

I couldn't stand it. Ed was talking in that ultra-patient, just-trying-to-explain-the-facts-to-moronic-little-you voice that he used to lecture me with all the time when we were married. It was either scream my head off or interrupt. I chose the one that would be, unfortunately, the least fun. "Ed," I said, cutting him off, "I didn't break and enter. I just entered. I don't think there are any laws against just entering."

Ed was already shaking his head before I even finished. "Oh, yes, there are," he said, giving me a withering look. "I'll have you know that what you just did is called trespassing—"

Do tell.

"Ed," I said.

"—because neither one of the boys is here, they're both at work, so you can't just walk in here. The police are pretty conscientious about—"

"Ed!" I said again.

"—enforcing this kind of thing. I mean, all I'd have to do is pick up the phone and report you and—"

"ED!" I said still again.

"—you'd be in big trouble."

That one stopped me for a second or two. Big trouble? Ed was hiding out from the police because they thought he might've murdered somebody, and yet he thought *trespassing* could get me into big trouble? Good Lord, didn't he ever listen to himself? Not to mention, did he really think that I'd believe for an instant that he would ever pick up the phone and report me? I mean, wouldn't that involve him getting in touch with the very people he was so anxious to avoid that he was in danger of becoming a permanent resident of a closet?

"Ed," I said, "I'm trying to tell you something important. Will you listen to me for five seconds?"

I mentally congratulated myself for not losing my cool entirely, and shouting, "Shut UP!" Never let it be said that I'm not a Southern lady.

Ed evidently didn't realize that there were other ways I could've chosen to express myself. He ran his hand through his sandy hair, and looked long-suffering. "All right, Schuyler," he said with an elaborate sigh, "what do you want to tell me, for God's sake?"

Now that I had his attention, I wasn't sure how to begin. "Well, it's about Kimberly."

As soon as I said her name, Ed's eyes narrowed.

I looked away. "I just talked to a guy by the name of Carl McGraw," I went on, "and he had some very interesting things to tell me. That I thought you really should know."

While Ed stood there, his face getting redder and redder, I told him all about Kimberly's little marriage scam. I told him what I'd found out from Paul. I told him everything that I could remember that McGraw had said. And I finished with, "Ed, I'm sorry." I meant it, too. At least, I meant it right up until Ed started yelling at me.

"How could you? *How* could you?" Ed was actually shouting. Evidently, he didn't particularly care what the neighbors heard.

I took a couple of steps away from him, and said, "Ed, keep your voice down, or somebody's going to hear."

"I don't care who hears! How could you?"

I just looked at him. "Ed," I said quietly, "you will care when the police show up."

That toned him down a little. "I want to know, how could you?" he said.

I really didn't know what he meant. How could *I* what? Obviously, he'd misunderstood me. "Ed, it wasn't me. Kimberly was the one who . . ."

I was just trying to make myself clear, for crying out loud. Ed, however, looked even more outraged. The man actually began to pace, flailing his arms in the air. Have I mentioned, I hate it when he does this? "How could you drag poor, sweet Kimberly's name through the mud like this?" Ed asked. "HOW?"

I gaped at him. I had not exactly been anticipating heartfelt gratitude for telling him what could only be bad news, but I certainly hadn't expected this. "Ed, I—"

He continued to pace. And interrupt. "I mean, I knew you were jealous, Schuyler—"

I caught my breath. Huh?

Ed stopped pacing, and just looked at me. "—but I never, *ever* thought you'd stoop this low."

I was speechless. Did Ed really believe that I'd been jealous of Kimberly? Good Lord. Why would he think such a thing, unless he also thought I might still be in love with him. My mouth was suddenly trying very hard not to laugh. I had to bite my bottom lip to avoid an outright guffaw.

"I mean," Ed was now saying, "*really,* Schuyler, poor Kimberly is dead."

I was still biting my lip. Which was just as well. The only thing that came to mind to say was, "And your *point*?" and I knew that would only start him pacing and flailing again.

"Haven't you ever heard you're not supposed to talk ill of the dead?"

I was getting irritated. That's why I sort of blurted out what I said next. Without thinking. "I'm not sure, Ed. Why don't you hum a few bars, and I'll see if—"

Ed cut me off, his eyes now looking as if little bonfires had been set off behind each one. "I can't believe you would tell jokes at a time like this."

Oh, brother. Ed was now doing his high-and-mighty routine. I took a deep breath. This man would try the patience of Job.

Wouldn't you know, he started pacing and flailing again. "I can't believe you would come in here and *attempt* to drag poor, sweet Kimberly's memory through the mud—"

I interrupted him. "Ed, I wasn't dragging Kimberly's memory anywhere. I'm just telling you what I—"

Ed was now pacing and flailing to beat the band. "I just can't believe—"

Okay. Okay. This was where I came in. "Ed," I said, cutting him off, "then what you're telling me is that you had no idea that Kimberly was pulling a scam?"

Ed stopped in his tracks. "She was not!"

I stared at him. Now I understood. He wasn't upset that I'd found out the truth. The fool didn't believe a word of what I'd told him. Ed thought I'd actually made up this story.

Or at least that's what he wanted me to think. Could he be acting this outraged just to throw me off? Just so that I'd believe that he'd never had any idea what Kimberly was really up to? "Look, Ed—" I began.

He didn't let me finish. "Kimberly would *never* do a thing like that. Never! I mean, to even suggest that one of *the* Metcalfs would—"

I just looked at him. Apparently, I had not made myself clear. "Ed, she was not one of *the* Metcalfs. Like I said, her parents work at a Wal-Mart—"

Can you believe, he cut me off again? "Nonsense!" Ed said. "Kimberly even had a framed color portrait of the Metcalfs on the mantel in her apartment. And, believe me, my dear—" here Ed actually did one of his smug, little laughs—"the Metcalfs were *not* standing in front of a Wal-Mart."

Have I mentioned how much I hate for Ed to call me "my dear" in that pompous, know-it-all voice? Have I also mentioned that I'd rather listen to a solid hour of fingernails scraping blackboards than one of his smug little laughs?

Ed was now waggling his finger at me. I *loathe* that. "Schuyler, my sweet Kimberly would never, never lie about a thing like that. I mean, this was her *family*."

I took another deep breath. I could not believe that Ed could actually be convinced that *his* Kimberly was one of the Metcalfs just on the basis of a photograph. Of course, it helped that Ed had *wanted* to be convinced that he was engaged to what amounted to royalty in Kentucky.

And yet, let's have a reality check here. *I* could have ten framed photographs of the Rockefellers on the mantel in my living room, and that still wouldn't make me a Rockefeller.

The bad thing was I couldn't have Ed call and talk to McGraw so that he could verify what I was saying. I couldn't have Ed call *anybody,* or else they might turn him in. So, for right now, all he had was my word. And, clearly, that wasn't enough.

Have you ever noticed that people who lie always seem to think that other people are lying to them? Strange how that works.

I took still another deep breath. "Ed, Kimberly didn't just lie about her family, she lied about everything."

Oh, Lord. That sent him pacing and flailing again.

"No, she didn't! You're the one who's lying!" Ed's pacing was now taking him past the window on my right.

I turned in that direction. "Ed, will you keep your—"

This time it wasn't Ed that interrupted me. There was suddenly a sound like an angry bee whizzing past my ear. And immediately after that, the sound of shattering glass.

It all happened so fast, for a second I just stood there. Not sure what had happened.

Then, of course, I realized. And dropped like a rock to the floor.

Ed, my hero, was already down there, covering his head with his hands.

"Somebody's shooting at us," he whispered. His tone implied that it was my fault.

"Are you hit?" I whispered back.

"No," he whispered. "Did you let somebody follow you here?"

"I'm not hit either," I said. "Thanks for asking."

Ed made a noise that did not sound kind. *"Did you let somebody follow you here?"* he said in a loud stage whisper.

Now how was I supposed to answer that? "How would I know?" I whispered. "I didn't see anybody."

Lying on his stomach, Ed managed to take a long, irritated breath. "I can't believe you would just drive over here, as casually as can be, without once checking in your rearview mirror or anything. It's probably the police out there. They've probably got the place surrounded. But did you check? No, you probably didn't even look once to see if—"

That did it.

"Ed, will you SHUT UP!" I got to my feet and dusted

off my skirt. It needed dusting, believe me. In fact, I was fairly certain that the floor on which I'd just been lying had not been cleaned since the turn of the century. I stepped around Ed, who was still lying facedown, resisted the impulse to kick him while he was down, and went over to the lamp on the table. And snapped it off.

I know all this sounds either extremely brave, or absolutely foolhardy, but what it really was was neither. I'd just had all I could take of Ed. On some level I must've decided I'd rather be shot than listen to him another minute. I mean, please, shooter, put me out of my misery.

I headed straight for the window while Ed, of course, whispered, "For crying out loud! What the hell are you doing? Get down!"

I ignored him. Peeking out the side of the shattered glass through miniblinds coated in more turn-of-the-century dust, I saw absolutely no one. Not even anybody walking by on the sidewalk. Just the usual traffic on Third Street.

It was getting dark outside, and the lamp on the end table had been on. So I guess Ed would've been easy to see, from any one of several vantage points. Behind the shrubs across the street, from one of several windows in the three-story buildings across the street. Hell, he could've even been seen from this very building's front yard. Or even from a car slowing down for just a moment.

Good Lord. Could Ed be right? For maybe once in his life? Had Paul Hettinger followed me, intending to make good his promise to kill Ed? I would've thought that when I left him Paul had been too intoxicated to drive, but let's face it, that unfortunately has not stopped an awful lot of people. Not to mention, when you're on the way to commit murder, you might not much care about being arrested for D.U.I. Maybe Paul could even have been faking when he'd acted as if he didn't notice when I left. So that it wouldn't occur to me that he could've hurried to his own car and followed me.

I turned then, and I could see where the bullet that

broke the window had buried itself in the plaster across the room. Just looking at it made me cold.

"Ed," I said, "you've got to give up."

I don't know what the man thought I said, but he answered, still lying on his stomach, "I don't have to do anything. I'll get up when I'm good and—"

I shook my head. "I didn't say *get up,* I said, give up. You've got to give yourself up."

That prompted Ed to sit up and stare at me as if I were insane. "You're joking."

I shook my head again. "Ed, somebody's shooting at you. You've got to call the police!"

"How do you know they're shooting at me? *You* were here!"

I should not have resisted the impulse to kick him. "Ed, do you seriously think that somebody is—"

Ed, what a surprise, interrupted me. "It could be somebody you sold a house for—somebody who thinks you sold it for too little. Or maybe somebody whose loan got turned down, or—"

I just looked at him. Evidently, Ed thought I did such a good job in the real estate biz that I had mobs of previous clients gunning for me.

I'd heard enough. "Ed," I said, cutting him off, "why don't we let the police decide who was being shot at? Okay?"

Crossing his arms across his chest, Ed shook his head. Still sitting on the floor. "I'm not calling the police." Oh, God. He had that stubborn set to his mouth that always meant he was never going to give in. "Hell," Ed said, "maybe they weren't shooting at either one of us. This isn't the best neighborhood in the world, you know. Maybe it was one of those drive-by things they're always having in L.A."

Before Ed got me into an idiotic discussion regarding the similarities between Louisville, Kentucky, and Los Angeles, California—which would be like discussing the similarities between Nome, Alaska, and Miami, Florida—I changed the subject. "Ed, I know you don't want to turn yourself in, but listen to me, you'll be a lot safer in jail than you will be out here in a shooting gallery."

I thought I'd made a valid point. Almost immediately, however, I got the idea that Ed didn't agree. For one thing, he laughed. "You have *got* to be kidding!" He laughed again, and then he actually went on and on for a while, telling me just how *not* valid my point was. I didn't really follow all of it, but the gist of what Ed had to say was that he apparently really liked the quiet ambiance of a shooting gallery.

Once again, I'd had it. "Ed, if you won't turn yourself in, you can't stay here. The boys will be back soon, and I'm not going to put them in any more danger than they're already in."

Ed seemed to feel that he was at a distinct disadvantage, arguing with me while sitting more or less at my feet. He slowly stood up, glancing nervously over at the window. "Whoever was shooting is long gone," he said. Without conviction, I might add.

"You don't know that, and neither do I," I said. "Now if you don't leave this apartment right now, I'm going to call the police myself and tell them where you are."

Ed's face went bright red, and a few of the veins started pulsing in his neck. *"You said I had forty-eight hours!"*

"I lied."

I know it was mean of me, but I actually enjoyed saying this to him.

"You have never stood by me!" Ed said.

"I'm not having Daniel and Nathan shot at. That's *it*." I glared at him, hoping that I had an expression on my face that clearly said I also was not ever going to give in.

I guess I did, because Ed's face turned even redder. *"You have always put the kids before me. Always!"*

I nodded. "Of course I have," I said. "Adults do put children before adults. That's the way parenthood is supposed to work."

"Well, Daniel and Nathan are not children anymore." Ed actually said this as if it were news.

"So what does that mean? That I should let them get shot?" I stared at him. *"You're* kidding, right?"

I think Ed must've known then that it was hopeless. Ten minutes later, he and I were walking into the garage in the back of the boys' apartment building. Sure enough, there was Ed'$ Toy right where I'd thought it would be.

Ed had borrowed Daniel's jean jacket with the ragged holes in both sleeves and the Grateful Dead iron-on peeling off the back. He was also borrowing Daniel's ancient Thunderbird, the one that is in the garage so often I have nicknamed it the Couch with Wheels. Ed, of course, was taking the Couch with Wheels because the police would, no doubt, be on the lookout for Ed'$ Toy.

"Well," he said, right after he'd backed the Couch out of the garage and rolled the window down on the driver's side, "I'll be in touch. I'm not sure what I'm going to do."

He stared at me, his face forlorn. I think I was supposed to feel guilty for throwing him out of his safe haven.

"Drive safely," I said cheerily.

"I guess I'll just keep on the move," Ed said.

I just looked at him, In *that* car? The way I saw it, moving at all was fifty-fifty. *Keeping* on the move would be a miracle.

"Don't forget," I said, "you promised you'd turn yourself in to the police in forty-eight hours."

Ed was shaking his head before I'd even finished. "Oh, no. If you won't let me stay with the boys, the deal is off."

I folded my arms across my chest and glared at him. "Ed, you've got to turn yourself in. It's too dangerous to be wandering around the streets. Somebody could take another shot at—"

Ed cut me off, his expression long-suffering. "Okay, Okay, I'll turn myself in."

"Tomorrow," I added for him. "You'll turn yourself in tomorrow."

Ed nodded, looking straight at me. "I'll turn myself in tomorrow."

"You promise?"

Ed still looked straight at me. "I promise."

I nodded and turned to go.

There wasn't a doubt in my mind that he was lying.

Chapter 18

Nathan has a tendency to panic, so on the way home, I made a quick stop at Poppa's Pizza where Nathan is—as he will readily tell you—"pursuing a career in pizza delivery." The sad thing about his telling people this is that he's serious. Nathan was out on a delivery, but I left him a note, letting him know pretty much what to expect when he got home.

As soon as I walked in my front door, I made a beeline for the cordless phone lying on an end table in my living room. I gave Daniel a call at the Burger Bite, where he's been pursuing a career doing as little as possible for the last six months, as best as I've been able to tell. Always laid-back, Daniel took the news regarding his shattered window and his dad's abrupt departure with more emotion than I'd expected. "Yo," he said. "Bummer."

What could I say? My heart broke for him.

I got off the phone right after that, and it was just as well, since I could hear somebody in the background yelling Daniel's name and something about why haven't the floors been mopped. I was sure I didn't want to hear the rest of what they had to say.

I was also sure I didn't want to hear whatever messages I'd gotten during the day, but my answering machine, sitting on the end table next to my phone, was blinking like Christmas tree lights. I pressed Play and was treated to message after message from, who else, Jarvis Arndoerfer of Arndoerfer Realty fame. They started at a fairly high decibel level and went even higher. Most of them said pretty much the same thing. "What the hell is going on? Have you gotten yourself involved in a murder AGAIN? This is NOT good for business." Jarvis always acts as if I go around telling all potential clients, "Look, if you plan to kill anybody anytime soon, and then plan to relocate, I'm your real estate agent. I have a lot of experience in that particular area." I mean, what did he think? I wasn't any happier about all this than he was.

In fact, I think I was considerably less happy about it than he was. I knew I should immediately pick up the phone and try to calm Jarvis down, but to tell you the truth, I wasn't in the mood.

I also wasn't in the mood to go to this dumb dinner at Mother Harriet's, either, but I had promised Matthias. And food did sound nice. With all the running around I'd done, the only thing I'd really had all day was Coke. Although I really do like the Real Thing, I believe going on a total Coke diet was probably not a great idea.

I glanced at my watch, wondering if I had time to make me a little snack before I went to dinner.

And my mouth dropped open. Good Lord. It was a *lot* later than I'd thought. Where in the hell had this day gone? I had no idea how much time a person could consume talking to possible murder suspects and getting shot at. According to my watch, which I fervently hoped was fast, I had about fifteen minutes before Matthias rang my doorbell.

On the up side, I didn't have time to call Jarvis back anyway. Or even to check in with my office. In fact, it looked as if this was going to be a showerless, test-out-the-deodorant night. The good thing was, it was highly unlikely that Matthias and I were going to get to spend any intimate time together in the immediate future, so if my underarms could stand a little shaving, who would know?

I ran upstairs, shedding clothes as I went. The worst part about not taking a shower was that my hair always looks its best right after it's washed. It always looks its worst when it hasn't been washed in over a day. Which, as luck would have it, was its condition right now. My hair, in all honesty, looked a great deal like Paul Hettinger's had looked earlier.

Only his had more curl.

I plugged in my hair curler in the bathroom, and I ran to my closet. I hadn't even thought about what I was going to wear, so for an entire minute, I just stood there, staring at the contents of my closet

Have I mentioned that every time I get extremely rattled, my neck breaks out in these large red blotches? This was why, before I married Ed, I'd spent months trying to find a turtleneck wedding dress. Which, by the way, I never did find.

Tonight there wasn't a doubt in my mind that I was going to be rattled, so let's face it, a turtleneck it was going to have to be. Fortunately, I'd had this problem before, so I had quite a few turtleneck things.

I looked at every one of them. All of them needed ironing.

Oh, God. There wasn't time to iron, so I settled for a burgundy silk blouse with a fairly high lace collar. My thinking was that the collar would cover some of the blotches—and those that it didn't cover might just look as if they were a part of the collar.

With the burgundy blouse, I decided on a Liz Claiborne jacket in a gold and burgundy tweed that wasn't too wrinkled, and a black silk skirt that was wrinkled at the waist but the coat would cover it. The skirt was ankle-length.

I know. I know. Nuns wear more flamboyant outfits. And yet under the circumstances, I thought I should probably go with a conservative look. I wasn't sure, of course, since I was more or less charting new territory here. Oddly enough, none of the etiquette books I've read have ever mentioned what would be appropriate attire for a special occasion such as this one—going to dinner at the home of a woman who's convinced you were having an affair with her late husband, after which you murdered him and took up with her son. The books don't even mention if you should bring wine.

I doused myself with extra deodorant and scrambled into the clothes I'd selected, leaving the hangers on the floor. Then, literally running to my bathroom, I curled my hair under so that I no longer looked like Paul Hettinger, I looked like Prince Valiant. Then I started putting on makeup as fast as I could. Foundation over what little foundation had not worn off my face during the day. A little blush so I didn't look dead. A lot of lipstick so it wouldn't wear off during dinner. Lip liner so that my lips looked fuller on top than they really are. Cover-up on blemishes and moles and freckles so I wouldn't have anybody staring at me over dinner, wondering what the hell is that on her face? Eyeliner so I wouldn't look as tired as I felt. Eye shadow to cover the eyeliner, so it wouldn't look as if I had any eyeliner on. Mascara to look as if I actually had eyelashes. Under-eye concealer crap, so I wouldn't look any older than Matthias than I was—a mere year, that was all. And, finally, hair spray to keep my hair in place and make it feel like tiny wires all over my head.

When I finally got all that done, I took a deep breath. In my opinion, the next multibillionaire won't be a computer software genius, like a lot of people seem to think. It'll be the guy who invents the disposable peel-off makeup mask. The mask will have all your makeup on the inside, so that you can just fit the thing to your face, pat it all down, and then peel it off, leaving all your makeup in place. I alone would buy a truckload of the things.

I was just rinsing and reinserting my contacts so that maybe I could wear them all night long without my eyes turning red—when I heard the noise out front.

Matthias drives a green 1964 MG that he insists he's restoring. I myself have never been sure that this was the right word for what he was doing to this thing. Since to restore something, I believe, pretty much requires that something be there in the first place.

I don't think this is the case with Matthias's MG. On its best day it's still a bucket of bolts. And a noisy bucket at that. The thing always sounds as if a few of its bolts have shaken loose and are rattling around inside the engine. In the past I have actually cringed a little when Matthias's MG rattled to a stop in front of my house. I know it sounds shallow, but I haven't particularly wanted my neighbors to see me getting into or exiting a vehicle that looks and sounds like the Bolt Bucket. If nothing else, I've been afraid my neighbors might start going door-to-door, taking up a collection for me.

I have not only cringed, I have outright frowned on days when it's been hot, air conditioning being one of the things that was never there in the first place that Matthias has yet to restore.

Tonight, however, hearing the familiar death rattle outside, I smiled, and yes, my heart did this silly, little leap of joy. I couldn't believe it, but I was actually looking *forward* to riding in the old Bolt Bucket. I didn't even care that both bucket seats moved forward an inch or so every time you hit a bump in the road. I didn't even care that there was nothing but wires where the glove compartment was supposed to be. I didn't even care that there were holes in the floorboard through which you could actually see the road whizzing by under us.

When my front doorbell sounded, I stopped right in the middle of putting in a contact lens, and I hurried downstairs. I did this even though by then I'd only gotten one contact in. I guess I expected Matthias to be a sight for sore eyes, even if half of him was blurry. I also knew very well that even though the upcoming dinner would probably be about as much fun as the Inquisition—only less friendly—at least Matthias and I would have some time alone together on the ride over to his mother's house.

I suppose as I ran downstairs to answer the door I bore a remarkable resemblance to that woman in the classic television commercial—the one who runs ecstatically in slow motion through a meadow and finally leaps into the arms of her lover. When I got to my front door, I must've been even more excited about seeing Matthias than I thought. My hands were actually shaking a little, so it took me a minute to get the door unlocked and open. "Matthias," I said the moment I saw him. My voice had this idiotic lilt.

If this really had been a commercial—or a scene from virtually any romantic movie—Matthias would have responded with "Schuyler." Said in a hushed but adoring tone. And then he would've taken me into his arms. This, however, was clearly neither a commercial nor a movie, because Matthias just stood there on my porch, looking oddly uncomfortable.

To give him the benefit of the doubt, he could've been looking uncomfortable because he was wearing something I almost never see him in—a suit. Matthias usually considers himself dressed up if he's wearing a clean pair of blue jeans. Now he was wearing a dark gray suit I'd never laid eyes on before, and an ivory shirt with one of those collars like Tom Cruise wore in *Rain Man*. The kind that look a little like a priest's collar, that you don't wear a tie with, you just button.

"Ready to go?" Matthias said. His voice was tense.

I just looked at him. No kiss?

"Sure," I said uncertainly. I tried to get a good look at his face, but with only one contact in, it was pretty difficult. With both eyes open, his face looked a little fuzzy, and I didn't want to shut one eye and peer at him as if I were looking through a microscope. Not with him looking straight at me, anyway.

"I, um, read about the thing," Matthias said. "You know, about Ed and all."

Uh-oh. So this was it. I didn't know why it hadn't occurred to me before. Of course. He would've read the article in the *Courier-Journal* this morning.

And—oh, my dear Lord in heaven—*everybody* in Matthias's family would probably have read it, too. His mother. Barbara. And probably their cook. And their housekeeper. Hell, their mailman probably knew that my ex-husband was a suspect in the murder of his fiancée.

I actually felt a little sick. I wondered if it was too late to find whoever it was who'd shot out the boys' window earlier, and beg him to kill me.

Some of what was going through my mind must've shown on my face, because Matthias said, "Are you okay? It sounded pretty awful."

I pasted a smile on my face. "I'm fine," I lied.

"I wish you'd told me," Matthias said.

I stared at him. He was just standing there, making no

motion to come inside. Was he mad I hadn't told him all about the Ed mess on the phone last night?

"You already had a lot on your mind," I said.

"Yeah," Matthias said, "well—"

I have no idea what else he'd been about to say. At that moment a quick movement on my right caught my eye, and I glanced in that direction. The Bolt Bucket was now parked in my driveway, and the motion that had attracted my attention was on the passenger side. I stared at it. More specifically, because I was looking through my bad eye— the right one without a contact—I stared at the blurry shape in the front seat. The blurry shape that seemed to be powdering its blurry nose.

I turned my head more to the right so that I could focus on the blurry shape with my good eye—the left one with the contact—and I immediately wished I hadn't.

The now-no-longer-blurry shape sitting in the Bolt Bucket was Barbara. What's more, she looked terrific.

I couldn't see any more of her than her shoulders and head, but she'd obviously changed her hairstyle since those photographs I'd seen of her were taken. Now Barbara's hair was chin-length, feathered back from her face, and to be painfully honest, extremely flattering. Barbara, I couldn't help but notice, did not look at all like Prince Valiant.

I felt even sicker.

I turned to look back at Matthias, and that was apparently his cue to begin talking very fast. "Barbara didn't want to drive her car over to my mother's. She says since she's been up in Boston she's developed night blindness, so that after dark her vision is significantly impaired."

Significantly impaired? Matthias must've been quoting Barbara verbatim. Who must've been quoting some medical journal verbatim. Not that I didn't believe the night blindness story. Oh, no. I believed every damn word of it. What's more, I was sure if Barbara wanted to discuss selling me Louisville's Second Street bridge, I'd believe every damn word of that, too. I'm trusting that way.

Sure I am.

Matthias was hurrying on. "That means—"

I held up my hand. I knew what it meant. It meant that Barbara was not about to let me and Matthias have even so much as a minute to ourselves. I forced myself to smile. "Well, of *course* you couldn't let her drive," I said. "My goodness, if the poor thing can't see, she could get herself killed." Fat chance, I added mentally. "We couldn't have that."

To keep Matthias from seeing in my eyes exactly what I was thinking, I turned and looked back over at the MG. That, of course, was when it hit me. Wait a minute. There were only two bucket seats in the MG, one for the driver and one for a passenger. A single passenger.

So what exactly was Matthias intending to do, strap me on top? Tie me to the luggage rack with bungee cords?

Even without looking in my eyes, Matthias must've picked up on some of what I was thinking. He cleared his throat. "I hope you don't mind," he said, "following me to my mother's in your car."

I just looked at him. His eyes were very, very green. My neck was suddenly very, very hot. Oh, my, yes, I'd say I'd just arrived at Blotch City.

No wonder Matthias had been looking so tense. It hadn't been the story about Ed, it had been the story Matthias knew he was going to have to tell *me*.

"You don't mind, do you, Sky?" Matthias was now saying.

"Matthias," I began, "let me tell you how I feel." At this point I might've lost it altogether and told Matthias in a loud voice just exactly how much I appreciated this change of plans. But then it occurred to me that Barbara was without a doubt staring straight at me. I could almost feel her eyes, as she quietly waited for me to explode.

I turned back to Matthias. He was standing there, staring straight at me, looking totally miserable. I knew I could probably get him to change the riding arrangements, but what would that really get me? I'd end up looking like the petty, possessive, demanding girlfriend. What was it that Matthias had said about Barbara? She expects the world to revolve around her, that all she has to do is say the word, and everybody jumps. Did I want to act just like her?

I gritted my teeth and gave Matthias a smile. "I don't mind at all. Not a bit. Here, let me get my purse, and I'll be right with you."

Matthias, can you believe, didn't even follow me inside. Instead, he just kept standing out there on my porch, still looking unhappy.

I immediately headed for my bedroom. Mumbling to myself, of course. "I should just tell him I'm not going, that's what I should do. I should just say, this is it, I've had it, hasta la vista, baby, I'm outta here. That's what I should say, all right. Then I wouldn't have to face questions from every single person in his whole damn family about the news in today's paper. Oh, yes, I ought to tell him that I've just remembered that I'm busy tonight. I have to wash my hair."

Which, believe me, was the absolute truth.

And yet, once again, it was Barbara who stopped me. Because there was not a doubt in my mind that my deciding not to go was exactly what Barbara would want me to do. That alone was enough to make me reach for my purse, square my shoulders, and march resolutely right back downstairs to my front porch. Where Matthias was still standing, looking as if he'd rather be doing just about anything but this.

"Okay," I said, and I did my best to sound cheerful, "let's go." I guess the smile I gave Matthias this time was a little too bright. He looked a little startled when he saw it.

I turned to lock my door.

And that's when Matthias reached for my hand. "Just a second," he said, his fingers closing around mine. "I think you've forgotten something."

I gave him a look, mainly to let him know that he was mistaken, I'd forgotten nothing. In fact, I was pretty sure I was going to remember the way he'd pretty much booted me out of his car in favor of the pseudo-ailing but very attractive Barbara for a long, long time.

Matthias, however, was not looking at me. He was

looking over at Barbara and holding up an index finger, wordlessly signaling: *Just a minute.*

Turning back to me, he tightened his hold on my hand and pulled me back inside, shutting the door firmly behind us.

As soon as the door slammed shut, Matthias said, "I think you've forgotten this." And then he pulled me into his arms and bent his head to kiss me.

My first impulse was to pull away. After all, this was the guy who'd just canceled my ticket to ride in the Bolt Bucket. The guy who'd spent last night with his ex instead of me. The guy who'd run out yesterday afternoon to get his ex's favorite wine.

Almost the instant all this flashed through my mind, though, something else also occurred to me: *This was also the guy I loved.* The man who made me feel happy just to look at him. Who had sexy green eyes and a wonderful laugh, and who actually loaded my dishwasher after dinner.

Not to mention, was it really good planning at this point to give Matthias the cold shoulder, treat him like dirt, and make him feel like I didn't want him to touch me? I mean, for God's sake, why didn't I just go out to the Bolt Bucket and tell Barbara she owes me a thank-you note, because I've just handed Matthias over to her, gift-wrapped?

To hell with that. If I were going to lose this man to his ex-wife, then I was most certainly going to give him something to remember me by. I wrapped my arms around his neck, buried my fingers in his thick, shaggy hair, and I gave him a kiss that I could feel all the way down to my toes.

Matthias must've felt something, too, because when we finally pulled away from each other, he stared at me as if maybe he didn't quite recognize me. He also seemed to be having a little trouble getting his breath. "Damn," he finally said, shaking his head. "I sure wish to hell we didn't have to go to this stupid party."

I could have kissed him again.

I would have, too, but would you believe, right then

there was this little tap, tap, tap on my front door? The kind of tap, tap, tap made by long fingernails?

I looked at Matthias. He stared back at me, a muscle jumping in his jaw.

I supposed then that this was probably not the Avon lady.

Sure enough, when I opened my front door, Barbara was standing there. "Well, well, well," she said, with a broad smile, "we meet at last."

"Yes," I said. "We do." That was about all I could think of to say, since my brain was suddenly processing a great deal of new information. Like, for example, Barbara apparently had not made the same decision I had with regard to conservative dress. As a matter of fact, compared to Barbara, Joan Collins would've looked dowdy. Barbara was wearing a strapless cocktail dress in a rich teal blue, spike heels to match, and a wrap around her shoulders in a rainbow of colors, from a deep teal to a rich magenta.

I couldn't help noticing that Barbara must've spent a significant portion of her life recently in a tanning bed. Her skin looked luminous and golden against the rich colors.

I also couldn't help noticing that Barbara had lost a lot of weight since she had those snapshots taken that I believe I've mentioned before. To be brutally honest, the woman was now at least ten pounds thinner than me. Barbara's face was no longer round, but was now more oval-shaped, with high cheekbones and hollows in each cheek. Her hair had not only been shaped and feathered back, she'd also had it lightened around her face. So that what you first focused on were her eyes. Large and brown and tilted at the ends, they looked like Sophia Loren's.

I actually felt a little ill as I stared at the woman who used to be married to the man I loved. The woman who was now saying, "I really hate to hurry everybody along like this, but, well, I was just sitting out in the car, watching the time just tick away, and worrying that we might be late."

I stared at her. Yes, I just bet you were.

"And, well, Matthias," Barbara said, lowering her voice

and reaching out to lay her hand on his arm, "you know how Mother Cross is about being on time." Barbara gave him a look up through her lashes, as if the two of them shared some kind of secret knowledge.

And then she turned back to me. "Oh, what am I thinking?" Barbara said with a little smile. "Of course, you must know that yourself by now."

I just looked at her. I now had no doubt that she knew very well that I did not exactly socialize with Mother Harriet. How sweet of Barbara to rub it in.

Barbara was smiling at me again. "Our Matthias here is so casual about such things. Why, can you believe it, Matthias almost missed our own daughter's birth, he took so long to get to the hospital." Barbara looked over at Matthias again, this time with an indulgent smile. "Of course, he *would* be at work when my labor started, so I had to meet him at—"

As much fun as we were all having, wandering down Memory Lane, I really hated to interrupt. "You know, you're right, it *is* getting late."

I looked over at Matthias, but he was looking at Barbara. "That's right, Barb, we really should be getting a move on. Mother will be expecting us."

Barbara immediately shut her mouth and turned quickly toward the door. "Oh. Certainly. That's right."

I wasn't sure, but she might've said this last through her teeth.

Oh, God. This was going to be *such* a fun evening.

Chapter 19

Mother Harriet was waiting for us at the door. She was smiling broadly. Of course, I wasn't sure if she was smiling because she was playing the gracious hostess, or if it was just because she was tickled pink to see that Matthias and I were indeed arriving in separate cars—much like she and Barbara had planned.

Matthias—that incredibly sweet man—stopped and waited for me to get out of my car and join him before he headed inside. Otherwise, I do believe Barbara would've dragged him bodily inside, leaving me behind still making sure I'd turned off my headlights and locked my car.

In this neighborhood, locking my car was probably a waste of time. After all, there were BMWs, Porsches, Lexuses, and Mercedes in nearly every driveway within a five-mile radius. In Mother Harriet's driveway alone I counted three BMWs, two Cadillacs, and two Lincolns. Did I really think that a car thief would take a fast look around and go for the Tercel?

Of course, I wasn't surprised to see all the luxury automobiles. Mother Harriet, you see, now lived in a prestigious area off Brownsboro Road called Manor Hills. Actually, calling this area prestigious would be an understatement. What would not be an understatement would be to say that everybody who lived back here was at the very least a millionaire.

Not surprisingly, the entire area was unbelievably beautiful, particularly this time of year, with the long, winding roads lined with huge oaks and maples rich with autumn color. It was also unbelievably expensive back here. Houses started in the seven-hundred-and-fifty-thousand-dollar range, and climbed steeply.

The houses were huge and majestic, and they all sat well back off the road, mostly on hills, so that their occupants could look down on professionally landscaped grounds, circular driveways—and, not incidentally, just about everybody else in Louisville.

The styles of the houses ranged from extremely modern to classically elegant, and most real estate agents in this area knew that it was in Manor Hills that you could find the most extreme architectural styles in the entire state. Mainly because, let's face it, if you have enough money, you can build anything you like. Back here you could build a gingerbread house if you wanted, provided that it was huge, surrounded by trees, and you weren't intending to imprison Hansel and Gretel inside the thing.

Mother Harriet, after the death of Matthias's father, multimillionaire Ephraim Cross, had definitely had enough money to build anything she pleased. She'd chosen, however, to build the kind of home you see a lot of in the Kentuckiana area—the stately Southern colonial mansion with the standard two-story-tall white columns out front reminiscent of Tara in *Gone With the Wind*.

It's a style that, frankly, my dear, I've seen so often, it makes me want to gag.

It also makes the word *pretentious* come to mind. I mean, sure, all the lots in Manor Hills are pretty big—some even as large as an acre—but Southern plantations they're not.

I liked the old Cross house much better than this one, but according to Matthias, the house that Harriet had shared with Matthias's dad had held too many sad memories. That's why she'd decided to build this new house only months after Mr. Cross was killed. At least that's what Harriet had told Matthias.

I've always secretly wondered if someone might've told old Harriet what I myself had discovered while trying to prove that I was innocent of Ephraim Cross's murder—that Ephraim had enjoyed the company of a certain young lady several times in the very bedroom he'd shared with Harriet. Oh, yes, that might've soured Harriet on the old homestead a little.

When I finally finished with my car, got my purse, and joined Matthias, Barbara was actually rubbing her arms, as if trying to save them from frostbite. "Goodness," she said, looking pointedly at me, "it *is* terribly cold this time of year, isn't it?"

Apparently, I was supposed to feel guilty for making her wait out here in the elements while I locked up my car. What I felt instead was puzzled. The woman was from Boston, and she thought that it was cold *here*?

"Hmm," I said.

Barbara moved closer to Matthias, shivering noticeably. I could've been wrong here, but it seemed to me as if Barbara was expecting him to put his arm around her. To keep her from succumbing to hypothermia, of course.

Matthias, Lord love him, either missed the cue or chose to ignore it. He stepped away from Barbara and took my arm. "You didn't have to wait on us, Barb," he said. "You could've gone on ahead. Then maybe you wouldn't have gotten so cold."

Have I mentioned that Matthias was an adorable man?

Barbara's mouth immediately tightened, but undaunted, she closed the gap between them and quickly took Matthias's other arm. "And deprive you of the opportunity to make a grand entrance with a lady on each arm?" Barbara said, smiling sweetly. "Not on your life, hon."

After that, we all marched toward Mother Harriet, three abreast. I imagine we probably looked a lot like the beginning of that old TV show, *Bonanza,* with the three brothers lining up and heading straight toward the camera. Only— thank God, I might add—Barbara, Matthias, and I weren't on horses.

Harriet's smile had gotten even wider by the time we got up to her. Tall, with short silver hair worn upswept around her face, she had the high cheekbones and fine features of a model. Tonight she was wearing an ankle-length, blue-silver silk dress that made her large eyes look positively luminous.

To be honest, when Harriet is not extremely angry, she is a very beautiful woman. Oddly enough, however, I have personally rarely seen her when she was not fit to be tied.

"Matthias!" she now said, her voice shrill with excitement. You'd have thought she hadn't seen him since before the Vietnam War. "I'm so GLAD to see you. So GLAD to see you." She gave Matthias a hug and a kiss on both cheeks. Matthias winked at me over the top of his mother's head.

Next, Mother Harriet approached Barbara. Watching this little greeting was a lot like watching one of those reunion scenes on *Unsolved Mysteries*. In fact, I believe the *Unsolved Mysteries* episode where the woman finally meets the total stranger who'd pulled her and her infant son from a burning building fifty years before, and then vanished into the night, was significantly less emotional. "So good to see you, my dear," Harriet kept saying. "So good. So good."

I looked over at Matthias, who was now also looking a little taken aback at this display. Hadn't these two already seen each other this week? Or was Harriet getting senile and beginning to forget things?

I halfway expected Harriet to suggest that I carry Barbara's purse for her, or maybe do a little dishwashing once I got inside, but to give credit where credit was due, Harriet was cordial. She even reached out and actually took my very own hand. "And Schuyler," she said. Her eyes were slits, but her mouth continued to smile. "I want to thank you so much for coming." Harriet's hands did, of course, feel as if maybe earlier in the day she'd screwed them off, like a mannequin's, and left them to chill in the refrigerator for a few hours, but at least she'd made the gesture.

I would've been surprised that I'd gotten such a reception if Matthias had not been standing right there, looking stern. I glanced over at him, and he was staring straight at his mother, his mouth almost a perfect straight line. I couldn't help wondering if he and his mother had recently had words. In which, oh, say, he'd told her that she'd better be nice to me, or else.

Harriet led us all into the living room, directing someone in a black-and-white uniform to take our coats. I, of course, held on to mine, lest everyone present see just how wrinkled my skirt really was. Matthias looked at me, a question in his eyes.

I stared right back at him. "I get chilled," I said.

Matthias responded by looking amused. Sometimes I think that man can see right through me.

Once the coat issue was settled, we all followed Harriet into yet another room. This one was about five times the size of my own living room, and inside there were quite a few people standing in groups of three and four, all holding drinks. The sound of ice clinking against glass supplied background music to the constant drone of conversation.

I took a quick look around, and butterflies started tickling my stomach. Apparently what Matthias had referred to as "my mother's closest friends" included an ex-mayor, the current lieutenant governor, and the president of the University of Louisville. It also included several men and women whose faces looked so familiar, I knew I probably should know who they were.

Oh, my, yes, this was most certainly going to be a fun evening.

For the next god-awful half hour, I stood in the middle of some of the biggest wigs in Louisville and tried to make small talk while the huge, brightly lit chandeliers overhead made me feel like an ant under a sunlamp. I also silently thanked God that I'd decided to go with the ankle-length skirt. Of course, some of the other ankle-length skirts in that room looked as if they probably cost slightly more than the down payment on my house, but hey, my skirt *was* the right length, I'll have you know.

In addition to silently thanking God, I also silently prayed that every single bigwig in that room was far too busy and far too important to bother reading a little thing like the Louisville paper. Surely it was the *Wall Street Journal* or nothing.

As it turned out, it wasn't quite as bad as I'd expected. Other than the time when Barbara recounted in a gleeful voice how Emily's first word had been "Da-Da." And when Barbara went on and on about this "wonderful" antique sofa she and Matthias had found at a garage sale just a couple streets over from their first apartment. And the time she droned on about this dumb cruise she and Matthias had taken to the Bahamas. Other than those times, I hardly felt nauseated at all.

I did feel that choosing the burgundy blouse had been a good idea. Since by the time Barbara had gone on to recount in an extremely loud voice how she and Matthias had discovered this quaint inn in Maine that had been the perfect romantic hideaway, I knew my neck was, without a doubt, one big burgundy blotch.

I also truly enjoyed Barbara's warm and touching story about her and Matthias teaching Em to roller-skate. What do you know, the kid had fallen several times, and once she'd even taken Matthias and Barbara down with her. What a hoot.

"I mean, can you imagine?" Barbara finished, looking over at me. "All three of us on the ground!"

I just shook my head. "No kidding," I said. "Really."

Barbara again told the one about how Matthias had been late for Emily's birth. After that, Barbara had looked straight at me, laughing. "What a hoot," she said.

I'd smiled right back. "A hoot," I said. "An absolute hoot."

Matthias then jumped in, telling something or another about one of his printing students, and for a moment, I could actually stop smiling.

It was a good thing. My mouth was starting to hurt so bad, I was wondering if I'd be able to eat.

When dinner was finally served, Matthias offered me his arm. By then, I'd drunk an entire Bloody Mary, and I almost kissed him on the mouth right then and there.

Over dinner, Barbara had a few more merry tales to tell—or should I say, married tales. She chattered on about everything from Emily's childhood to Matthias's first job. When she started talking about where they'd gone on their honeymoon, Matthias cut her off.

By that time I felt as if my smile were glued on.

At the head of the table, Mother Cross's smile looked as if maybe hers had been stapled on. She definitely looked in pain. Particularly every time Matthias looked over at me and winked.

Finally, when the plates were cleared away—and I could not have told you what in the world I'd eaten—Harriet turned to me. "Oh, by the way, it seems you made the papers again."

She got the reaction she wanted. Everybody at the table, including the lieutenant governor, looked over at me.

"It seems you're involved in another murder."

I just concentrated on Harriet's face, without looking at anybody else. "Well, unfortunately, yes," I said. "One of my clients."

Harriet dabbed at her lips and said to the room at large, "My, my, Schuyler here leads *such* an exciting life."

She made this little comment, of course, in much the same way as you might say, *My, my, Schuyler here has anthrax.*

I tried to smile. "Well, I'm not sure if I'd call it exciting."

"Oh, I would!" This, of course, was Barbara putting in her two cents' worth. "I mean, isn't your ex-husband the one that they think did it?"

Once again every head at the table turned to stare at me.

Once again I didn't look at any of them. I concentrated on Barbara. "I'm not sure about that, either," I said.

Barbara looked over at Harriet for support. "Oh, I do hope I haven't said anything I shouldn't."

Harriet was already waving any cares that Barbara had away, but I thought I should relieve her mind.

"Oh, no," I said sweetly, "I believe everybody here knows that murder is an appropriate topic for dinner conversation."

I immediately wished I hadn't said anything, because right after that, there was this awful silence.

Until Matthias finally jumped in with another story about another one of his printmaking students. Which I'm not sure anybody listened to.

I know I didn't.

The evening eventually ended with a whimper instead of anything else, if you get my drift. Matthias did walk me to my car, but clearly he had to drive Barbara home. To his house.

After Matthias gave me a quick kiss and said in my ear, "Thanks, Sky. I mean it. I owe you," every word of which I agreed with, he gave my elbow a squeeze, and I got into my Tercel and drove home. I was almost there when I realized I was crying.

Lord. Maybe I really should have agreed to move in with Matthias, back when I had the chance. Was I a total idiot or what?

I all but fell into bed, and the next morning I was almost glad to be heading in to the office. At least listening to Jarvis scream would be a welcome diversion from all the other things I had on my mind.

When I pulled into the Arndoerfer parking lot, I was happy to discover that no one was there. I have my own key, so I unlocked the door, dropped my purse on the desk, and immediately headed toward the kitchen in the back.

To get brunch, of course—a large Coke, extremely heavy on the ice.

When I returned to my desk, I thought I was seeing things. Standing there at my desk were Adrienne and Frank Henderson. Holding hands and grinning at me.

I stared. The two of them looked cheerful enough. So why did I think this was *not* going to be good news?

Chapter 20

For a moment I thought that the Hendersons had just stopped by to find out what the status of the sale of their house was, since one of the buyers could obviously no longer go through with the deal.

Right after Frank started talking, though, I realized that this was a moot point. "We really appreciate all you've done, Schuyler," he said, "but we're taking the house off the market."

I looked from one of them to the other. "Was it something I—"

Adrienne interrupted me, her eyes dancing with excitement. "The truth is, we're no longer getting a divorce," she said.

I'm not sure why I was so surprised. For a moment I just stared at them. When I finally found my voice, I got to my feet and said, "Well, how wonderful." I reached out to pat Adrienne's arm. "That's just great." I turned to Frank and shook his hand, feeling a little awkward. "I am really happy for you both. Really."

Frank was smiling. Adrienne was smiling. And I was smiling.

"Well, we just wanted to drop by and tell you in person," Frank said. "And now I'd better take Adrienne on home and get to the office."

I nodded. "Of course," I said. It really was nice of them to come by and tell me face-to-face. When they're firing you, most clients do it by phone.

Adrienne, Frank, and I all smiled at each other again. In

fact, everything seemed okay. If you overlooked the part where I'd just lost a listing. Which was, I realized, a bit self-centered of me to be thinking. After all, it was perfectly okay for the Hendersons to decide not to sell their house after all. They had every right to do that. And it wasn't as if I personally had done anything wrong. Their decision had clearly had nothing to do with me.

And yet, when the two of them turned to walk out the front door, I felt an odd twinge of uneasiness. Which was dumb, when I thought about it.

I mean, I'd said I was happy for them both. And I really was. I mean, how could you not be? I knew that I'd just lost a listing, but in spite of that, I had to feel glad that Adrienne was no longer wandering around, looking lost. So what was wrong with me? I sat there at my desk, staring after Adrienne and Frank, and a cold kernel seemed to be forming in the pit of my stomach. What was it about this little Kodak moment that bothered me?

At first I thought that it had to be because, in this instance, the wife had won. She'd gotten her husband back again. So it certainly wasn't hard to extrapolate from this that Barbara could do the same thing. Barbara could very easily get Matthias back, too. The two of them, after all, had a child together. And a shared history.

And yet as I continued to watch Adrienne, still arm-in-arm with Frank going out the front door, I realized that it wasn't the wife-as-victor image that bothered me. I didn't mind that Adrienne had won Frank back. In fact, more power to her. It was high time that the wife won for once.

No, it was something else—something I couldn't quite put my finger on. I scooted my chair back and went to the front window. There I parted the blinds, and I watched Adrienne and Frank again. They were about halfway across the parking lot by then, and I could only see their backs.

That's when it hit me. Good Lord. Adrienne, from the back, looked an awful lot like Kimberly. The two women had to be just about the same height, the same weight. They were both petite blonds with shoulder-length hair, curled under at the ends.

Frank had unlocked the car and was now holding the passenger door open for his wife. Adrienne patted him on the chest, said something, and then smiled up at him as she got in the car.

Frank returned her smile. At least he did right up until Adrienne's head was inside the car and he'd closed the passenger door. Then his smile disappeared as fast as if it were a lamp that had just been switched off. His shoulders slumped a little as he walked slowly around to the driver's side of the Volvo, opened the door, and got in.

I, of course, was still at the front window, shamelessly staring. My goodness, if you didn't know better, you could get the idea that Frank was not nearly as happy about this latest turn of events as his wife was. And yet, he'd obviously agreed to stay with her.

So what could've caused him to change his mind?

I stood there at the window, once again picturing Adrienne walking away from me, crossing the parking lot. Looking from the back so much like Kimberly.

And then it hit me.

Good Lord. What if the murderer had not intended to kill Kimberly at all?

Suddenly, I could see just exactly how it could all fit. I could see, as easily as if it were being played out in front of me, how it all could've happened. Adrienne and Kimberly could've quarreled that morning. They might've had an argument over the new wallpaper that Kimberly had picked out, or the new carpet, or any of a number of changes that Kimberly had told me she intended to make to Adrienne's beloved house. This would certainly explain Kimberly's phone call to me early Tuesday morning. Kimberly had wanted me, as the listing agent, to handle it for her, and to keep Adrienne out of her hair.

If this were the case, it would also explain what Kimberly had meant by "Ed is going to be mad." If this little scenario was correct, Kimberly would have indeed thought that Ed was going to be mad. In fact, he was going to be furious *at Adrienne* and the way she was acting. As if the house *were* still hers.

My scenario also could explain why Adrienne had left.

Adrienne had seen what Kimberly intended to do to her precious house, and unable to stand it, she'd just taken off. She could've driven around for a while, calming down, and then returned to the house just in time to see her husband attack Kimberly by mistake. Realizing that Adrienne would never really let him go, Frank had come up the back stairs. He'd approached the petite blonde from behind, and thinking the woman in front of him was Adrienne, he'd hit her in the head with the flashlight.

There was no reason for Frank to have thought anybody else was in the house. Kimberly had not driven her own car, and Ed himself had not arrived until later. So there would've been no cars in the driveway. Frank could've easily assumed that his wife's car was in the garage, and that Adrienne was inside.

Kimberly had fallen headfirst down the stairs, and died when she'd hit the floor below.

And Adrienne could have seen it all, and realized immediately that Frank had mistaken Kimberly for her. Adrienne could also have realized that this was her big chance to get everything back that she'd lost—her husband and her house. She could've told Frank that if he didn't come back to her, she would tell the police what she'd seen. And Frank would suddenly find himself in prison—or worse, awaiting execution on death row.

Frank, still reeling from his discovery that he'd killed the wrong woman, would have agreed. Adrienne or Frank could have put the piece of magazine cover in Kimberly's hand, implicating Ed, and then she and Frank could have driven off, only to return a little while later. *After,* of course, Ed had arrived. Shortly thereafter, I myself had come onto the scene.

It did all seem to fit.

The angry phone call to Paul Hettinger from someone sounding like Ed could even be explained. When you're screaming, everybody with a deep voice sounds pretty much the same. It could easily have been McGraw who'd phoned Paul. McGraw would've known Paul's real name, too. He'd have been told what it was by the detective he'd hired. McGraw could have spotted Kimberly at the same time as she spotted him, realized she was scamming somebody else, and had his detective find out where Paul and Kimberly were now living. McGraw could have then called Paul up to scare them both.

I now needed to find out for sure if what I suspected was true. I went back to my desk, sat down, and tried to come up with a plan.

It didn't take long.

Jarvis, of course, would not be happy if I left the office unmanned again, and yet, let's face it, after the story in the *Courier-Journal,* leaving the office empty would be the least of my sins.

I reached for the phone.

Chapter 21

Frank Henderson's office was in one of the new office complexes just off Hurstbourne Lane. Ultramodern, with lots of glass and weathered wood, the building had a spacious parking lot right out front, so I could see even before I pulled in that Frank's car was there.

I parked and hurried inside. There was no secretary seated out at the front desk, but I spotted Frank's name on a door to the left of the desk. It was half-open, so I gave it a little push and walked on in.

Frank was in there, looking through a manila folder and frowning. He must not have heard me come in, because when he finally noticed me standing there, he gave a little start.

"Schuyler?" He glanced toward the desk out front, and frowned again when he saw that the desk was at present unoccupied. Turning back to me, he smiled. "What can I do for you? I do hope this isn't about our pulling our house off the market, because I'm afraid that's a done deal. It's not anything you did. I can assure you—"

I shook my head, and tried to look pitying. "Frank, Frank, Frank," I said. I'd heard somebody say somebody's name like this on *NYPD Blue* recently, with a mixture of pity and scorn. "I just talked to Adrienne on the phone, and she told me everything."

Frank must've seen somebody on TV look both puzzled and faintly amused recently, because that's what he tried to do. "Everything?" he said, an uneasy smile playing about his mouth. "I'm afraid I don't understand—"

If he was going to smile, I was, too. "Oh, I think you understand perfectly. After you dropped Adrienne off on your way to work, I guess she had a chance to think things over. Your wife just told me that she had an attack of conscience. She told me that she suddenly realized that she didn't want to be an accessory to murder."

Frank's eyes bulged at that one. He put his hands flat on his desk, and said, "She *what*?"

If Frank had not looked so alarmed, I might've thought that I was way off base. But obviously I was not. I took a step forward and said slowly, enunciating every word, "Your wife—Adrienne? She told me everything. In fact, I believe her exact words were, 'I'm on my way to the police station right now. I'm going to turn myself in, and tell them everything.' "

It was strange, watching Frank's face. Not a muscle seemed to move, and yet it hardened somehow, even as I watched. In a matter of moments, his face looked as cold and hard as if it had been carved from ice. "You're making all this up," he said. "You're angry we fired you, and you're out to get even." Having said this, he gave me a level look, as if to say, *See? You spread this around town, and I'll tell them you're lying and why.*

I almost laughed. "I don't care what you tell anybody. I'm not making any of this up, and you know it."

"Hell if I do," he said. He was trying for bravado and he didn't quite make it.

"Adrienne told me everything," I said again. "And now she's on her way to the police."

Frank made a scoffing noise in the back of his throat. Not a nice sound. "Adrienne would never tell you—" Frank realized right then what he was saying, because he stopped in midsentence. "I mean, she had nothing to tell, of course . . ." His voice trailed off.

Uh-huh. Right. I crossed the room to the telephone on his desk, picked up the receiver, and held it out to him. "If you don't believe me, why don't you give your wife a call?"

Frank just stood there for a long moment, a muscle working in his jaw. His eyes moved from my face to the telephone and back again, like a cornered animal looking for a way out. Then he got up so fast, I thought for a moment his desk chair was going to tip over backward. He grabbed the phone out of my hand, and started dialing.

I could hear the faint sound of the phone ringing and ringing and ringing even from where I was standing.

Frank, I must say, was not the most patient person in the world. He listened to the distant ringing, the color draining from his face. Then, with an exasperated look in my direction, he broke the connection and dialed again. "I don't understand. I do NOT understand!" He was all but mumbling this to himself. "I told her to stay by the phone, just in case I needed to reach her. I told her. *I told her.*" This last he said through gritted teeth.

Still, I could hear the persistent ringing of the phone.

I folded my arms across my chest. "Like I said, Adrienne's on her way to the police station," I said. "And, unless she's got a car phone, you're not going to—"

Frank slammed the receiver down. "That damned bitch!" Frank said. He ran his hands through his hair, and even across the desk from him, I could see that his hands were shaking. "Goddamnit, how I wish it *had* been her!"

What a sweet sentiment, I thought. And to think if it hadn't been for a little thing like murder, the Henderson marriage would've been one of the ones that had stood the test of time.

It was a chilling thought.

Particularly since Frank was so touchingly loyal to his wife. He'd barely hung up the phone when he started filling me in on all the details about how it had been Adrienne who'd taken the shot at Ed.

"She wasn't just shooting to scare him, either. Oh, no," Frank went on eagerly, "Adrienne had been trying to kill him."

My mouth went dry. My God. Somebody had really been trying to kill *Ed.* What's more, Adrienne had almost succeeded.

Frank evidently picked up on my horrified look, because he rushed to add, "Hell, I tried to talk her out of it, I really did. I mean, what I did was an accident, for God's sake. An *accident*. I never meant to hurt Kimberly."

I stared at him. He might not have intended to hurt Kimberly, all right, but he clearly had intended to murder his wife. That didn't sound like an accident to me.

Frank was hurrying on. "I didn't have any choice. Kimberly saw me. I came up behind her and gave her a shove. And then she fell. Landing facedown." He took a ragged breath. "But she was still conscious. She lifted her head and looked straight at me. She would've told. I had to make sure she didn't tell."

I stared at him. He made it sound like nothing more than a business decision. "So you hit her with the flashlight?"

"I had to," Frank said. "I didn't want to."

Somehow, I didn't think that would get him any extra credit.

"But Adrienne?" Frank was going on. "Now that bitch is something else again. She's cold-blooded."

I swallowed, feeling a little sick. Frank was calling Adrienne cold-blooded, and yet he'd calmly gone along with the scheme to frame Ed for a murder that Ed had not committed. If the plan had worked, Ed would've been spending a significant portion of the rest of his life behind bars. Hell, he might even have gone to the electric chair. And all for nothing.

I guess I looked as if I were rapidly losing any shreds of sympathy I might've had for him, because Frank started talking even faster. "Adrienne's the one who thought of everything. She decided that if she got rid of your ex-husband, he wouldn't be able to deny that he was the one who'd killed Kimberly. And once he was dead, everybody would be convinced that he was guilty. Adrienne was sure that if Ed Ridgway turned up dead, the police would think that Kimberly's brother must've done it, avenging her murder." Frank held his hands out. "We would be in the clear."

Frank was just standing there, looking at me. But I could see what was now going through his mind. For a man who was not cold-blooded, he was calmly considering killing me. Just as if it were yet another business decision. I didn't even have time to get scared, though, because you could tell he realized right away that it would be no use. If Adrienne was already turning herself in, then killing me would accomplish nothing. Except perhaps to eliminate any possibility of his avoiding the electric chair.

"Schuyler," Frank said, "I don't suppose you'd just let me walk out of here? Maybe give me a little head start?"

I just stared at him. Over the years, working as a real estate agent, I've been asked to do some unbelievable things. Like, could I possibly forget that the house didn't quite pass the termite inspection? And, would I please only show the property to people of the Caucasian persuasion? Oh, yes, right here in Louisville, in the oh-so-modern nineties, these things still happen. I've even been asked to rig an appraisal so that the house would qualify for a larger loan.

All of these things, I must admit, I more or less expected. I never, however, expected to have a murderer ask me to give him a head start. I looked Frank right in the eye. "You're bigger than I am, so I don't think I can stop you. But if I were you, I wouldn't run. Running just—"

I had been about to tell him how running always makes you look very bad. In fact, I'd intended to more or less repeat what I'd tried to tell Ed earlier.

Frank, however, didn't give me the chance.

He grabbed the cord of the phone on his desk and gave it a jerk that pulled the connection out of the wall. That done, he threw the thing on the floor and took off for the door.

I just stood there, shaking my head. What was it with men? Didn't they watch *any* made-for-TV movies?

Chapter 22

Frank didn't even make it out of Louisville. Mainly, because I hurried out to the front desk, dialed Constello, and told him everything as fast as I could.

It wasn't long before Constello put me on hold to make a call of his own. Evidently, in a matter of minutes he had every squad car in Louisville looking for Frank. They pulled him over just as he was heading down Interstate 65, just this side of the Bullitt County line.

Once Adrienne heard that Frank had told all, she immediately followed her husband's example. Frank's and Adrienne's stories were pretty much the same, except for one thing. Each blamed the other one for what had happened.

Frank insisted that if it hadn't been for Adrienne being such a bitch, he would never have been driven to commit murder. "I was just trying to get away from her, for God's sake, but she wouldn't let me go."

It occurred to me when I heard this that Frank now had his wish. He had finally gotten away from Adrienne, all right. He had gotten away for life. With no possibility of parole.

Adrienne, even I had to admit, was not the least bit sympathetic. "I mean, really," she said, "would you KILL somebody without first getting a good look at her face? Just to make sure you were killing the right person. I mean, how dumb can you be?"

She actually said this. Right in front of Tony Constello, who reported it to me.

What Frank didn't know, of course, was that he had not been able to contact Adrienne that afternoon because I'd had Nathan do me a little favor. Lord knows, after the way he had not stayed in the car at Paul's apartment like we'd agreed, he owed me a favor. I hadn't even had to remind him, either. I'd phoned Nathan, told him what I wanted him to do, and Nathan had been eager to help me out. Oddly enough.

When I got off the phone with him, Nathan immediately phoned Adrienne and told her what I'd told him to say. That there had been an automobile accident—that, in fact, he and her husband, Frank Henderson, had been in a little fender bender, and that Frank needed her to come pick him up. Nathan told her that Frank was talking to the police right now, and that Frank had asked him to call her on Nathan's car phone.

Strangely enough, the address Nathan gave Adrienne didn't exist.

Evidently, she spent quite some time looking for it.

Ed, I must say, was rather grateful to me for having helped get him out of all this mess. He never did turn himself in like he'd promised, of course. But he did hear on the news on the radio in the Couch with Wheels that Frank and Adrienne had been arrested. So he'd immediately come in from the cold, so to speak.

In actuality, Ed had almost been too grateful. One day not too long after the Hendersons were arrested, he'd dropped by Arndoerfer Realty. Wearing my favorite men's cologne, Aramis. Which, I believe, I might've mentioned to either him or the boys I like so much its fragrance makes me feel a little dizzy. When worn by the right person.

Which Ed, believe me, was not.

Ed had leaned toward me, taken my hand in his, and looked deeply into my eyes. Then he'd started going on and on about how much he appreciated me standing by him. In, yes, "his hour of need."

An exact quote.

I'd been sipping a Coke, of course, and to extract my hand from Ed's, I'd reached for it and taken a sip. Ed had just smiled. "You know, kid," he said, leaning over and touching my cheek, "you and I make a good team."

I had to smile. "You know, kid," I said, getting up and going over to him, "there is nobody in the world like you." I didn't even add, *I hope.* That's how relieved I was that all this was over. I leaned close and gave Ed a genuinely affectionate kiss, pulling away, of course, when he tried predictably to make it something more than I had intended. "But, Ed," I went on, "we do *not* make a good team. We never have. We never will."

I think Ed expected it. He just looked at me and smiled again. "You'll change your mind," he said. "Someday you'll realize we really do make a great team."

I was still shaking my head when Ed went out the door.

Ed and I may not make a good team, but I was pretty sure that Matthias and I did.

What I wasn't sure about was how Matthias felt about it. Especially lately, with Barbara clearly on the prowl. I guess that's why my heart jumped to my mouth when Matthias phoned right after I'd gotten back from the police station. Can you believe, even with the Hendersons in custody, the salt-and-pepper shakers still wanted to talk everything over? And over. And over.

By the time I got back to my house, I was exhausted. When the phone rang, I was afraid it was Jarvis calling me, so I'd let my answering machine pick up. When I heard Matthias's voice, I grabbed the receiver.

"Sky?" Matthias said. "We need to talk."

His voice sounded odd.

"We need to talk?" I repeated. I meant that as a question, but Matthias seemed to think that I was simply reiterating what he'd just said.

"How about if I pick you up in about fifteen minutes?"

Oh, God. This sounded urgent. My stomach felt as if it had just taken the express elevator to the basement.

I had just enough time to run a comb through my hair and put on lipstick before the Bolt Bucket rattled to a stop out front.

Matthias and I immediately headed toward Cherokee Park, a municipal park minutes from my house. At the place everybody around here calls Big Rock—mainly because there happened to be, yes, a *big rock* there in the middle of the creek—Matthias pulled off the road, switched off the death rattles, and turned to face me. He looked uncomfortable. "Well, I guess you've probably guessed what's been going on."

I just looked at him. "I have?"

Matthias ran a big hand over his beard. "I really had no idea. I mean, you could've knocked me over with a feather."

"What?" I said.

"It just came out of the blue. I would've never in my wildest dreams have ever—"

I couldn't help it. "WHAT?"

Matthias ran his hand over his beard again. "Barbara, that's what. She wants us to give our marriage another try. Really. She's been trying to get us back together."

I stared at him, my mouth going dry.

"And, Sky, you don't want to know what she did after Mother's party. I was sitting in my living room, watching TV, and Barbara came out of her room, wearing, well, she was wearing—um, she had on one of those little—you know, with the garters and the holes in—"

I held up my hand. "You're right," I said, "I don't want to know." I swallowed, staring at him. So what was he saying, exactly? Was he going back to his wife? Was that what this was all about?

I could feel hot tears already stinging the back of my eyes.

Oh, God.

Matthias really did have the greenest eyes I'd ever seen.

Oh, God.

"Sky," he was now saying, "I've got to tell you—"

Oh, God.

"I have never been so embarrassed," Matthias said. "I had to practically shove her off me. And then when I tried to tell her about us, Barb screamed at me. She called me a son of a bitch."

I stared at him, suddenly feeling lighter than air.

Barbara had called him a son of a bitch! What a wonderful thing for her to do!

"Then," Matthias hurried on, "when Barb insisted that I drive her to the airport so that she could take the first flight home, she didn't say one word. Not until she was going up the ramp. Then right in front of everybody, she turned to me, gave me the finger, and yelled 'Fuck you, Matthias!'" He ran his hand over his beard one more time. "Have you ever heard of anything so awful?"

I wrapped my arms around his neck. And tried not to laugh. "Awful," I repeated and kissed him.

When we finally pulled away, Matthias told me the rest of it. How Barb had been making him jump through hoops ever since she'd gotten into town. It had been her idea for him to run out immediately and get her some wine. "I didn't get the right one the first time, either. So she made me return to the store to get her very favorite," Matthias said. "Lord. That woman drives me nuts. If it weren't for Emily, I'd be happy to never see her again."

I didn't know what to say. He actually looked guilty. Guilty that he no longer loved the mother of his child. That he no longer even liked her.

No wonder Barbara had been able to get him to run all over town for her. And no wonder Mother Harriet had been able to get him to agree to let Barbara stay with him.

I reached over and squeezed his hand. Matthias really was the sweetest man.

Matthias responded by pulling me close again. "Look, maybe this is bad timing, but Sky, I really do want us to be together."

He kissed me again, so tenderly. I knew he had to feel my body trembling against his, and I didn't even care.

"I'm asking you again to move in with me, Sky. We can get married right away, or we can wait. Whatever you want."

I tilted my head back and just looked at him. He did have the greenest eyes I'd ever seen. And, have I mentioned, a wonderfully thick beard, peppered here and there with gray, that I love running my fingers through?

And a slow, lazy smile that could turn my knees to jelly. He was smiling at me now.

I returned his smile. My heart was pounding so loud, I could barely hear myself think.

A simple yes, that's all it would take, and I wouldn't have to worry about where Barbara was going to stay the next time she came to town. I'd finally have Matthias all to myself.

And then, without really intending to, I suddenly flashed on all the things I'd agreed to recently just because of the pressure of the moment. All the choices I'd made that I hadn't really wanted to.

And I thought of Elena. Her choices had been limited because of circumstance and economics. I didn't even have that excuse.

In fact, the only thing limiting *my* choices was me.

While all this was going through my mind, I reached over almost absently and took Matthias's hand in mine. His hand felt so strong, so comforting. It was a hand I could be happy holding for the rest of my life.

Moving even closer to him, I took a deep breath.

"Matthias, I love you with all my heart," I said.

And then, once again, I told him no.

MYSTERY FAVORITES